Early Praise for *Functional Programming Patterns*

This book is an absolute gem and should be required reading for anybody looking to transition from OO to FP. It is an extremely well-built safety rope for those crossing the bridge between two very different worlds. Consider this mandatory reading.

➤ Colin Yates, technical team leader at QFI Consulting, LLP

This book sticks to the meat and potatoes of what functional programming can do for the object-oriented JVM programmer. The functional patterns are sectioned in the back of the book separate from the functional replacements of the object-oriented patterns, making the book handy reference material. As a Scala programmer, I even picked up some new tricks along the read.

➤ Justin James, developer with Full Stack Apps

This book is good for those who have dabbled a bit in Clojure or Scala but are not really comfortable with it; the ideal audience is seasoned OO programmers looking to adopt a functional style, as it gives those programmers a guide for transitioning away from the patterns they are comfortable with.

➤ Rod Hilton, Java developer and PhD candidate at the University of Colorado

Functional Programming Patterns
in Scala and Clojure
Write Lean Programs for the JVM

Michael Bevilacqua-Linn

The Pragmatic Bookshelf

Dallas, Texas • Raleigh, North Carolina

Many of the designations used by manufacturers and sellers to distinguish their products are claimed as trademarks. Where those designations appear in this book, and The Pragmatic Programmers, LLC was aware of a trademark claim, the designations have been printed in initial capital letters or in all capitals. The Pragmatic Starter Kit, The Pragmatic Programmer, Pragmatic Programming, Pragmatic Bookshelf, PragProg and the linking *g* device are trademarks of The Pragmatic Programmers, LLC.

Every precaution was taken in the preparation of this book. However, the publisher assumes no responsibility for errors or omissions, or for damages that may result from the use of information (including program listings) contained herein.

Our Pragmatic courses, workshops, and other products can help you and your team create better software and have more fun. For more information, as well as the latest Pragmatic titles, please visit us at *http://pragprog.com*.

The team that produced this book includes:

Fahmida Rashid (editor)
Potomac Indexing, LLC (indexer)
Molly McBeath (copyeditor)
David J Kelly (typesetter)
Janet Furlow (producer)
Juliet Benda (rights)
Ellie Callahan (support)

Printed in the United States of America.
ISBN-13: 978-1-937785-47-5
Printed on acid-free paper.
Book version: P2.0—July 2014

Contents

Acknowledgments

I'd like to thank my parents, without whom I would not exist.

Thanks also go to my wonderful girlfriend, who put up with many a night and weekend listening to me mutter about code samples, inconsistent tenses, and run-on sentences.

This book would have suffered greatly without a great group of technical reviewers. My thanks to Rod Hilton, Michajlo "Mishu" Matijkiw, Venkat Subramaniam, Justin James, Dave Cleaver, Ted Neward, Neal Ford, Richard Minerich, Dustin Campbell, Dave Copeland, Josh Carter, Fred Daoud, and Chris Smith.

Finally, I'd like to thank Dave Thomas and Andy Hunt. Their book, *The Pragmatic Programmer*, is one of the first books I read when I started my career. It made a tremendous impact, and I've still got my original dog-eared, fingerprint-covered, bruised and battered copy. In the Pragmatic Bookshelf, they've created a publisher that's truly dedicated to producing high-quality technical books and supporting the authors who write them.

Preface

This book is about patterns and functional programming in Scala and Clojure. It shows how to replace, or greatly simplify, many of the common patterns we use in object-oriented programming, and it introduces some patterns commonly used in the functional world.

Used together, these patterns let programmers solve problems faster and in a more concise, declarative style than with object-oriented programming alone. If you're using Java and want to see how functional programming can help you work more efficiently, or if you've started using Scala and Clojure and can't quite wrap your head around functional problem-solving, this is the book for you.

Before we dig in, I'd like to start off with a story. This story is true, though some names have been changed to protect the not-so-innocent.

A Tale of Functional Programming

by: Michael Bevilacqua-Linn, software firefighter

The site isn't down, but an awful lot of alarms are going off. We trace the problems to changes someone made to a third-party API we use. The changes are causing major data problems on our side; namely, we don't know what the changes are and we can't find anyone who can tell us. It also turns out the system that talks to the API uses legacy code, and the only guy who knows how to work on it happens to be away on vacation. This a big system: 500,000-lines-of-Java-and-OSGI big.

Support calls are flooding in, lots of them. Expensive support calls from frustrated customers. We need to fix the problem quickly. I start up a Clojure REPL and use it to poke around the problem API.

My boss pokes his head into my office. "How's it going?" he asks. "Working on it," I say. Ten minutes later, my grandboss pokes his head into my office. "How's it going?" he asks. "Working on it," I say. Another ten minutes pass by when my great-grandboss pokes his head into my office. "How's it going?" he asks. "Working on it," I say. I get a half hour of silence before the CTO pokes his head into my office. "Working on it," I say before he opens his mouth.

An hour passes, and I figure out what's changed. I whip up a way to keep the data clean until the legacy developer gets back and can put together a proper fix. I hand my little program off

> to the operations team, which gets it up and running in a JVM, somewhere safe. The support calls stop coming in, and everyone relaxes a bit.
>
> A week or so later at an all-hands meeting, the great-grandboss thanks me for the Java program I wrote that saved the day. I smile and say, "That wasn't Java."

The REPL, Clojure's interactive programming environment, helped a lot in this story. However, lots of languages that aren't particularly functional have similar interactive programming environments, so that's not all there is to it.

Two of the patterns that we'll see in this book, Pattern 21, *Domain-Specific Language*, on page 218, and Pattern 15, *Chain of Operations*, on page 159, contributed greatly to this story's happy ending.

Earlier on, I had written a small instance of domain-specific language for working with these particular APIs that helped me explore them very quickly even though they're very large and it was difficult to figure out where the problem might lie. In addition, the powerful data transformation facilities that functional programming relies on, such as the examples we'll see in Pattern 15, *Chain of Operations*, on page 159, helped me quickly write code to clean up the mess.

How This Book Is Organized

We'll start with an introduction to patterns and how they relate to functional programming. Then we'll take a look at an extended example, a small web framework called TinyWeb. We'll first show TinyWeb written using classic object-oriented patterns in Java. We'll then rewrite it, piece by piece, to a hybrid style that is object oriented and functional, using Scala. We'll then write in a functional style using Clojure.

The TinyWeb extended example serves a few purposes. It will let us see how several of the patterns we cover in this book fit together in a comprehensive manner. We also use it to introduce the basics of Scala and Clojure. Finally, since we'll transform TinyWeb from Java to Scala and Clojure bit by bit, it gives us a chance to explore how to easily integrate Java code with Scala and Clojure.

The remainder of the book is organized into two sections. The first, Chapter 3, *Replacing Object-Oriented Patterns*, on page 39, describes functional replacements for object-oriented patterns. These take weighty object-oriented patterns and replace them with concise functional solutions.

Peter Norvig, author of the classic Lisp text *Paradigms of Artificial Intelligence Programming: Case Studies in Common Lisp [Nor92]*, current director of research at Google, and all-around very smart guy, pointed out in *Design*

Patterns in Dynamic Languages that expressive languages like Lisp could turn classic object-oriented patterns invisible.[1]

Unfortunately, not many people in the mainstream software development world seem to have read Norvig, but when we can replace a complicated pattern with something simpler, it makes sense that we should. It makes our code more concise, easier to understand, and easier to maintain.

The second section, Chapter 4, *Functional Patterns*, on page 137, describes patterns that are native to the functional world. These patterns run the gamut from tiny—patterns consisting of a line or two of code—to very large—ones that deal with entire programs.

Sometimes these patterns have first-class language support, which means that someone else has done the hard work of implementing them for us. Even when they don't, we can often use an extremely powerful pattern, Pattern 21, *Domain-Specific Language*, on page 218, to add it. This means that functional patterns are more lightweight than object-oriented patterns. You still need to understand the pattern before you can use it, but the implementation becomes as simple as a few lines of code.

Pattern Template

The patterns are laid out using the following format, with some exceptions. For example, a pattern that doesn't have any other common name would not have the Also Known As subsection, and the Functional Replacement subsections only apply to the patterns in Chapter 3, *Replacing Object-Oriented Patterns*, on page 39.

Intent

The Intent subsection provides a quick explanation of the intent of this pattern and the problem it solves.

Overview

Here is where you'll find a deeper motivation for the pattern and an explanation of how it works.

Also Known As

This subsection lists other common names for the pattern.

---

1.   http://norvig.com/design-patterns/

Functional Replacement

Here you'll find how to replace this pattern with functional programming techniques—sometimes object-oriented patterns can be replaced with basic functional language features and sometimes with simpler patterns.

Example Code

This subsection contains samples of the pattern—for object-oriented patterns, we first show a sketch of the object-oriented solution using either class diagrams or a sketch of the Java code before showing how to replace them in Clojure and Scala. Functional patterns will be shown in Clojure and Scala only.

Discussion

This area provides a summary and discussion of interesting points about the pattern.

For Further Reading

Look here for a list of references for further information on the pattern.

Related Patterns

This provides a list of other patterns in this book that are related to the current one.

Why Scala and Clojure

Many of the patterns in this book can be applied using other languages with functional features, but we will focus on Clojure and Scala for our examples. We focus on these two languages for quite a few reasons, but first and foremost because they're both practical languages suitable for coding in production environments.

Both Scala and Clojure run on a Java virtual machine (JVM), so they interoperate well with existing Java libraries and have no issues being dropped into the JVM infrastructure. This makes them ideal to run alongside existing Java codebases. Finally, while both Scala and Clojure have functional features, they're quite different from each other. Learning to use both of them exposes us to a very broad range of functional programming paradigms.

Scala is a hybrid object-oriented/functional language. It's statically typed and combines a very sophisticated type system with local type inference, which allows us to often omit explicit type annotations in our code.

Clojure is a modern take on Lisp. It has Lisp's powerful macro system and dynamic typing, but Clojure has added some new features not seen in older Lisps. Most important is its unique way of dealing with state change by using reference types, a software transactional memory system, and efficient immutable data structures.

While Clojure is not an object-oriented language, it does give us some good features that are common in object-oriented languages, just not in the way we may be familiar with. For instance, we can still get polymorphism through Clojure's multimethods and protocols, and we can get hierarchies through Clojure's ad hoc hierarchies.

As we introduce the patterns, we'll explore both of these languages and their features, so this book serves as a good introduction to both Scala and Clojure. For further detail on either language, my favorite books are *Programming Clojure [HB12]* and *The Joy of Clojure [FH11]* for Clojure, and *Programming Scala: Tackle Multi-Core Complexity on the Java Virtual Machine [Sub09]* and *Scala In Depth [Sue12]* for Scala.

How to Read This Book

The best place to start is with Chapter 1, *Patterns and Functional Programming*, on page 1, which goes over the basics of functional programming and its relation to patterns. Next, Chapter 2, *TinyWeb: Patterns Working Together*, on page 9, introduces basic concepts in Scala and Clojure and shows how several of the patterns in this book fit together.

From there you can jump around, pattern by pattern, as needed. The patterns covered earlier in Chapter 3, *Replacing Object-Oriented Patterns*, on page 39, and Chapter 4, *Functional Patterns*, on page 137, tend to be more basic than later ones, so they're worth reading first if you have no previous functional experience.

A quick summary of each pattern can be found in Section 1.2, *Pattern Glossary*, on page 4, for easy browsing. Once you're through the introduction, you can use it to look up a pattern that solves the particular problem you need to solve.

However, if you are completely new to functional programming, you should start with Pattern 1, *Replacing Functional Interface*, on page 40, Pattern 2, *Replacing State-Carrying Functional Interface*, on page 47, and Pattern 12, *Tail Recursion*, on page 138.

Online Resources

As you work through the book, you can download all the included code files from http://pragprog.com/titles/mbfpp/source_code. On the book's home page at http://pragprog.com/book/mbfpp, you can find links to the book forum and to report errata. Also, for ebook buyers, clicking on the box above the code downloads the code for that extract for you.

CHAPTER 1

Patterns and Functional Programming

Patterns and functional programming go together in two ways. First, many object-oriented design patterns are simpler to implement with functional programming. This is true for several reasons. Functional languages give us a concise way of passing around a bit of computation without having to create a new class. Also, using expressions rather than statements lets us eliminate extraneous variables, and the declarative nature of many functional solutions lets us do in a single line of code what might take five lines in the imperative style. Some object-oriented patterns can even be replaced with a straightforward application of functional language features.

Second, the functional world also has its own set of useful patterns. These patterns focus on writing code that avoids mutability and favors a declarative style, which helps us write simpler, more maintainable code. The two main sections of this book cover these two sets of patterns.

You may be surprised to see the first set. Don't the patterns we know and love extend across languages? Aren't they supposed to provide common solutions to common problems regardless of what language you are using? The answer to both questions is yes, so long as the language you are using looks something like Java or its ancestor, C++.

With the emergence of more expressive language features, many of these patterns fade away. Classic Java itself has a great example of a language feature replacing a pattern: foreach. The introduction of foreach loops to Java 1.5 reduced the usefulness of the explicit Iterator pattern described in *Design Patterns: Elements of Reusable Object-Oriented Software [GHJV95]*, even though foreach loops use it behind the scenes.

That's not to say that foreach loops are exactly equivalent to the Iterator. A foreach won't replace an Iterator in all cases. The problems they do address are solved in a simpler way. Developers prefer the built-in foreach loops for the common-sense reasons that they are less work to implement and are less error prone.

Many functional language features and techniques have a similar effect on coding projects. While they may not be the exact equivalent to a pattern, they often provide developers with a built-in alternative that solves the same problem. Similar to the foreach-Iterator example, other language features give programmers techniques that are less work and often produce code that is more concise and easier to understand than the original.

Adding functional features and techniques adds more tools to our programming toolbox, just as Java 1.5 did with its foreach loop but on a grander scale. These tools often complement the tools we already know and love from the object-oriented world.

The second set of patterns we cover in this book, native functional patterns, describes the patterns that evolved out of the functional style. These functional patterns differ from the object-oriented patterns you may be familiar with in a few key ways. The first, and most obvious, is that functions are the primary unit of composition, just as objects are in the object-oriented world.

Another key difference lies in the patterns' granularity. The patterns from *Design Patterns: Elements of Reusable Object-Oriented Software [GHJV95]* (one of the original drivers of the software patterns movement) are generally templates that define a few classes and specify how they fit together. Most of them are medium size. They often don't concern themselves either with very small issues that encompass just a few lines of code or with very large issues that encompass entire programs.

The functional patterns in this book cover a much broader range, as some of them can be implemented in a line or two of code. Others tackle very big problems, such as creating new, miniature programming languages.

The range is in line with the book that started the patterns movement in general, *A Pattern Language [AIS77]*. This book on architectural patterns starts off with the very big "1—Independent Regions" pattern, which outlines why the planet should be organized into political entities of about 10,000 people, and goes all the way down to "248—Soft Tile and Brick," which explains how to make your own bricks.

Before we dig into the various patterns in this book, let's spend some time getting familiar with functional programming itself.

1.1 What Is Functional Programming?

At its core, functional programming is about immutability and about composing functions rather than objects. Many related characteristics fall out of this style.

Functional programs do the following:

Have first-class functions: *First-class functions* are functions that can be passed around, dynamically created, stored in data structures, and treated like any other first-class object in the language.

Favor pure functions: *Pure functions* are functions that have no side effects. A *side effect* is an action that the function does that modifies state outside the function.

Compose functions: Functional programming favors building programs from the bottom up by composing functions together.

Use expressions: Functional programming favors expressions over statements. Expressions yield values. Statements do not and exist only to control the flow of a program.

Use Immutability: Since functional programming favors pure functions, which can't mutate data, it also makes heavy use of immutable data. Instead of modifying an existing data structure, a new one is efficiently created.

Transform, rather than mutate, data: Functional programming uses functions to transform immutable data. One data structure is put into the function, and a new immutable data structure comes out. This is in explicit contrast with the popular object-oriented model, which views objects as little packets of mutable state and behavior.

A focus on immutable data leads to programs that are written in a more declarative style, since we can't modify a data structure piece by piece. Here's an iterative way to filter the odd numbers out of a list, written in Java. Notice how it relies on mutation to add odd numbers to filteredList one at a time.

```
JavaExamples/src/main/java/com/mblinn/mbfpp/intro/FilterOdds.java
public List<Integer> filterOdds(List<Integer> list) {
        List<Integer> filteredList = new ArrayList<Integer>();
        for (Integer current : list) {
                if (isOdd(current)) {
                        filteredList.add(current);
                }
        }
        return filteredList;
}
```

```
private boolean isOdd(Integer integer) {
        return 0 != integer % 2;
}
```

And here's a functional version, written in Clojure.

```
(filter odd? list-of-ints)
```

The functional version is obviously much shorter than the object-oriented version. As mentioned previously, this is because functional programming is declarative. That is, it specifies what should be done rather than how to do it. For many problems we encounter in programming, this style lets us work at a higher level of abstraction.

However, other problems are hard, if not impossible, to solve using strict functional programming techniques. A compiler is a pure function. If you put a program in, you expect to get the same machine code out every time. If you don't, it's probably a compiler bug. Google's search engine, however, is not a pure function. If we got the same results from a Google search query every time, we'd be stuck with a late 1990s view of the Web, which would be quite tragic.

For this reason, functional programming languages tend to lie on a spectrum of strictness. Some are more functionally pure than others. Of the two languages we're using in this book, Clojure is purer on the functional spectrum; at least, it is if we avoid its Java interoperability features.

For example, in idiomatic Clojure, we don't mutate data as we do in Java. Instead, we rely on an efficient set of immutable data structures, a set of reference types, and a software transactional memory system. This allows us to get the benefits of mutability without the dangers. We'll introduce these techniques in Section 2.4, *TinyWeb in Clojure*, on page 28.

Scala has more support for mutable data, but immutable data is preferred. For instance, Scala has both mutable and immutable versions of its collections library, but the immutable data structures are imported and used by default.

1.2   Pattern Glossary

Here is where we introduce all of the patterns we cover in the book and give a brief overview of each. This is a great list to skim if you already have a specific problem you need to solve in a functional way.

Replacing Object-Oriented Patterns

This section shows how to replace common object-oriented patterns with functional language features. This generally cuts down on the amount of code we have to write while giving us a more concise code to maintain.

Pattern 1, *Replacing Functional Interface*, on page 40

Here we replace common types of functional interfaces, such as Runnable or Comparator, with native functional features.

This section introduces two basic types of functional features. The first type, higher-order functions, allows us to pass functions around as first-class data. The second, anonymous functions, allows us to write quick one-off functions without giving them a name. These features combine to let us replace most instances of Functional Interface very concisely.

Pattern 2, *Replacing State-Carrying Functional Interface*, on page 47

With this pattern we replace instances of Functional Interface that need to carry around some bit of state—we introduce another new functional feature, closures, which lets us wrap up a function and some state to pass around.

Pattern 3, *Replacing Command*, on page 54

Replacing Command encapsulates an action in an object—here we'll take a look at how we can replace the object-oriented version using the techniques introduced in the previous two patterns.

Pattern 4, *Replacing Builder for Immutable Object*, on page 62

Here we carry data using the classic Java convention, a class full of getters and setters—this approach is intimately tied up with mutability. Here we'll show how to get the convenience of a Java Bean along with the benefits of immutability.

Pattern 5, *Replacing Iterator*, on page 72

Replacing Iterator gives us a way to access items in a collection sequentially—here we'll see how we can solve many of the problems we'd solve with Iterator using higher-order functions and sequence comprehensions, which give us solutions that are more declarative.

Pattern 6, *Replacing Template Method*, on page 83

This pattern defines the outline of an algorithm in a superclass, leaving subclasses to implement its details. Here we'll see how to use higher-order functions and function composition to replace this inheritance-based pattern.

Pattern 7, *Replacing Strategy*, on page 92

In this pattern we define a set of algorithms that all implement a common interface. This allows a programmer to easily swap out one implementation of an algorithm for another.

Pattern 8, *Replacing Null Object*, on page 99

In this pattern we discuss how to replace Null Object and talk about other types of null handling—in Scala, we take advantage of the type system using Option. In Clojure, we rely on nil and some language support to make it more convenient to deal with.

Pattern 9, *Replacing Decorator*, on page 109

Replacing Decorator adds new behavior to an object without changing the original class. Here we'll see how to achieve the same effect with function composition.

Pattern 10, *Replacing Visitor*, on page 113

Replacing Visitor makes it easy to add operations to a data type but difficult to add new implementations of the type. Here we show solutions in Scala and Clojure that make it possible to do both.

Pattern 11, *Replacing Dependency Injection*, on page 128

This pattern injects an object's dependencies into it, rather than instantiating them inline—this allows us to swap out their implementations. We'll explore Scala's Cake pattern, which gives us a DI-like pattern.

Introducing Functional Patterns

Pattern 12, *Tail Recursion*, on page 138

Tail Recursion is functionally equivalent to iteration and provides a way to write a recursive algorithm without requiring a stack frame for each recursive call. While we'll prefer more declarative solutions throughout the book, sometimes the most straightforward way to solve a problem is more iterative. Here we'll show how to use Tail Recursion for those situations.

Pattern 13, *Mutual Recursion*, on page 146

Mutual Recursion is a pattern where recursive functions call one another. As with Tail Recursion, we need a way to do this without consuming stack frames for it to be practical. Here we'll show how to use a feature called *trampolining* to do just that.

Pattern 14, *Filter-Map-Reduce,* **on page 155**

Filter, map, and reduce are three of the most commonly used higher-order functions. Used together, they're a very powerful tool for data manipulation and are the inspiration for the popular MapReduce data-processing paradigm. In this pattern, we'll see how they can be used on a smaller scale.

Pattern 15, *Chain of Operations,* **on page 159**

Functional programming eschews mutability; so instead of mutating a data structure, we take one immutable data structure, operate on it, and produce a new one. Chain of Operations examines the differing ways to do so in Scala and Clojure.

Pattern 16, *Function Builder,* **on page 167**

Higher-order functions can create other functions using the Function Builder pattern. Here we'll show some common instances of the pattern that are built into many functional languages, and we'll explore a few custom ones.

Pattern 17, *Memoization,* **on page 182**

This pattern caches the results of a pure function invocation to avoid having to do an expensive computation more than once.

Pattern 18, *Lazy Sequence,* **on page 186**

Lazy Sequence is a pattern where a sequence is realized bit by bit only as it's needed. This allows us to create infinitely long sequences and to easily work with streams of data.

Pattern 19, *Focused Mutability,* **on page 196**

Focused Mutability makes a small critical section of code use mutable data structures to optimize performance. The need for this is less common than you might think. Clojure and Scala, backed by the JVM, provide very efficient mechanisms for working with immutable data, so immutability is rarely the bottleneck.

Pattern 20, *Customized Control Flow,* **on page 206**

With most languages, it's impossible to add a new way of doing control flow to the language without modifying the language itself. Functional languages, however, usually provide a way to create custom control abstractions tailored for specific uses.

Pattern 21, *Domain-Specific Language*, on page 218

The Domain-Specific Language pattern allows us to create a language that is purpose-built for solving a specific problem. Using a well-designed implementation of domain-specific language is the ultimate solution for often-solved problems, as it lets us program close to the problem domain. This reduces the amount of code we have to write and the mental friction in transforming our thoughts into code.

CHAPTER 2

TinyWeb: Patterns Working Together

2.1 Introducing TinyWeb

We'll start our journey with a look at an example of a program that makes heavy use of classic object-oriented patterns, a small web framework called TinyWeb. After introducing TinyWeb, we'll see how to rewrite it in a hybrid object-oriented and functional style using Scala. Finally, we'll move on to a more fully functional style in Clojure.

Let's focus on a few goals for this example. The first is to see several patterns working together in one codebase before we go into them in more detail.

The second is to introduce basic Scala and Clojure concepts for those unfamiliar with either, or both, of the languages. A full introduction to the languages is beyond the scope of this book, but this section gives you enough of the basics to understand the majority of the remaining code.

Finally, we'll work existing Java code into a Scala or Clojure codebase. We'll do this by taking the Java version of TinyWeb and transforming it into Scala and Clojure piece by piece.

TinyWeb itself is a small *model-view-controller* (MVC) web framework. It's far from complete, but it should feel familiar to anyone who has worked with any of the popular frameworks, such as Spring MVC. There's one little twist to TinyWeb: since this is a book on functional programming, we're going to do our best to work with immutable data, which can be quite challenging in Java.

2.2 TinyWeb in Java

The Java version of TinyWeb is a basic MVC web framework written in a classic object-oriented style. To handle requests we use a Controller implemented using the Template method, which we cover in detail in Pattern 6, *Replacing*

Template Method, on page 83. Views are implemented using the Strategy pattern, covered in Pattern 7, *Replacing Strategy,* on page 92.

Our framework is built around core pieces of data objects, HttpRequest and HttpResponse. We want these to be immutable and easy to work with, so we are going to build them using the Builder pattern discussed in Pattern 4, *Replacing Builder for Immutable Object,* on page 62. Builder is a standard way of getting immutable objects in Java.

Finally, we've got request filters that run before a request is handled and that do some work on the request, such as modifying it. We will implement these filters using the Filter class, a simple example of Pattern 1, *Replacing Functional Interface,* on page 40. Our filters also show how to handle changing data using immutable objects.

The whole system is summarized in the following figure.

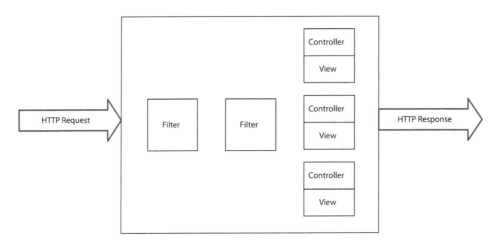

Figure 1—A TinyWeb Overview. A graphical overview of TinyWeb

We'll start off with a look at our core data types, HttpRequest and HttpResponse.

HttpRequest and HttpResponse

Let's dig into the code, starting with HttpResponse. In this example we'll only need a body and a response code in our response, so those are the only attributes we'll add. The following code block shows how we can implement the class. Here we use the fluent builder of the type made popular in the Java classic, *Effective Java [Blo08].*

JavaExamples/src/main/java/com/mblinn/oo/tinyweb/HttpResponse.java

```
package com.mblinn.oo.tinyweb;

public class HttpResponse {
        private final String body;
        private final Integer responseCode;

        public String getBody() {
                return body;
        }

        public Integer getResponseCode() {
                return responseCode;
        }

        private HttpResponse(Builder builder) {
                body = builder.body;
                responseCode = builder.responseCode;
        }

        public static class Builder {
                private String body;
                private Integer responseCode;

                public Builder body(String body) {
                        this.body = body;
                        return this;
                }

                public Builder responseCode(Integer responseCode) {
                        this.responseCode = responseCode;
                        return this;
                }

                public HttpResponse build() {
                        return new HttpResponse(this);
                }

                public static Builder newBuilder() {
                        return new Builder();
                }
        }
}
```

This approach encapsulates all mutability inside of a Builder object, which then builds an immutable HttpResponse. While this gives us a clean way of working with immutable data, it's quite verbose. For example, we could create a simple test request using this code:

```
HttpResponse testResponse = HttpResponse.Builder.newBuilder()
        .responseCode(200)
        .body("responseBody")
        .build();
```

Without using Builder we'd need to pass all of our arguments in the constructor. This is okay for our small example, but this practice grows unwieldy when working with larger classes. Another option would be to use a Java Bean–style class with getters and setters, but that would require mutability.

Let's move on and take a quick look at HttpRequest. Since the class is similar to HttpResponse (though it lets us set a request body, headers, and a path), we won't repeat the code in full. One feature is worth mentioning, though.

In order to support request filters that "modify" the incoming request, we need to create a new request based off the existing one, since our request objects aren't mutable. We'll use builderFrom() to do so. This method takes an existing HttpRequest and uses it to set starting values for a new builder. The code for builderFrom() follows:

JavaExamples/src/main/java/com/mblinn/oo/tinyweb/HttpRequest.java
```
public static Builder builderFrom(HttpRequest request) {
        Builder builder = new Builder();
        builder.path(request.getPath());
        builder.body(request.getBody());

        Map<String, String> headers = request.getHeaders();
        for (String headerName : headers.keySet())
                builder.addHeader(headerName,
                                    headers.get(headerName));

        return builder;
}
```

This may seem wasteful, but the JVM is a miracle of modern software engineering. It's able to garbage-collect short-lived objects very efficiently, so this style of programming performs admirably well in most domains.

Views and Strategy

Let's continue our tour of TinyWeb with a look at view handling. In a fully featured framework, we'd include some ways to plug template engines into our view, but for TinyWeb we'll just assume we're generating our response bodies entirely in code using string manipulation.

First we'll need a View interface, which has a single method, render(). render() takes in a model in the form of a Map<String, List<String>>, which represents the

Immutability: Not Just for Functional Programmers

The experienced object-oriented programmer might grumble about extra effort to get immutable objects, especially if we're doing it "just to be functional." However, immutable data doesn't just fall out of functional programming; it's a good practice that can help us write cleaner code.

A large class of software bugs boil down to one section of code modifying data in another section in an unexpected way. This type of bug becomes even more heinous in the multicore world we all live in now. By making our data immutable, we can avoid this class of bugs altogether.

Using immutable data is an oft-repeated bit of advice in the Java world; it's mentioned in *Effective Java [Blo08]—Item 15: Minimize Mutability*, among other places, but it is rarely followed. This is largely due to the fact that Java wasn't designed with immutability in mind, so it takes a lot of programmer effort to get it.

Still, some popular, high-quality libraries, such as Joda-Time and Google's collections library, provide excellent support for programming with immutable data. The fact that both of these popular libraries provide replacements for functionality available in Java's standard library speaks to the usefulness of immutable data.

Thankfully, both Scala and Clojure have much more first-class support for immutable data, to the extent that it's often harder to use mutable data than immutable.

model attributes and values. We'll use a List<String> for our values so that a single attribute can have multiple values. It returns a String representing the rendered view.

The View interface is in the following code:

```
JavaExamples/src/main/java/com/mblinn/oo/tinyweb/View.java
package com.mblinn.oo.tinyweb;

import java.util.List;
import java.util.Map;

public interface View {
        public String render(Map<String, List<String>> model);
}
```

Next we need two classes that are designed to work together using the Strategy pattern: StrategyView and RenderingStrategy.

RenderingStrategy is responsible for doing the actual work of rendering a view as implemented by the framework user. It's an instance of a Strategy class from the Strategy pattern, and its code follows:

JavaExamples/src/main/java/com/mblinn/oo/tinyweb/RenderingStrategy.java
```java
package com.mblinn.oo.tinyweb;

import java.util.List;
import java.util.Map;

public interface RenderingStrategy {

        public String renderView(Map<String, List<String>> model);

}
```

Now let's examine the class that delegates to RenderingStrategy, StrategyView. This class is implemented by the framework and takes care of properly handing exceptions thrown out of the RenderingStrategy. Its code follows:

JavaExamples/src/main/java/com/mblinn/oo/tinyweb/StrategyView.java
```java
package com.mblinn.oo.tinyweb;

import java.util.List;
import java.util.Map;

public class StrategyView implements View {

        private RenderingStrategy viewRenderer;

        public StrategyView(RenderingStrategy viewRenderer) {
                this.viewRenderer = viewRenderer;
        }

        @Override
        public String render(Map<String, List<String>> model) {
                try {
                        return viewRenderer.renderView(model);
                } catch (Exception e) {
                        throw new RenderingException(e);
                }
        }
}
```

To implement a view, the framework user creates a new subclass of RenderingStrategy with the right view-rendering logic, and the framework injects it into StrategyView.

In this simple example, StrategyView plays a minimal role. It simply swallows exceptions and wraps them in RenderingException so that they can be handled properly at a higher level. A more complete framework might use StrategyView as an integration point for various rendering engines, among other things, but we'll keep it simple here.

Controllers and Template Method

Next up is our Controller. The Controller itself is a simple interface with a single method, handleRequest(), which takes an HttpRequest and returns an HttpResponse. The code for the interface follows:

JavaExamples/src/main/java/com/mblinn/oo/tinyweb/Controller.java
```java
package com.mblinn.oo.tinyweb;

public interface Controller {
        public HttpResponse handleRequest(HttpRequest httpRequest);
}
```

We'll use the Template Method pattern so that users can implement their own controllers. The central class for this implementation is TemplateController, which has an abstract doRequest(), as shown in the following code:

JavaExamples/src/main/java/com/mblinn/oo/tinyweb/TemplateController.java
```java
package com.mblinn.oo.tinyweb;

import java.util.List;
import java.util.Map;

public abstract class TemplateController implements Controller {
        private View view;
        public TemplateController(View view) {
                this.view = view;
        }

        public HttpResponse handleRequest(HttpRequest request) {
                Integer responseCode = 200;
                String responseBody = "";

                try {
                        Map<String, List<String>> model = doRequest(request);
                        responseBody = view.render(model);
                } catch (ControllerException e) {
                        responseCode = e.getStatusCode();
                } catch (RenderingException e) {
                        responseCode = 500;
                        responseBody = "Exception while rendering.";
                } catch (Exception e) {
                        responseCode = 500;
                }

                return HttpResponse.Builder.newBuilder().body(responseBody)
                    .responseCode(responseCode).build();
        }
        protected abstract Map<String, List<String>> doRequest(HttpRequest request);
}
```

To implement a controller, a user of the framework extends TemplateController and implements its doRequest() method.

Both the Template Method pattern we used for our controllers and the Strategy pattern we used for our views support similar tasks. They let some general code, perhaps in a library or framework, delegate out to another bit of code intended to perform a specific task. The Template Method pattern does it using inheritance, while the Strategy pattern does it using composition.

In the functional world, we'll rely heavily on composition, which also happens be good practice in the object-oriented world. However, it'll be a composition of functions rather than a composition of objects.

Filter and Functional Interface

Finally, let's examine Filter. The Filter class is a Functional Interface that lets us perform some action on HttpRequest before it's processed. For instance, we may want to log some information about the request or even add a header. It has a single method, doFilter(), takes HttpRequest, and returns a filtered instance of it.

If an individual Filter needs to do something that modifies a request, it simply creates a new one based on the existing request and returns it. This lets us work with an immutable HttpRequest but gives us the illusion that it can be changed.

The code for Filter follows:

JavaExamples/src/main/java/com/mblinn/oo/tinyweb/Filter.java
```java
package com.mblinn.oo.tinyweb;

public interface Filter {
        public HttpRequest doFilter(HttpRequest request);
}
```

Now that we've seen all of the pieces of TinyWeb, let's see how they fit together.

Tying It All Together

To tie it all together, we'll use the main class, TinyWeb. This class takes two constructor arguments. The first is a Map, where the keys are Strings representing request paths and the values are Controller objects. The second argument is a list of Filters to run on all requests before they are passed to the appropriate controller.

The TinyWeb class has a single public method, handleRequest(), which takes HttpRequest. The handleRequest() method then runs the request through the filters, looks up the appropriate controller to handle it, and returns the resulting HttpResponse. The code is below:

JavaExamples/src/main/java/com/mblinn/oo/tinyweb/TinyWeb.java

```java
package com.mblinn.oo.tinyweb;

import java.util.List;
import java.util.Map;

public class TinyWeb {
        private Map<String, Controller> controllers;
        private List<Filter> filters;

        public TinyWeb(Map<String, Controller> controllers, List<Filter> filters) {
                this.controllers = controllers;
                this.filters = filters;
        }

        public HttpResponse handleRequest(HttpRequest httpRequest) {

                HttpRequest currentRequest = httpRequest;
                for (Filter filter : filters) {
                        currentRequest = filter.doFilter(currentRequest);
                }

                Controller controller = controllers.get(currentRequest.getPath());

                if (null == controller)
                        return null;

                return controller.handleRequest(currentRequest);
        }
}
```

A full-featured Java web framework wouldn't expose a class like this directly as its framework plumbing. Instead it would use some set of configuration files and annotations to wire things together. However, we'll stop adding to TinyWeb here and move on to an example that uses it.

Using TinyWeb

Let's implement an example program that takes an HttpRequest with a comma-separated list of names as its value and returns a body that's full of friendly greetings for those names. We'll also add a filter that logs the path that was requested.

We'll start by looking at GreetingController. When the controller receives an HttpRequest, it picks out the body of the request, splits it on commas, and treats each element in the split body as a name. It then generates a random friendly greeting for each name and puts the names into the model under the key greetings. The code for GreetingController follows:

JavaExamples/src/main/java/com/mblinn/oo/tinyweb/example/GreetingController.java

```java
package com.mblinn.oo.tinyweb.example;
import java.util.ArrayList;
import java.util.HashMap;
import java.util.List;
import java.util.Map;
import java.util.Random;

import com.mblinn.oo.tinyweb.HttpRequest;
import com.mblinn.oo.tinyweb.TemplateController;
import com.mblinn.oo.tinyweb.View;

public class GreetingController extends TemplateController {
        private Random random;
        public GreetingController(View view) {
                super(view);
                random = new Random();
        }

        @Override
        public Map<String, List<String>> doRequest(HttpRequest httpRequest) {
                Map<String, List<String>> helloModel =
                                new HashMap<String, List<String>>();
                helloModel.put("greetings",
                                generateGreetings(httpRequest.getBody()));
                return helloModel;
        }

        private List<String> generateGreetings(String namesCommaSeparated) {
                String[] names = namesCommaSeparated.split(",");
                List<String> greetings = new ArrayList<String>();
                for (String name : names) {
                        greetings.add(makeGreeting(name));
                }
                return greetings;
        }

        private String makeGreeting(String name) {
                String[] greetings =
                        { "Hello", "Greetings", "Salutations", "Hola" };
                String greetingPrefix = greetings[random.nextInt(4)];
                return String.format("%s, %s", greetingPrefix, name);
        }
}
```

Next up, let's take a look at GreetingRenderingStrategy. This class iterates through the list of friendly greetings generated by the controller and places each into an <h2> tag. Then it prepends the greetings with an <h1> containing "Friendly Greetings:", as the following code shows:

JavaExamples/src/main/java/com/mblinn/oo/tinyweb/example/GreetingRenderingStrategy.java

```java
package com.mblinn.oo.tinyweb.example;

import java.util.List;
import java.util.Map;

import com.mblinn.oo.tinyweb.RenderingStrategy;

public class GreetingRenderingStrategy implements RenderingStrategy {

    @Override
    public String renderView(Map<String, List<String>> model) {
        List<String> greetings = model.get("greetings");
        StringBuffer responseBody = new StringBuffer();
        responseBody.append("<h1>Friendly Greetings:</h1>\n");
        for (String greeting : greetings) {
            responseBody.append(
                    String.format("<h2>%s</h2>\n", greeting));

        }
        return responseBody.toString();
    }

}
```

Finally, let's look at an example filter. The LoggingFilter class just logs out the path of the request it's being run on. Its code follows:

JavaExamples/src/main/java/com/mblinn/oo/tinyweb/example/LoggingFilter.java

```java
package com.mblinn.oo.tinyweb.example;

import com.mblinn.oo.tinyweb.Filter;
import com.mblinn.oo.tinyweb.HttpRequest;

public class LoggingFilter implements Filter {

    @Override
    public HttpRequest doFilter(HttpRequest request) {
        System.out.println("In Logging Filter - request for path: "
            + request.getPath());
        return request;
    }

}
```

Wiring up a simple test harness that connects everything together into a TinyWeb, throws an HttpRequest at it, and then prints the response to the console gets us the following output. This indicates that everything is working properly:

```
In Logging Filter - request for path: greeting/
responseCode: 200
responseBody:
<h1>Friendly Greetings:</h1>
<h2>Hola, Mike</h2>
<h2>Greetings, Joe</h2>
<h2>Hola, John</h2>
<h2>Salutations, Steve</h2>
```

Now that we've seen the TinyWeb framework in Java, let's take a look at how we'll use some of the functional replacements for the object-oriented patterns we'll explore in this book. This will give us a TinyWeb that's functionally equivalent but written with fewer lines of code and in a more declarative, easier-to-read style.

2.3 TinyWeb in Scala

Let's take TinyWeb and transform it into Scala. We'll do this a bit at a time so we can show how our Scala code can work with the existing Java code. The overall shape of the framework will be similar to the Java version, but we'll take advantage of some of Scala's functional features to make the code more concise.

Step One: Changing Views

We'll start with our view code. In Java, we used the classic Strategy pattern. In Scala, we'll stick with the Strategy pattern, but we'll use *higher-order functions* for our strategy implementations. We'll also see some of the benefits of expressions over statements for control flow.

The biggest change we'll make is to the view-rendering code. Instead of using Functional Interface in the form of RenderingStrategy, we'll use a higher-order function. We go over this replacement in great detail in Pattern 1, *Replacing Functional Interface*, on page 40.

Here's our modified view code in its full functional glory:

ScalaExamples/src/main/scala/com/mblinn/mbfpp/oo/tinyweb/stepone/View.scala
```scala
package com.mblinn.mbfpp.oo.tinyweb.stepone
import com.mblinn.oo.tinyweb.RenderingException

trait View {
  def render(model: Map[String, List[String]]): String
}
```

```scala
class FunctionView(viewRenderer: (Map[String, List[String]]) => String)
        extends View {
  def render(model: Map[String, List[String]]) =
    try
        viewRenderer(model)
    catch {
        case e: Exception => throw new RenderingException(e)
    }
}
```

We start off with our View trait. It defines a single method, render(), which takes a map representing the data in our model and returns a rendered String.

```scala
trait View {
  def render(model: Map[String, List[String]]): String
}
```

Next up, let's take a look at the body of FunctionView. The code below declares a class that has a constructor with a single argument, viewRenderer, which sets an immutable field of the same name.

```scala
class FunctionView(viewRenderer: (Map[String, List[String]]) => String)
        extends View {
  «classBody»
}
```

The viewRenderer function parameter has a rather strange-looking type annotation, (Map[String, String]) => String. This is a function type. It says that viewRenderer is a function that takes a Map[String, String] and returns a String, just like the renderView() on our Java RenderingStrategy.

Next, let's take a look at the render() method itself. As we can see from the code below, it takes in a model and runs it through the viewRender() function.

```scala
def render(model: Map[String, List[String]]) =
  try
    viewRenderer(model)
  catch {
    case e: Exception => throw new RenderingException(e)
  }
```

Notice how there's no return keyword anywhere in this code snippet? This illustrates another important aspect of functional programming. In the functional world, we program primarily with expressions. The value of a function is just the value of the last expression in it.

In this example, that expression happens to be a try block. If no exception is thrown, the try block takes on the value of its main branch; otherwise it takes on the value of the appropriate case clause in the catch branch.

If we wanted to supply a default value rather than wrap the exception up into a RenderException, we can do so just by having the appropriate case branch take on our default, as illustrated in the following code:

```
try
  viewRenderer(model)
catch {
  case e: Exception => ""
}
```

Now when an exception is caught, the try block takes on the value of the empty string.

Step Two: A Controller First Cut

Now let's take a look at transforming our controller code into Scala. In Java we used the Controller interface and the TemplateController class. Individual controllers were implemented by subclassing TemplateController.

In Scala, we rely on function composition just like we did with our views by passing in a doRequest() function when we create a Controller:

ScalaExamples/src/main/scala/com/mblinn/mbfpp/oo/tinyweb/steptwo/Controller.scala
```
package com.mblinn.mbfpp.oo.tinyweb.steptwo

import com.mblinn.oo.tinyweb.HttpRequest
import com.mblinn.oo.tinyweb.HttpResponse
import com.mblinn.oo.tinyweb.ControllerException
import com.mblinn.oo.tinyweb.RenderingException

trait Controller {
  def handleRequest(httpRequest: HttpRequest): HttpResponse
}

class FunctionController(view: View, doRequest: (HttpRequest) =>
  Map[String, List[String]] ) extends Controller {

  def handleRequest(request: HttpRequest): HttpResponse = {
    var responseCode = 200;
    var responseBody = "";

    try {
      val model = doRequest(request)
      responseBody = view.render(model)
    } catch {
      case e: ControllerException =>
        responseCode = e.getStatusCode()
      case e: RenderingException =>
        responseCode = 500
        responseBody = "Exception while rendering."
```

```
    case e: Exception =>
      responseCode = 500
  }

  HttpResponse.Builder.newBuilder()
                .body(responseBody).responseCode(responseCode).build()
  }
}
```

This code should look fairly similar to our view code. This is a fairly literal translation of Java into Scala, but it's not terribly functional because we're using the try-catch as a statement to set the values of responseCode and responseBody.

We're also reusing our Java HttpRequest and HttpResponse. Scala provides a more concise way to create these data-carrying classes, called *case classes*. Using the try-catch as an expression, as well as using case classes, can help cut down on our code significantly.

We'll make both of these changes in our next transformation.

Immutable HttpRequest and HttpResponse

Let's start by switching over to case classes instead of using the Builder pattern. It's as simple as the code below:

ScalaExamples/src/main/scala/com/mblinn/mbfpp/oo/tinyweb/stepthree/HttpData.scala
```
package com.mblinn.mbfpp.oo.tinyweb.stepthree

case class HttpRequest(headers: Map[String, String], body: String, path: String)
case class HttpResponse(body: String, responseCode: Integer)
```

We can create new HttpRequest and HttpResponse objects easily, as the following REPL output shows:

```
scala> val request = HttpRequest(Map("X-Test" -> "Value"), "requestBody", "/test")
request: com.mblinn.mbfpp.oo.tinyweb.stepfour.HttpRequest =
      HttpRequest(Map(X-Test -> Value),requestBody,/test)

scala> val response = HttpResponse("requestBody", 200)
response: com.mblinn.mbfpp.oo.tinyweb.stepfour.HttpResponse =
      HttpResponse(requestBody,200)
```

At first glance, this might seem similar to using a Java class with constructor arguments, except that we don't need to use the new keyword. However, in Pattern 4, *Replacing Builder for Immutable Object*, on page 62, we dig deeper and see how Scala's ability to provide default arguments in a constructor, the natural immutability of case classes, and the ability to easily create a new instance of a case class from an existing instance lets them satisfy the intent of the Builder pattern.

Let's take a look at our second change. Since a try-catch block in Scala has a value, we can use it as an expression rather than as a statement. This might seem a bit odd at first, but the upshot is that we can use the fact that Scala's try-catch is an expression to simply have the try-catch block take on the value of the HttpResponse we're returning. The code to do so is below:

ScalaExamples/src/main/scala/com/mblinn/mbfpp/oo/tinyweb/stepthree/Controller.scala

```scala
package com.mblinn.mbfpp.oo.tinyweb.stepthree
import com.mblinn.oo.tinyweb.ControllerException
import com.mblinn.oo.tinyweb.RenderingException

trait Controller {
  def handleRequest(httpRequest: HttpRequest): HttpResponse
}
class FunctionController(view: View, doRequest: (HttpRequest) =>
  Map[String, List[String]] ) extends Controller {
  def handleRequest(request: HttpRequest): HttpResponse =
    try {
      val model = doRequest(request)
      val responseBody = view.render(model)
      HttpResponse(responseBody, 200)
    } catch {
      case e: ControllerException =>
        HttpResponse("", e.getStatusCode)
      case e: RenderingException =>
        HttpResponse("Exception while rendering.", 500)
      case e: Exception =>
        HttpResponse("", 500)
    }
}
```

This style of programming has a couple of benefits. First, we've eliminated a couple of extraneous variables, responseCode and responseBody. Second, we've reduced the number of lines of code a programmer needs to scan to understand which HttpResponse we're returning from the entire method to a single line.

Rather than tracing the values of responseCode and responseBody from the top of the method through the try block and finally into the HttpResponse, we only need to look at the appropriate piece of the try block to understand the final value of the HttpResponse. These changes combine to give us code that's more readable and concise.

Tying It Together

Now let's add in the class that ties it all together, TinyWeb. Like its Java counterpart, TinyWeb is instantiated with a map of Controllers and a map of filters. Unlike Java, we don't define a class for filter; we simply use a list of higher-order functions!

Also like the Java version, the Scala TinyWeb has a single method, handleRequest(), which takes in an HttpRequest. Instead of returning an HttpResponse directly, we return an Option[HttpResponse], which gives us a clean way of handling the case when we can't find a controller for a particular request. The code for the Scala TinyWeb is below:

```
ScalaExamples/src/main/scala/com/mblinn/mbfpp/oo/tinyweb/stepfour/Tinyweb.scala
package com.mblinn.mbfpp.oo.tinyweb.stepfour
class TinyWeb(controllers: Map[String, Controller],
    filters: List[(HttpRequest) => HttpRequest]) {

  def handleRequest(httpRequest: HttpRequest): Option[HttpResponse] = {
    val composedFilter = filters.reverse.reduceLeft(
        (composed, next) => composed compose next)
    val filteredRequest = composedFilter(httpRequest)
    val controllerOption = controllers.get(filteredRequest.path)
    controllerOption map { controller => controller.handleRequest(filteredRequest) }
  }
}
```

Let's take a look at it in greater detail starting with the class definition.

```
class TinyWeb(controllers: Map[String, Controller],
    filters: List[(HttpRequest) => HttpRequest]) {
        «classBody»
}
```

Here we're defining a class that takes two constructor arguments, a map of controllers and a list of filters. Note the type of the filters argument, List[(HttpRequest) => HttpRequest]. This says that filters is a list of functions from HttpRequest to HttpRequest.

Next up, let's look at the signature of the handleRequest() method:

```
def handleRequest(httpRequest: HttpRequest): Option[HttpResponse] = {
        «functionBody»
}
```

As advertised, we're returning an Option[HttpResponse] instead of an HttpResponse. The Option type is a container type with two subtypes, Some and None. If we've got a value to store in it, we can store it in an instance of Some; otherwise we use None to indicate that we've got no real value. We'll cover Option in greater detail in Pattern 8, *Replacing Null Object*, on page 99.

Now that we've seen the TinyWeb framework, let's take a look at it in action. We'll use the same example from the Java section, returning a list of friendly greetings. However, since it's Scala, we can poke at our example in the REPL as we go. Let's get started with our view code.

Using Scala TinyWeb

Let's take a look at using our Scala TinyWeb framework.

We'll start by creating a FunctionView and the rendering function we'll compose into it. The following code creates this function, which we'll name greetingViewRenderer(), and the FunctionView that goes along with it:

ScalaExamples/src/main/scala/com/mblinn/mbfpp/oo/tinyweb/example/Example.scala
```scala
def greetingViewRenderer(model: Map[String, List[String]]) =
  "<h1>Friendly Greetings:%s".format(
      model
      getOrElse("greetings", List[String]())
      map(renderGreeting)
      mkString ", ")

private def renderGreeting(greeting: String) =
  "<h2>%s</h2>".format(greeting)


def greetingView = new FunctionView(greetingViewRenderer)
```

We're using a couple of new bits of Scala here. First, we introduce the map() method, which lets us map a function over all the elements in a sequence and returns a new sequence. Second, we're using a bit of syntactic sugar that Scala provides that allows us to treat any method with a single argument as an infix operator. The object on the left side of the operator is treated as the receiver of the method call, and the object on the right is the argument.

This bit of syntax means that we can omit the familiar dot syntax when working in Scala. For instance, the two usages of map() below are equivalent:

```scala
scala> val greetings = List("Hi!", "Hola", "Aloha")
greetings: List[java.lang.String]

scala> greetings.map(renderGreeting)
res0: List[String] = List(<h2>Hi!</h2>, <h2>Hola</h2>, <h2>Aloha</h2>)

scala> greetings map renderGreeting
res1: List[String] = List(<h2>Hi!</h2>, <h2>Hola</h2>, <h2>Aloha</h2>)
```

Now let's take a look at our controller code. Here we create the handleGreetingRequest() function to pass into our Controller. As a helper, we use makeGreeting(), which takes in a name and generates a random friendly greeting.

Inside of handleGreetingRequest() we create a list of names by splitting the request body, which returns an array like in Java, converting that array into a Scala list and mapping the makeGreeting() method over it. We then use that list as the value for the "greetings" key in our model map:

Scala Functions and Methods

Since Scala is a hybrid language, it's got both functions and methods. Methods are defined using the def keyword, as we do in the following code snippet:

```
scala> def addOneMethod(num: Int) = num + 1
addOneMethod: (num: Int)Int
```

We can create a function and name it by using Scala's anonymous function syntax, assigning the resulting function to a val, like we do in this code snippet:

```
scala> val addOneFunction = (num: Int) => num + 1
addOneFunction: Int => Int = <function1>
```

We can almost always use methods as higher-order functions. For instance, here we pass both the method and the function version of addOne() into map().

```
scala> val someInts = List(1, 2, 3)
someInts: List[Int] = List(1, 2, 3)

scala> someInts map addOneMethod
res1: List[Int] = List(2, 3, 4)

scala> someInts map addOneFunction
res2: List[Int] = List(2, 3, 4)
```

Since method definitions have a cleaner syntax, we use them when we need to define a function, rather than using the function syntax. When we need to manually convert a method into a function, we can do so with the underscore operator, as we do in the following REPL session:

```
scala> addOneMethod _
res3: Int => Int = <function1>
```

The need to do this is very rare, though; for the most part Scala is smart enough to do the conversion automatically.

ScalaExamples/src/main/scala/com/mblinn/mbfpp/oo/tinyweb/example/Example.scala

```
def handleGreetingRequest(request: HttpRequest) =
  Map("greetings" -> request.body.split(",").toList.map(makeGreeting))

private def random = new Random()
private def greetings = Vector("Hello", "Greetings", "Salutations", "Hola")
private def makeGreeting(name: String) =
  "%s, %s".format(greetings(random.nextInt(greetings.size)), name)

def greetingController = new FunctionController(greetingView, handleGreetingRequest)
```

Finally, let's take a look at our logging filter. This function simply writes the path that it finds in the passed-in HttpRequest to the console and then returns the path unmodified:

ScalaExamples/src/main/scala/com/mblinn/mbfpp/oo/tinyweb/example/Example.scala

```
private def loggingFilter(request: HttpRequest) = {
  println("In Logging Filter - request for path: %s".format(request.path))
  request
}
```

To finish up the example, we need to create an instance of TinyWeb with the controller, the view, and the filter we defined earlier, and we need to create a test HttpResponse:

ScalaExamples/src/main/scala/com/mblinn/mbfpp/oo/tinyweb/example/Example.scala

```
def tinyweb = new TinyWeb(
    Map("/greeting" -> greetingController),
    List(loggingFilter))
def testHttpRequest = HttpRequest(
    body="Mike,Joe,John,Steve",
    path="/greeting")
```

We can now run the test request through TinyWeb's handleRequest() method in the REPL and view the corresponding HttpResponse:

```
scala> tinyweb.handleRequest(testHttpRequest)
In Logging Filter - request for path: /greeting
res0: Option[com.mblinn.mbfpp.oo.tinyweb.stepfour.HttpResponse] =
Some(HttpResponse(<h1>Friendly Greetings:<h2>Mike</h2>, <h2>Nam</h2>, <h2>John</h2>,
200))
```

That wraps up our Scala version of TinyWeb. We've made a few changes to the style that we used in our Java version. First, we replaced most of our iterative code with code that's more declarative. Second, we've replaced our bulky builders with Scala's case classes, which give us a built-in way to handle immutable data. Finally, we've replaced our use of Functional Interface with plain old functions.

Taken together, these small changes save us quite a bit of code and give us a solution that's shorter and easier to read. Next up, we'll take a look at TinyWeb in Clojure.

2.4 TinyWeb in Clojure

Now let's take TinyWeb and translate it into Clojure. This is going to be a bigger leap than the translation from Java to Scala, so we'll take it slowly.

The most obvious difference between Clojure and Java is the syntax. It's very different than the C-inspired syntax found in most modern programming languages. This isn't incidental: the syntax enables one of Clojure's most powerful features, *macros*, which we'll cover in Pattern 21, *Domain-Specific Language*, on page 218.

A Gentle Introduction to Clojure

For now let's just have a gentle introduction. Clojure uses *prefix syntax*, which just means that the function name comes before the function arguments in a function call. Here we call the count function to get the size of a vector, one of Clojure's immutable data structures:

```
=> (count [1 2 3 4])
4
```

Like Scala, Clojure has excellent interoperability with existing Java code. Calling a method on a Java class looks almost exactly like calling a Clojure function; you just need to prepend the method name with a period and put it before the class instance rather than after. For instance, this is how we call the length() method on an instance of a Java String:

```
=> (.length "Clojure")
7
```

Instead of organizing Clojure code into objects and methods in Java or into objects, methods, and functions in Scala, Clojure code is organized into functions and namespaces. Our Clojure version of TinyWeb is based on models, views, controllers, and filters, just like the Java and Scala versions; however, these components will take quite a different form.

Our views, controllers, and filter codes are simply functions, and our models are maps. To tie everything together, we use a function named TinyWeb, which takes in all our components and returns a function that takes in an HTTP request, runs it through the filters, and then routes it to the proper controller and view.

Controllers in Clojure

Let's start our look at the Clojure code with the controllers. Below, we implement a simple controller that takes the body of an incoming HTTP request and uses it to set a name in a model. For this first iteration, we'll use the same HttpRequest as our Java code. We'll change it to be more idiomatic Clojure later on:

ClojureExamples/src/mbfpp/oo/tinyweb/stepone.clj

```
(ns mbfpp.oo.tinyweb.stepone
  (:import (com.mblinn.oo.tinyweb HttpRequest HttpRequest$Builder)))
(defn test-controller [http-request]
  {:name (.getBody http-request)})
(def test-builder (HttpRequest$Builder/newBuilder))
(def test-http-request (.. test-builder (body "Mike") (path "/say-hello") build))
(defn test-controller-with-map [http-request]
  {:name (http-request :body)})
```

Let's take a look at this code piece by piece, starting with the namespace declaration.

ClojureExamples/src/mbfpp/oo/tinyweb/stepone.clj
```
(ns mbfpp.oo.tinyweb.stepone
  (:import (com.mblinn.oo.tinyweb HttpRequest HttpRequest$Builder)))
```

Here we define a namespace called mbfpp.oo.tinyweb.stepone. A namespace is simply a collection of functions that form a library that can be imported in full or in part by another namespace.

As part of the definition, we import a couple of Java classes, HttpRequest and HttpRequest$Builder. The second one might look a little strange, but it's just the full name for the static inner Builder class we created as part of our HttpRequest. Clojure doesn't have any special syntax for referring to static inner classes, so we need to use the full class name.

The keyword :import is an example of a Clojure keyword. A keyword is just an identifier that provides very fast equality checks and is always prepended with a colon. Here we're using the :import keyword to indicate what classes should be imported into the namespace we've just declared, but keywords have many other uses. They're often used as keys in a map, for instance.

Now let's take a look at our controller, which takes an HttpRequest from the original Java solution and produces a Clojure map as a model:

ClojureExamples/src/mbfpp/oo/tinyweb/stepone.clj
```
(defn test-controller [http-request]
  {:name (.getBody http-request)})
```

Here we call the getBody() method on the HttpRequest to get the body of the request, and we use it to create a map with a single key-value pair. The key is the keyword :name, and the value is the String body of the HttpRequest.

Before we move on, let's look at Clojure maps in greater detail. In Clojure, it's common to use maps to pass around data. The syntax for creating a map in Clojure is to enclose key-value pairs inside curly braces. For instance, here we're creating a map with two key-value pairs. The first key is the keyword :name, and the value is the String "Mike". The second is the keyword :sex, and the value is another keyword, :male>:

```
=> {:name "Mike" :sex :male}
{:name "Mike" :sex :male}
```

Maps in Clojure are functions of their keys. This means that we can call a map as a function, passing a key we expect to be in the map, and the map will return the value. If the key isn't in the map, nil is returned, as the code below shows:

```
=> (def test-map {:name "Mike"})
#'mbfpp.oo.tinyweb.stepone/test-map
=> (test-map :name)
"Mike"
=> (test-map :orange)
nil
```

Keywords in Clojure are also functions. When they are passed a map, they will look themselves up in it, as in the following snippet, which shows the most common way to look up a value from a map:

```
=> (def test-map {:name "Mike"})
#'mbfpp.oo.tinyweb.stepone/test-map
=> (:name test-map)
"Mike"
=> (:orange test-map)
nil
```

Now let's create some test data. Below, we create an HttpRequest$Builder and use it to create a new HttpRequest:

ClojureExamples/src/mbfpp/oo/tinyweb/stepone.clj
```
(def test-builder (HttpRequest$Builder/newBuilder))
(def test-http-request (.. test-builder (body "Mike") (path "/say-hello") build))
```

This code features two more Clojure/Java interop features. First, the forward slash lets us call a static method or reference a static variable on a class. So the snippet (HttpRequest$Builder/newBuilder) is calling the newBuilder() method on the HttpRequest$Builder class. As another example, we can use this syntax to parse an integer from a String using the parseInt() method on the Integer class:

```
=> (Integer/parseInt "42")
42
```

Next up is the .. macro, a handy interop feature that makes calling a series of methods on a Java object easy. It works by taking the first argument to .. and threading it through calls to the rest of the arguments.

The snippet (.. test-builder (body "Mike") (path "/say-hello") build) first calls the body() method on test-builder with the argument "Mike". Then it takes that result and calls the path() method on it with the argument "say-hello" and finally calls build() on that result to return an instance of HttpResult.

Here's another example of using the .. macro to uppercase the string "mike" and then take the first character of it:

```
=> (.. "mike" toUpperCase (substring 0 1))
"M"
```

Maps for Data

Now that we've seen some basic Clojure and Clojure/Java interoperability, let's take the next step in transforming TinyWeb into Clojure. Here we'll change test-controller so that the HTTP request it takes in is also a map, just like the model it returns. We'll also introduce a view function and a render function that's responsible for calling views. The code for our next iteration is below:

ClojureExamples/src/mbfpp/oo/tinyweb/steptwo.clj
```clojure
(ns mbfpp.oo.tinyweb.steptwo
  (:import (com.mblinn.oo.tinyweb RenderingException)))

(defn test-controller [http-request]
  {:name (http-request :body)})

(defn test-view [model]
  (str "<h1>Hello, " (model :name) "</h1>"))

(defn- render [view model]
  (try
    (view model)
    (catch Exception e (throw (RenderingException. e)))))
```

Let's take a closer look at the pieces, starting with our new test-controller. As we can see in the code, we're expecting http-request to be a map with a :body key that represents the body of the HTTP request. We're pulling out the value for that key and putting it into a new map that represents our model:

ClojureExamples/src/mbfpp/oo/tinyweb/steptwo.clj
```clojure
(defn test-controller [http-request]
  {:name (http-request :body)})
```

We can explore how test-controller works very easily using the REPL. All we need to do is define a test-http-request map and pass it into test-controller, which we do in this REPL output:

```clojure
=> (def test-http-request {:body "Mike" :path "/say-hello" :headers {}})
#'mbfpp.oo.tinyweb.steptwo/test-http-request
=> (test-controller test-http-request)
{:name "Mike"}
```

Views in Clojure

Now that we've got our controller approach buttoned up, let's take a look at some view code. Just like our controllers, views will be functions. They take a map that represents the model they operate on and return a String that represents the output of the view.

Here is some code for a simple test-view that just wraps a name in an <h1> tag:

ClojureExamples/src/mbfpp/oo/tinyweb/steptwo.clj

```
(defn test-view [model]
  (str "<h1>Hello, " (model :name) "</h1>"))
```

Again, we can try this out simply in the REPL by defining a test model and passing it into the function:

```
=> (def test-model {:name "Mike"})
#'mbfpp.oo.tinyweb.steptwo/test-model
=> (test-view test-model)
"<h1>Hello, Mike</h1>"
```

We need one more piece to finish our view-handling code. In Java, we used Pattern 7, *Replacing Strategy*, on page 92, to ensure that any exceptions in view-handling code were properly wrapped up in a RenderingException. In Clojure we'll do something similar with higher-order functions. As the code below shows, all we need to do is pass our view function into the render function, which takes care of running the view and wrapping any exceptions:

ClojureExamples/src/mbfpp/oo/tinyweb/steptwo.clj

```
(defn- render [view model]
  (try
    (view model)
    (catch Exception e (throw (RenderingException. e)))))
```

Tying It All Together

Now that we've got a handle on our Clojure views and controllers, let's finish up the example by adding in filters and the glue code that ties everything together. We'll do this final step in a namespace called core. This is the standard core namespace that Clojure's build tool Leiningen creates when you create a new project, so it's become the de facto standard core namespace for Clojure projects.

To do this, we'll add an execute-request function, which is responsible for executing an http-request. The function takes an http-request and a request handler. The request handler is simply a map containing the controller and view that should be used to handle the request.

We'll also need apply-filters, which takes an http-request, applies a series of filters to it, and returns a new http-request. Finally, we'll need the tinyweb function.

The tinyweb function is what ties everything together. It takes in two arguments: a map of request handlers keyed off the path each should handle and a sequence of filters. It then returns a function that takes an http-request, applies the sequence of filters to it, routes it to the appropriate request handler, and returns the result.

Here is the code for the full Clojure TinyWeb library:

ClojureExamples/src/mbfpp/oo/tinyweb/core.clj
```
(ns mbfpp.oo.tinyweb.core
  (:require [clojure.string :as str])
  (:import (com.mblinn.oo.tinyweb RenderingException ControllerException)))
(defn- render [view model]
  (try
    (view model)
    (catch Exception e (throw (RenderingException. e)))))
(defn- execute-request [http-request handler]
  (let [controller (handler :controller)
        view (handler :view)]
    (try
      {:status-code 200
       :body
       (render
         view
         (controller http-request))}
      (catch ControllerException e {:status-code (.getStatusCode e) :body ""})
      (catch RenderingException e {:status-code  500
                                   :body "Exception while rendering"})
      (catch Exception e (.printStackTrace e) {:status-code 500 :body ""}))))
(defn- apply-filters [filters http-request]
  (let [composed-filter (reduce comp (reverse filters))]
    (composed-filter http-request)))
(defn tinyweb [request-handlers filters]
  (fn [http-request]
    (let [filtered-request (apply-filters filters http-request)
          path (http-request :path)
          handler (request-handlers path)]
      (execute-request filtered-request handler))))
```

The render method is unchanged from the previous iteration, so let's start by examining the execute-request function. We have already defined the function in the full Clojure TinyWeb library. To start picking apart the execute-request function, let's first define some test data in the REPL. We'll need the test-controller and test-view we defined in our last iteration to create a test request handler, which we do below:

```
=> (defn test-controller [http-request]
{:name (http-request :body)})

(defn test-view [model]
(str "<h1>Hello, " (model :name) "</h1>"))
#'mbfpp.oo.tinyweb.core/test-controller
#'mbfpp.oo.tinyweb.core/test-view
=> (def test-request-handler {:controller test-controller
                              :view test-view})
#'mbfpp.oo.tinyweb.core/test-request-handler
```

Now we just need our test-http-request, and we can verify that execute-request runs the passed-in request-handler on the passed-in http-request, as we'd expect:

```
=> (def test-http-request {:body "Mike" :path "/say-hello" :headers {}})
#'mbfpp.oo.tinyweb.steptwo/test-http-request
=> (execute-request test-http-request test-request-handler)
{:status-code 200, :body "<h1>Hello, Mike</h1>"}
```

Let's look at the pieces of execute-request in more detail by trying them out in the REPL, starting with the let statement that picks the controller and view out of request-handler, which we've outlined here:

```
(let [controller (handler :controller)
      view (handler :view)]
«let-body»)
```

A let statement is how you assign local names in Clojure, somewhat like a local variable in Java. However, unlike a variable, the value these names refer to isn't meant to be changed. In the let statement above, we're picking the view and controller functions out of the request-handler map and naming them controller and view. We can then refer to them by those names inside the let statement.

Let's take a look at a simpler example of a let expression. Below, we use let to bind name to the String "Mike" and to bind greeting to the String "Hello". Then, inside the body of the let expression, we use them to create a greeting:

```
=> (let [name "Mike"
         greeting "Hello"]
     (str greeting ", " name))
"Hello, Mike"
```

Now that we've got let under our belts, let's take a look at the try expression, which we've repeated below. Much like in Scala, try is an expression with a value. If no exception is thrown, try takes on the value of the body of the expression itself; otherwise it takes on the value of a catch clause:

```
(try
  {:status-code 200
   :body
     (render
       view
       (controller http-request))}
(catch ControllerException e {:status-code (.getStatusCode e) :body ""})
(catch RenderingException e {:status-code  500
                              :body "Exception while rendering"})
(catch Exception e (.printStackTrace e) {:status-code 500 :body ""}))
```

If no exception is thrown, then the try expression takes the value of a map with two key-value pairs, which represents our HTTP response. The first key is the :status-code with a value of 200. The second is :body. Its value is computed by passing the http-request into the controller and then passing that result into the render function along with the view to be rendered.

We can see this in action using our test-view and test-controller below:

```
=> (render test-view (test-controller test-http-request))
"<h1>Hello, Mike</h1>"
```

Before we move on, let's take a bit of a closer look at Clojure's exception handling using a couple of simpler examples. Below, we see an example of a try expression where the body is just the String "hello, world", so the value of the whole expression is "hello, world":

```
=> (try
    "hello, world"
   (catch Exception e (.message e)))
"hello, world"
```

Here's a simple example of how try expressions work when things go wrong. In the body of the try expression below, we're throwing a RuntimeException with the message "It's broke!". In the catch branch, we're catching Exception and just pulling the message out of it, which then becomes the value of the catch branch and thus the value of the entire try expression:

```
=> (try
     (throw (RuntimeException. "It's broke!"))
   (catch Exception e (.getMessage e)))
"It's broke!"
```

Next up, let's take a look at how we apply our filters. We use an apply-filters function, which takes a sequence of filters and an HTTP request, composes them into a single filter, and then applies it to the HTTP request. The code is below:

```
(defn- apply-filters [filters http-request]
  (let [composed-filter (reduce comp filters)]
       (composed-filter http-request)))
```

We explore the comp function further as part of Pattern 16, *Function Builder*, on page 167.

To finish off our Clojure TinyWeb implementation, we need a function, tinyweb, to tie everything together. This function takes in a map of request handlers and a sequence of filters. It returns a function that takes an HTTP request, using apply-filters to apply all the filters to the request.

Then it picks the path out of the HTTP request, looks in the map of request handlers to find the appropriate handler, and uses execute-request to execute it. The following is the code for tinyweb:

```
(defn tinyweb [request-handlers filters]
  (fn [http-request]
    (let [filtered-request (apply-filters filters http-request)
      path (:path http-request)
      handler (request-handlers path)]
        (execute-request filtered-request handler))))
```

Using TinyWeb

Let's take a look at using the Clojure version of TinyWeb. First let's define a test HTTP request:

```
=> (def request {:path "/greeting" :body "Mike,Joe,John,Steve"})
#'mbfpp.oo.tinyweb.core/request
```

Now let's take a look at our controller code, which is just a simple function and works much like our Scala version:

ClojureExamples/src/mbfpp/oo/tinyweb/example.clj
```
(defn make-greeting [name]
  (let [greetings ["Hello" "Greetings" "Salutations" "Hola"]
        greeting-count (count greetings)]
    (str (greetings (rand-int greeting-count)) ", " name)))

(defn handle-greeting [http-request]
  {:greetings (map make-greeting (str/split (:body http-request) #","))})
```

Running our test request through it returns the appropriate model map, as seen below:

```
=> (handle-greeting request)
{:greetings ("Greetings, Mike" "Hola, Joe" "Hola, John" "Hola, Steve")}
```

Next up is our view code. This code renders the model into HTML. It's just another function that takes in the appropriate model map and returns a string:

ClojureExamples/src/mbfpp/oo/tinyweb/example.clj
```
(defn render-greeting [greeting]
  (str "<h2>"greeting"</h2>"))

(defn greeting-view [model]
  (let [rendered-greetings (str/join " " (map render-greeting (:greetings model)))]
    (str "<h1>Friendly Greetings</h1> " rendered-greetings)))
```

If we run greeting-view over the output of handle-greeting, we get our rendered HTML:

```
=> (greeting-view (handle-greeting request))
"<h1>Friendly Greetings</h1>
<h2>Hola, Mike</h2>
<h2>Hello, Joe</h2>
<h2>Greetings, John</h2>
<h2>Salutations, Steve</h2>"
```

Next let's look at our logging-filter. This is just a simple function that logs out the path of the request before returning it:

ClojureExamples/src/mbfpp/oo/tinyweb/example.clj
```
(defn logging-filter [http-request]
  (println (str "In Logging Filter - request for path: " (:path http-request)))
  http-request)
```

Finally, we'll wire everything together into an instance of TinyWeb, as we do in the following code:

ClojureExamples/src/mbfpp/oo/tinyweb/example.clj
```
(def request-handlers
  {"/greeting" {:controller handle-greeting :view greeting-view}})
(def filters [logging-filter])
(def tinyweb-instance (tinyweb request-handlers filters))
```

If we run our test request through the instance of TinyWeb, it's filtered and processed as it should be:

```
=> (tinyweb-instance request)
In Logging Filter - request for path: /greeting
{:status-code 200,
:body "<h1>Friendly Greetings</h1>
<h2>Greetings, Mike</h2>
<h2>Greetings, Joe</h2>
<h2>Hello, John</h2>
<h2>Hola, Steve</h2>"}
```

That wraps up our look at TinyWeb! The code in this chapter has been kept simple; we've stuck to a minimal set of language features and omitted much error handling and many useful features. However, it does show how quite a few of the patterns we'll examine in this book fit together.

Throughout the remainder of the book, we'll take a closer look at these patterns and many others as we continue our journey through functional programming.

CHAPTER 3

Replacing Object-Oriented Patterns

3.1 Introduction

Object-oriented patterns are a staple of modern software engineering. In this chapter, we'll take a look at some of the most common ones and the problems they solve. Then we'll introduce more functional solutions that solve the same sorts of problems that the object-oriented patterns solve.

For each pattern that we introduce, we'll first look at it in Java. Then we'll look at a Scala approach that solves the same problems, and finally we'll wrap up with a look at a Clojure version that does as well.

Sometimes the Scala and Clojure replacements will be quite similar. For instance, the Scala and Clojure solutions in both Pattern 1, *Replacing Functional Interface*, on page 40, and Pattern 7, *Replacing Strategy*, on page 92, are largely the same. Other times the solutions we explore in these two languages will be quite different but still embody the same functional concept.

The solutions we look at in Pattern 4, *Replacing Builder for Immutable Object*, on page 62, for instance, are very different in Scala and Clojure. However, in both cases they show straightforward ways of working with immutable data.

By exploring both the similarities and the differences between Scala and Clojure, you should get a good feel for how each language approaches functional programming and how it differs from the traditional imperative style you may be used to.

Let's get started with our first pattern, Functional Interface!

Pattern 1

Replacing Functional Interface

Intent

To encapsulate a bit of program logic so that it can be passed around, stored in data structures, and generally treated like any other first-class construct

Overview

Functional Interface is a basic object-oriented design pattern. It consists of an interface with a single method with a name like run, execute, perform, apply, or some other generic verb. Implementations of Functional Interface perform a single well-defined action, as any method should.

Functional Interface lets us call an object as if it were a function, which lets us pass verbs around our program rather than nouns. This turns the traditional object-oriented view of the world on its head a bit. In the strict object-oriented view, objects, which are nouns, are king. Verbs, or methods, are second-class citizens, always attached to an object, doomed to a life of servitude to their noun overlords.

Also Known As

Function Object
Functoid
Functor

Functional Replacement

A strict view of object orientation makes some problems clumsier to solve. I've lost track of the number of times I've written five or six lines of boilerplate to wrap a single line of useful code into Runnable or Callable, two of Java's most popular instances of Functional Interface.

To simplify things, we can replace Functional Interface with plain functions. It might seem strange that we can replace an object with seemingly more primitive functions, but functions in functional programming are much more powerful than functions in C or methods in Java.

In functional languages, functions are *higher order*: they can be returned from functions and used as arguments to others. They are *first-class constructs*, which means that in addition to being higher order they can also be assigned to variables, put into data structures, and generally manipulated. They can be unnamed, or *anonymous functions*, which are extremely handy for small, one-off pieces of code. In fact, Functional Interface (as its name might suggest) is a pattern that in the object-oriented world approximates the behavior of the functions of the functional world.

We'll cover a couple of different flavors of a Functional Interface replacement in this section. The first replaces smaller instances of the pattern—say ones that take a few lines of code—with an anonymous function. This is similar to using an anonymous inner class to implement Functional Interface in Java and is covered in *Sample Code: Anonymous Functions*, on page 41.

The second covers instances of the pattern that span more than a few lines. In Java, we'd implement these using a named rather than an anonymous class; in the functional world we use a named function, as we do in *Sample Code: Named Functions*, on page 43.

Sample Code: Anonymous Functions

Our first example demonstrates anonymous functions and how we can use them to replace small instances of Functional Interface. One common situation where we'd do this is when we need to sort a collection differently than its *natural ordering*, the way it's commonly ordered.

To do so, we need to create a custom comparison so that the sorting algorithm knows which elements come first. In classic Java, we need to create a Comparator implemented as an anonymous class. In Scala and Clojure, we get right to the point by using an anonymous function. We'll take a look at a simple example of sorting differently than the natural ordering for an object: sorting a Person by first name rather than last.

Classic Java

In classic Java, we'll use a Functional Interface named Comparator to help with our sort. We'll implement it as an anonymous function, since it's only a tiny bit of code, and we'll pass it into the sorting function. The kernel of the solution is here:

JavaExamples/src/main/java/com/mblinn/mbfpp/oo/fi/PersonFirstNameSort.java
```
Collections.sort(people, new Comparator<Person>() {
        public int compare(Person p1, Person p2) {
                return p1.getFirstName().compareTo(p2.getFirstName());
        }
});
```

This works, but most of the code is extra syntax to wrap our one line of actual logic into an anonymous class. Let's see how anonymous functions can help clean this up.

In Scala

Let's take a look at how we'd solve the problem of sorting by first rather than last name in Scala. We'll use a case class to represent people, and we'll do away with the Functional Interface Comparator. In its place, we'll use a plain old function.

Creating an anonymous function in Scala uses the following syntax:

```
(arg1: Type1, arg2: Type2) => FunctionBody
```

For instance, the following REPL session creates an anonymous function that takes two integer arguments and adds them together.

```
scala> (int1: Int, int2: Int) => int1 + int2
res0: (Int, Int) => Int = <function2>
```

Now that we've got the basic syntax down, let's see how to use an anonymous function to solve our person-sorting problem. To do so we use a method in Scala's collections library, sortWith(). The sortWith() method takes a comparison function and uses it to help sort a collection, much like Collections.sort() takes a Comparator to do the same.

Let's start with the code for our Person case class:

ScalaExamples/src/main/scala/com/mblinn/mbfpp/oo/fi/PersonExample.scala
```
case class Person(firstName: String, lastName: String)
```

Here's a vector full of them to use for test data:

ScalaExamples/src/main/scala/com/mblinn/mbfpp/oo/fi/PersonExample.scala
```
val p1 = Person("Michael", "Bevilacqua")
val p2 = Person("Pedro", "Vasquez")
val p3 = Person("Robert", "Aarons")

val people = Vector(p3, p2, p1)
```

The sortWith() method expects its comparison function to return a Boolean value that tells it whether the first argument is higher than the second argument. Scala's comparison operators < and > work on strings, so we can use them for this purpose.

The following code demonstrates this approach. We can omit the type annotations for the function parameters. Scala is able to infer them from the sortWith() method:

ScalaExamples/src/main/scala/com/mblinn/mbfpp/oo/fi/PersonExample.scala
```
people.sortWith((p1, p2) => p1.firstName < p2.firstName)
```

Running this in Scala's REPL gets us the following output.

```
res1: scala.collection.immutable.Vector[...] =
      Vector(
             Person(Michael,Bevilacqua),
             Person(Pedro,Vasquez),
             Person(Robert,Aarons))
```

This is shorter and simpler than using an equivalent implementation of Functional Interface!

In Clojure

We define an anonymous function in Clojure using the fn special form, as the following code outline shows.

```
(fn [arg1 arg2] function-body)
```

Let's start by creating some test people. In Clojure, we won't define a class to carry around data; we'll use a humble map:

ClojureExamples/src/mbfpp/rso/person.clj
```
(def p1 {:first-name "Michael" :last-name "Bevilacqua"})
(def p2 {:first-name "Pedro" :last-name "Vasquez"})
(def p3 {:first-name "Robert" :last-name "Aarons"})

(def people [p3 p2 p1])
```

Now we create an anonymous ordering function and pass it into the sort function along with the people we want to sort, as the following code demonstrates:

```
=> (sort (fn [p1 p2] (compare (p1 :first-name) (p2 :first-name))) people)
({:last-name "Bevilacqua", :first-name "Michael"}
 {:last-name "Vasquez", :first-name "Pedro"}
 {:last-name "Aarons", :first-name "Robert"})
```

By eliminating the extra syntax we need in Java to wrap our ordering function in a Comparator, we write code that gets right to the point.

Sample Code: Named Functions

Let's expand our person-sorting problem a bit. We'll add a middle name to each person in our list and modify our unusual sorting algorithm to sort by first name, then last name if the first names are the same, and finally middle name if the last names are also the same.

This makes the comparison code long enough that we should no longer embed it in the code that's using it. In Java we move the code out of an anonymous inner class and into a named class. In Clojure and Scala, we move it into a named function.

Classic Java

Anonymous classes and functions are great when the logic they're wrapping is small, but when it grows larger it gets messy to embed. In classic Java, we move to using a named class, as is sketched out below:

```java
public class ComplicatedNameComparator implements Comparator<Person> {
    public int compare(Person p1, Person p2) {
        «complicatedSortLogic»
    }
}
```

With higher-order functions, we use a named function.

In Scala

We start off by expanding our Scala case class to have a middle name and by defining some test data:

ScalaExamples/src/main/scala/com/mblinn/mbfpp/oo/fi/PersonExpanded.scala
```scala
case class Person(firstName: String, middleName: String, lastName: String)
val p1 = Person("Aaron", "Jeffrey", "Smith")
val p2 = Person("Aaron", "Bailey", "Zanthar")
val p3 = Person("Brian", "Adams", "Smith")
val people = Vector(p1, p2, p3)
```

Now we create a named comparison function and pass it into sortWith(), as the following code demonstrates:

ScalaExamples/src/main/scala/com/mblinn/mbfpp/oo/fi/PersonExpanded.scala
```scala
def complicatedSort(p1: Person, p2: Person) =
  if (p1.firstName != p2.firstName)
    p1.firstName < p2.firstName
  else if (p1.lastName != p2.lastName)
    p1.lastName < p2.lastName
  else
    p1.middleName < p2.middleName
```

And voilà! We can easily sort our people using an arbitrarily named function:

```scala
scala> people.sortWith(complicatedSort)
res0: scala.collection.immutable.Vector[...] =
        Vector(
                Person(Aaron,Jeffrey,Smith),
                Person(Aaron,Bailey,Zanthar),
                Person(Brian,Adams,Smith))
```

In Clojure

The Clojure solution is quite similar to the Scala one. We'll need a named function that can compare people according to our more complex set of rules, and we'll need to add middle names to our people.

Here's the code for our complicated sort algorithm:

```
ClojureExamples/src/mbfpp/rso/person_expanded.clj
(defn complicated-sort [p1 p2]
  (let [first-name-compare (compare (p1 :first-name) (p2 :first-name))
        middle-name-compare (compare (p1 :middle-name) (p2 :middle-name))
        last-name-compare (compare (p1 :last-name) (p2 :last-name))]
    (cond
      (not (= 0 first-name-compare)) first-name-compare
      (not (= 0 last-name-compare)) last-name-compare
      :else middle-name-compare)))
```

Now we can call sort as before, but instead of passing in an anonymous function, we pass the named function complicated-sort:

```
ClojureExamples/src/mbfpp/rso/person_expanded.clj
(def p1 {:first-name "Aaron" :middle-name "Jeffrey" :last-name "Smith"})
(def p2 {:first-name "Aaron" :middle-name "Bailey" :last-name "Zanthar"})
(def p3 {:first-name "Brian" :middle-name "Adams" :last-name "Smith"})
(def people [p1 p2 p3])

=> (sort complicated-sort people)
({:middle-name "Jeffrey", :last-name "Smith", :first-name "Aaron"}
{:middle-name "Bailey", :last-name "Zanthar", :first-name "Aaron"}
{:middle-name "Adams", :last-name "Smith", :first-name "Brian"})
```

That's all there is to it.

Discussion

Functional Interface is a bit odd. It comes from Java's current insistence on turning everything into an object, a noun. This is like having to use a ShoePutterOnner, a DoorOpener, and a Runner just to go for a run! Replacing the pattern with higher-order functions helps us in several ways. The first is that it reduces the syntactic overhead of many common tasks, cruft you have to write in order to write the code you want to write.

For instance, the first Comparator we came across in this section required five lines of Java code (formatted properly) to convey just one line of actual computation:

```
new Comparator<Person>() {
    public int compare(Person left, Person right) {
        return left.getFirstName().compareTo(right.getFirstName());
    }
}
```

Compare that to a single line of Clojure.

```
(fn [left right] (compare (left :first-name) (right :first-name)))
```

More importantly, using higher-order functions gives us a consistent way of passing around small bits of computation. With Functional Interface, you need to look up the right interface for every little problem you want to solve and figure out how to use it. We've seen Comparator in this chapter and mentioned a few other common uses of the pattern. Hundreds of others exist in Java's standard libraries and other popular libraries, each as unique as a snowflake, but more annoyingly different than beautiful.

Functional Interface and its replacements in this chapter have some differences that don't touch on the core problem that it's meant to solve. Since Functional Interface is implemented with a class, it defines a type and can use common object-oriented features such as subclassing and polymorphism. Higher-order functions cannot. This is actually a strength of higher-order functions over Functional Interface: you don't need a new type for each type of Functional Interface when just the existing function types will do.

For Further Reading

Effective Java [Blo08]—Item 21: Use Function Objects to Represent Strategies

JSR 335: Lambda Expressions for the Java Programming Language [Goe12] [1]

Related Patterns

Pattern 3, *Replacing Command*, on page 54

Pattern 6, *Replacing Template Method*, on page 83

Pattern 7, *Replacing Strategy*, on page 92

Pattern 16, *Function Builder*, on page 167

---

1.   http://cr.openjdk.java.net/~briangoetz/lambda/lambda-state-4.html

Replacing State-Carrying Functional Interface

Intent

To encapsulate a bit of state along with program logic so it can be passed around, stored in data structures, and generally treated like any other first-class construct

Overview

In Pattern 1, *Replacing Functional Interface*, on page 40, we saw how to replace Functional Interface with higher-order functions, but the instances we looked at didn't carry around any program state. In this pattern, we'll take a look at how we can replace Functional Interface implementations that need state using a powerful construct called a *closure*.

Also Known As

Function Object
Functoid
Functor

Functional Replacement

Functions in the functional world are part of a powerful construct called a *closure*. A closure wraps up a function along with the state available to it when it was created. This means that a function can reference any variable that was in scope when the function was created at the time it's called. The programmer doesn't have to do anything special to create a closure; the compiler and runtime take care of it, and the closure simply captures all the state that it needs automatically.

In classic Java, we'd carry state around by creating fields on the class and by providing setters for them or setting them through a constructor. In the functional world, we can take advantage of closures to handle this without any extra machinery. Closures are a bit magical, so it's worth examining them in more detail before we move on.

A closure is composed of a function and the state that was available to that function when it was created. Let's see what this might look like pictorially, as shown in the figure.

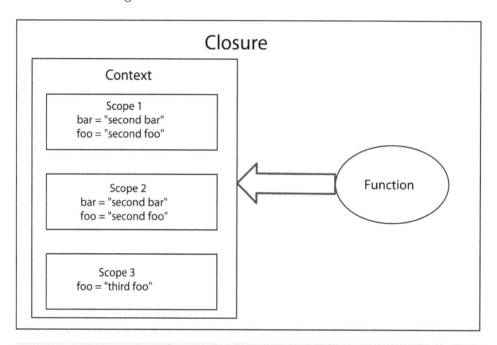

Figure 2—Structure of a Closure. A closure is a structure that consists of a function and its context at the time it was defined.

Here we can see that the closure has a function in it and a scope chain that lets it look up any variables that it needs to do its job. Translated into Clojure, it looks like this:

ClojureExamples/src/mbfpp/rso/closure_example.clj
```
(ns mbfpp.rso.closure-example)

; Scope 1 - Top Level
(def foo "first foo")
(def bar "first bar")
(def baz "first baz")

(defn make-printer [foo bar] ; Scope 2 - Function Arguments
  (fn []
    (let [foo "third foo"] ; Scope 3 - Let Statement
      (println foo)
      (println bar)
      (println baz))))
```

If we use this code to make a printer function and run it, it prints the foo, bar, and baz from the deepest scope that they're defined in, just as any experienced developer would expect:

```
=> (def a-printer (make-printer "second foo" "second bar"))
#'closure-example/a-printer
=> (a-printer)
third foo
second bar
first baz
nil
```

This may not seem surprising, but what if we took a-printer and passed it around our program, or stored it in a vector to retrieve and use later? It would still print the same values for foo, bar, and baz, which implies that those values stick around somewhere.

Behind the scenes, Clojure and Scala need to do an awful lot of magic to make that work. However, actually using a closure is as simple as declaring a function. I like to keep the previous figure in mind when working with closures because it's a good mental model of how they work.

Sample Code: Closure

To demonstrate closures, we'll take one last look at comparisons, with a bit of a twist. This time, we'll see how to create a comparison that's composed of a list of other comparisons, which means that we need someplace to store this list of comparisons.

In Java, we'll just pass them in as arguments to a constructor in our custom Comparator implementation, and we'll store them in a field. In Scala and Clojure, we can just use a closure. Let's jump into the Java example first.

Classic Java

In Java, we create a custom implementation of Comparator called ComposedComparator, with a single constructor that uses varargs to get an array of Comparators and stores them in a field.

When the compare() method on a ComposedComparator is called, it runs through all the comparators in its array and returns the first nonzero result. If all the results are zero, then it returns zero. An outline of this solution looks like so:

```
public class ComposedComparator<T> implements Comparator<T> {
        private Comparator<T>[] comparators;
        public ComposedComparator(Comparator<T>... comparators) {
                this.comparators = comparators;
        }
```

```
    @Override
    public int compare(T o1, T o2) {
      //Iterate through comparators and call each in turn.
    }

}
```

In the functional world, we can use closures instead of having to create new classes. Let's dig into how to do this in Scala.

In Scala

In Scala, we'll take advantage of closures to avoid explicitly keeping track of our list of comparisons in our composed comparison. Our Scala solution is centered around a higher-order function, makeComposedComparison(), which uses varargs to take in an array of comparison functions and returns a function that executes them in order.

One other difference between the Java and Scala solutions is in how we return the final result. In Java, we iterated through the list of Comparators, and as soon as we saw a nonzero comparison, we returned it.

We use map() to run our comparisons over our input. Then we search for the first one that's nonzero. If we don't find a nonzero value, all our comparisons were the same and we return zero. Here's the code for makeComposedComparison():

ScalaExamples/src/main/scala/com/mblinn/mbfpp/oo/fi/personexpanded/ClosureExample.scala
```scala
def makeComposedComparison(comparisons: (Person, Person) => Int*) =
  (p1: Person, p2: Person) =>
    comparisons.map(cmp => cmp(p1, p2)).find(_ != 0).getOrElse(0)
```

Now we can take two comparison functions and compose them together. In the code below, we define firstNameComparison() and lastNameComparison(), and then we compose them together into firstAndLastNameComparison():

ScalaExamples/src/main/scala/com/mblinn/mbfpp/oo/fi/personexpanded/ClosureExample.scala
```scala
def firstNameComparison(p1: Person, p2: Person) =
  p1.firstName.compareTo(p2.firstName)

def lastNameComparison(p1: Person, p2: Person) =
  p1.lastName.compareTo(p2.lastName)

val firstAndLastNameComparison = makeComposedComparison(
    firstNameComparison, lastNameComparison
)
```

Let's take a look at our composed comparison function in action by defining a couple of people and comparing them:

```
ScalaExamples/src/main/scala/com/mblinn/mbfpp/oo/fi/personexpanded/ClosureExample.scala
val p1 = Person("John", "", "Adams")
val p2 = Person("John", "Quincy", "Adams")

scala> firstAndLastNameComparison(p1, p2)
res0: Int = 0
```

One optimization we could make is to create a short-circuiting version of the composed comparison that stops running comparisons as soon as it comes across the first nonzero result. To do so, we could use a recursive function such as the ones we discuss in Pattern 12, *Tail Recursion*, on page 138, rather than the for comprehension we use here.

In Clojure

We'll wrap up the code samples for this pattern with a look at how we'd create composed comparisons in Clojure. We'll rely on a make-composed comparison, but it'll work a bit differently than the Scala version.

In Scala, we could use the find() method to find the first nonzero result; in Clojure we can use the some function. This is very different than Scala's Some type!

In Clojure, the some function takes a predicate and a sequence, and it returns the first value for which the predicate is true. Here we use Clojure's some and for to run all of the comparisons and select the correct final value:

```
ClojureExamples/src/mbfpp/rso/closure_comparison.clj
(defn make-composed-comparison [& comparisons]
  (fn [p1 p2]
    (let [results (for [comparison comparisons] (comparison p1 p2))
          first-non-zero-result
          (some (fn [result] (if (not (= 0 result)) result nil)) results)]
      (if (nil? first-non-zero-result)
        0
        first-non-zero-result))))
```

Now we can create our first-name-comparison and last-name-comparison and compose them together:

```
ClojureExamples/src/mbfpp/rso/closure_comparison.clj
(defn first-name-comparison [p1, p2]
  (compare (:first-name p1) (:first-name p2)))

(defn last-name-comparison [p1 p2]
  (compare (:last-name p1) (:last-name p2)))

(def first-and-last-name-comparison
  (make-composed-comparison
    first-name-comparison last-name-comparison))
```

And we'll use them to compare two people:

ClojureExamples/src/mbfpp/rso/closure_comparison.clj

```
(def p1 {:first-name "John" :middle-name "" :last-name "Adams"})
(def p2 {:first-name "John" :middle-name "Quincy" :last-name "Adams"})

=> (first-and-last-name-comparison p1 p2)
0
```

That wraps up our look at using closures to replace state-carrying Functional Interface implementations. Before we move on, let's discuss the relationship between closures and classes in a bit more detail.

Discussion

There's a joke about closures and classes: classes are a poor man's closure, and closures are a poor man's class. Besides demonstrating that functional programmers probably shouldn't go into standup comedy, this illustrates something interesting about the relationship between classes and closures.

In some ways, closures and classes are very similar. They can both carry around state and behavior. In others, they're quite different. Classes have a whole bunch of object-oriented machinery around them, they define types, they can be part of hierarchies, and so on. Closures are much simpler—they're just composed of a function and the context it was created in.

Having closures makes it much simpler to solve a whole host of common programming tasks, as we've seen in this section, which is why classes are a poor man's closure. However, classes have many programming features that closures don't, which is why closures are a poor man's class. Scala solves this problem by giving us both classes and closures, and Clojure solves it by deconstructing the good stuff from classes, such as polymorphism and type hierarchies, and giving it to programmers in other forms.

Having closures and higher-order functions can simplify many common patterns (Command, Template Method, and Strategy to name a few) to such an extent that they almost disappear. They're useful enough that closures and higher-order functions are one of the new major pieces of functionality in the upcoming Java 8 under the guise of JSR 335.

This is a big change to a mature language that absolutely has to be backwards-compatible, so it's not an easy task. It's not one that the stewards of Java undertook lightly; but because higher-order functions are such a big win, it was deemed important to include them. It's taken years of effort to specify and implement, but they're finally coming!

For Further Reading

Effective Java [Blo08]—Item 21: Use Function Objects to Represent Strategies

JSR 335: Lambda Expressions for the Java Programming Language [Goe12] [2]

Related Patterns

Pattern 3, *Replacing Command*, on page 54

Pattern 6, *Replacing Template Method*, on page 83

Pattern 7, *Replacing Strategy*, on page 92

Pattern 16, *Function Builder*, on page 167

---

2. http://cr.openjdk.java.net/~briangoetz/lambda/lambda-state-4.html

Pattern 3

Replacing Command

Intent

To turn a method invocation into an object and execute it in a central location so that we can keep track of invocations so they can be undone, logged, and so forth

Overview

Command encapsulates an action along with the information needed to perform it. Though it seems simple, the pattern has quite a few moving parts. In addition to the Command interface and its implementations, there's a client, which is responsible for creating the Command; an invoker, which is responsible for running it; and a receiver, on which the Command performs its action.

The invoker is worth talking about a little because it's often misunderstood. It helps to decouple the invocation of a method from the client asking for it to be invoked and gives us a central location in which all method invocations take place. This, combined with the fact that the invocation is represented by an object, lets us do handy things like log the method invocation so it can be undone or perhaps serialized to disk.

Figure 3, *Command Outline*, on page 55 sketches out how Command fits together.

A simple example is a logging Command. Here, the client is any class that needs to do logging and the receiver is a Logger instance. The invoker is the class that the client calls instead of calling the Logger directly.

Also Known As

Action

Functional Replacement

Command has a few moving parts, as does our functional replacement. The Command class itself is a Functional Interface that generally carries state, so we'll replace it with the closures we introduced in Pattern 2, *Replacing State-Carrying Functional Interface*, on page 47.

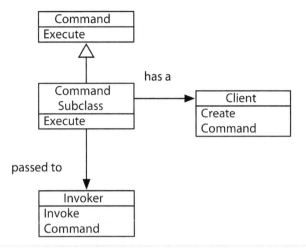

Figure 3—Command Outline. The outline of the Command pattern

Next we'll replace the invoker with a simple function responsible for executing commands, which I'll call the execution function. Just like the invoker, the execution function gives us a central place to control execution of our commands, so we can store or otherwise manipulate them as needed.

Finally, we'll create a *Function Builder* that's responsible for creating our commands so we can create them easily and consistently.

Sample Code: Cash Register

Let's look at how we'd implement a simple cash register with Command. Our cash register is very basic: it only handles whole dollars, and it contains a total amount of cash. Cash can only be added to the register.

We'll keep a log of transactions so that we can replay them. We'll take a look at how we'd do this with the traditional Command pattern first before moving on to the functional replacements in Scala and Clojure.

Classic Java

A Java implementation starts with defining a standard Command interface. This is an example of Pattern 1, *Replacing Functional Interface*, on page 40. We implement that interface with a Purchase class.

The receiver for our pattern is a CashRegister class. A Purchase will contain a reference to the CashRegister it should be executed against. To round out the pattern, we'll need an invoker, PurchaseInvoker, to actually execute our purchases.

A diagram of this implementation is below, and the full source can be found in this book's code samples.

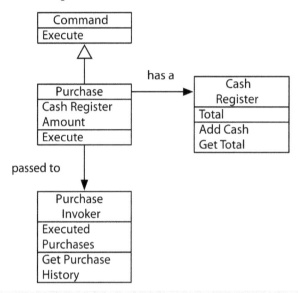

Figure 4—Cash Register Command. The structure of a cash register as a Command pattern in Java

Now that we've sketched out a Java implementation of the Command pattern, let's see how we can simplify it using functional programming.

In Scala

The cleanest replacement for Command in Scala takes advantage of Scala's hybrid nature. We'll retain a CashRegister class, just as in Java; however, instead of creating a Command interface and implementation, we'll simply use higher-order functions. Instead of creating a separate class to act as an invoker, we'll just create an execution function. Let's take a look at the code, starting with the CashRegister itself:

ScalaExamples/src/main/scala/com/mblinn/mbfpp/oo/command/register/Register.scala
```
class CashRegister(var total: Int) {
  def addCash(toAdd: Int) {
    total += toAdd
  }
}
```

Next we'll create the function makePurchase to create our purchase functions. It takes amount and register as arguments to add to it, and it returns a function that does the deed, as the following code shows:

```
ScalaExamples/src/main/scala/com/mblinn/mbfpp/oo/command/register/Register.scala
def makePurchase(register: CashRegister, amount: Int) = {
  () => {
    println("Purchase in amount: " + amount)
    register.addCash(amount)
  }
}
```

Finally, let's look at our execution function, executePurchase. It just adds the purchase function it was passed to a Vector to keep track of purchases we've made before executing it. Here's the code:

```
ScalaExamples/src/main/scala/com/mblinn/mbfpp/oo/command/register/Register.scala
var purchases: Vector[() => Unit] = Vector()
def executePurchase(purchase: () => Unit) = {
  purchases = purchases :+ purchase
  purchase()
}
```

What's That Var Doing in Here?

The code on page 57 has a mutable reference front and center.

```
var purchases: Vector[() => Unit] = Vector()
```

This might seem a bit odd in a book on functional programming. Shouldn't everything be immutable? It turns out that it's difficult, though not impossible, to model everything in a purely functional way. Keeping track of changing state is especially tricky.

Never fear though; all we're doing here is moving around a reference to a bit of immutable data. This gives us most of the benefits of immutability. For instance, we can safely create as many references to our original Vector without worrying about accidentally modifying the original, as the following code shows:

```
scala> var v1 = Vector("foo", "bar")
v1: scala.collection.immutable.Vector[String] = Vector(foo, bar)

scala> val v1Copy = v1
v1Copy: scala.collection.immutable.Vector[String] = Vector(foo, bar)

scala> v1 = v1 :+ "baz"
v1: scala.collection.immutable.Vector[String] = Vector(foo, bar, baz)

scala> v1Copy
res0: scala.collection.immutable.Vector[String] = Vector(foo, bar)
```

It's possible to program in a purely functional way using the excellent Scalaz library,[a] but this book focuses on a more pragmatic form of functional programming.

---

a.   https://code.google.com/p/scalaz/

Here's our solution in action:

```
scala> val register = new CashRegister(0)
register: CashRegister = CashRegister@53f7eb48

scala> val purchaseOne = makePurchase(register, 100)
purchaseOne: () => Unit = <function0>

scala> val purchaseTwo = makePurchase(register, 50)
purchaseTwo: () => Unit = <function0>

scala> executePurchase(purchaseOne)
Purchase in amount: 100

scala> executePurchase(purchaseTwo)
Purchase in amount: 50
```

As you can see, the register now has the correct total:

```
scala> register.total
res2: Int = 150
```

If we reset the register to 0, we can replay the purchases using the ones we've stored in the purchases vector:

```
scala> register.total = 0
register.total: Int = 0

scala> for(purchase <- purchases){ purchase.apply() }
Purchase in amount: 100
Purchase in amount: 50

scala> register.total
res4: Int = 150
```

Compared to the Java version, the Scala version is quite a bit more straightforward. No need for a Command, Purchase, or separate invoker class when you've got higher-order functions.

In Clojure

The overall structure of the Clojure solution is similar to the Scala one. We'll use higher-order functions for our commands, and we'll use an execution function to execute them. The biggest difference between the Scala and Clojure solutions is the cash register itself. Since Clojure doesn't have object-oriented features, we can't create a CashRegister class.

Instead, we'll simply use a Clojure atom to keep track of the cash in the register. To do so, we'll create a make-cash-register function that returns a fresh atom to represent a new register and an add-cash function that takes a register and an amount. We'll also create a reset function to reset our register to zero.

Here's the code for the Clojure cash register:

ClojureExamples/src/mbfpp/oo/command/cash_register.clj
```
(defn make-cash-register []
  (let [register (atom 0)]
    (set-validator! register (fn [new-total] (>= new-total 0)))
    register))

(defn add-cash [register to-add]
  (swap! register + to-add))

(defn reset [register]
  (swap! register (fn [oldval] 0)))
```

We can create an empty register:

```
=> (def register (make-cash-register))
#'mblinn.oo.command.ex1.version-one/register
```

And we'll add some cash:

```
=> (add-cash register 100)
100
```

Now that we've got our cash register, let's take a look at how we'll create commands. Remember, in Java this would require us to implement a Command interface. In Clojure we just use a function to represent purchases.

To create them, we'll use the make-purchase function, which takes a register and an amount and returns a function that adds amount to register. Here's the code:

ClojureExamples/src/mbfpp/oo/command/cash_register.clj
```
(defn make-purchase [register amount]
  (fn []
    (println (str "Purchase in amount: " amount))
    (add-cash register amount)))
```

Here we use it to create a couple of purchases:

```
=> (def register (make-cash-register))
#'mblinn.oo.command.ex1.version-one/register
=> @register
0
=> (def purchase-1 (make-purchase register 100))
#'mblinn.oo.command.ex1.version-one/purchase-1
=> (def purchase-2 (make-purchase register 50))
#'mblinn.oo.command.ex1.version-one/purchase-2
```

And here we run them:

```
=> (purchase-1)
Purchase in amount: 100
100
=> (purchase-2)
Purchase in amount: 50
150
```

To finish off the example, we'll need our execution function, execute-purchase, which stores the purchase commands before executing them. We'll use an atom, purchases, wrapped around a vector for that purpose. Here's the code we need:

ClojureExamples/src/mbfpp/oo/command/cash_register.clj
```
(def purchases (atom []))
(defn execute-purchase [purchase]
  (swap! purchases conj purchase)
  (purchase))
```

Now we can use execute-purchase to execute the purchases we defined above so that this time we'll get them in our purchase history. We'll reset register first:

```
=> (execute-purchase purchase-1)
Purchase in amount: 100
100
=> (execute-purchase purchase-2)
Purchase in amount: 50
150
```

Now if we reset the register again, we can run through our purchase history to rerun the purchases:

```
=> (reset register)
0
=> (doseq [purchase @purchases] (purchase))
Purchase in amount: 100
Purchase in amount: 50
nil
=> @register
150
```

That's our Clojure solution! One tidbit I find interesting about it is how we modeled our cash register without using objects by simply representing it as a bit of data and functions that operate on it. This is, of course, common in the functional world and it often leads to simpler code and smaller systems.

This might seem limiting to the experienced object-oriented programmer at first; for instance, what if you need polymorphism or hierarchies of types? Never fear, Clojure provides the programmer with all of the good stuff from the object-oriented world, just in a different, more decoupled form. For instance, Clojure has a way to create ad hoc hierarchies, and its multimethods and protocols give us polymorphism. We'll look at some of these tools in more detail in Pattern 10, *Replacing Visitor*, on page 113.

Discussion

I've found that Command, though it's used everywhere, is one of the most misunderstood patterns of *Design Patterns: Elements of Reusable Object-Oriented Software [GHJV95]*. People often conflate the Command interface with the Command pattern. The Command interface is only a small part of the overall pattern and is itself an example of Pattern 1, *Replacing Functional Interface*, on page 40. This isn't to say that the way it's commonly used is wrong, but it is often different than the way the Gang of Four describes it, which can lead to some confusion when talking about the pattern.

The examples in this section implemented a replacement for the full pattern in all its invoker/receiver/client glory, but it's easy enough to strip out unneeded parts. For example, if we didn't need our command to be able to work with multiple registers, we wouldn't have to pass a register into makePurchase.

For Further Reading

Design Patterns: Elements of Reusable Object-Oriented Software [GHJV95] —*Command*

Related Patterns

Pattern 1, *Replacing Functional Interface*, on page 40

Pattern 4

Replacing Builder for Immutable Object

Intent

To create an immutable object using a friendly syntax for setting attributes—because we can't modify them, we also need a simple way to create new objects based off existing ones, setting some attributes to new values as we do so.

Overview

In this section, we'll cover Fluent Builder, which produces immutable objects. This is a common pattern; Java's standard library uses it with its StringBuilder and StringBuffer. Many other common libraries use it as well, such as Google's protocol buffers framework.

Using immutable objects are a good practice that's often ignored in Java, where the most common way of carrying data around is in a class with a bunch of getters and setters. This forces data objects to be mutable, and mutability is the source of many common bugs.

The easiest way to get an immutable object in Java is just to create a class that takes in all the data it needs as constructor arguments. Unfortunately, as item 2 of the excellent *Effective Java [Blo08]* points out, this leads to a couple of problems when dealing with a large number of attributes.

The first is that a Java class with many constructor arguments is very hard to use. A programmer has to remember which argument goes in which position, rather than referring to it by name. The second is that there is no easy way to create defaults for attributes, since values for all attributes need to be passed into the constructor.

One way to get around that is to create several different constructors that take only a subset of values and that default the ones not passed in. For large objects this leads to the *telescoping constructor problem*, where a class has to implement many different constructors and pass values from the smaller constructors to ever larger ones.

The builder pattern we examine in this section, outlined in *Effective Java [Blo08]*, solves both of these problems at the cost of quite a bit of code.

Functional Replacement

The techniques used to replace these two patterns in Scala and Clojure are quite different, but both share the very important property that they make it extremely simple to create immutable objects. Let's take a look at Scala first.

In Scala

We'll cover three different techniques for creating immutable data structures in Scala, each of which has its own strengths and weaknesses.

First we'll cover creating a Scala class that consists entirely of immutable values. We'll show how to use named parameters and default values to achieve something very much like the fluent builder for an immutable object in Java but with a fraction of the overhead.

Next we'll take a look at Scala's case classes. Case classes are meant specifically for carrying data, so they come with some handy methods already implemented, like equals() and hashCode(), and they can be used with Scala's pattern matching to easily pick them apart. This makes them a good default choice for many data carrying uses.

In both instances, we'll use Scala's constructors to create objects. Scala's constructors don't have the same shortcomings as the Java constructors we discussed earlier, because we can name parameters and provide them with default values. This helps us avoid both the telescoping constructor problem and the problems involved with passing in several unnamed parameters and trying to remember which is which.

Finally, we'll cover Scala tuples, which are a handy way to pass around small composite data structures without having to create a new class.

In Clojure

Clojure has support for creating new classes, but it's intended to be used only for interop with Java. Instead, it's common to use plain old immutable maps to model aggregate data.

Coming from the Java world, it might seem like this is a bad idea, but since Clojure has excellent support for working with maps, it's actually very convenient. Using maps to model data allows us the full power of Clojure's sequence library in manipulating that data, which is a very powerful.

Many libraries rely on inspecting data objects to perform operations on their data, such as XStream, which serializes data objects to XML, or Hibernate, which can generate SQL queries using them. To do this sort of programming in Java, you need to use the reflection library. With Clojure, you can just use simple map operations.

The second way to model data in Clojure is to use a record. A record exposes a map-like interface; so you can still use the full power of Clojure's sequence library on it, but records have a few advantages over maps.

First, records are generally more performant. In addition, records define a type that can participate in Clojure's polymorphism. To use the old object-oriented chestnut, it allows us to define a make-noise that will bark when passed a dog and meow when passed a cat. In addition, records let us constrain the attributes that we can put into a data structure.

Generally, a good way to work in Clojure is to start off modeling your data using maps and then switch to records when you need the additional speed, you need to use polymorphism, or you just want to constrain the names of the attributes you're handling.

Sample Code: Immutable Data

In this section we'll take a look at how to represent data in Java using a builder for immutable objects. Then we'll take a look at three ways of replacing them in Clojure: regular classes with immutable attributes, case classes, and tuples. Finally, we'll take a look at two ways of replacing them in Clojure: plain old maps and records.

Classic Java

In classic Java, we can use a fluent builder to create an immutable object using nice syntax. To solve our problem, we create an ImmutablePerson that only has getters for its attributes. Nested inside of that class, we create a Builder class, which lets us construct an ImmutablePerson.

When we want to create an ImmutablePerson, we don't construct it directly; we create a new Builder, set the attributes we want to set, and then call build() to get an ImmutablePerson. This is outlined below:

```
public class ImmutablePerson {

    private final String firstName;
    // more attributes

    public String getFirstName() {
        return firstName;
    }
    // more getters
```

```java
        private ImmutablePerson(Builder builder) {
                firstName = builder.firstName;
                // set more attributes
        }

        public static class Builder {
                private String firstName;
                // more attributes

                public Builder firstName(String firstName) {
                        this.firstName = firstName;
                        return this;
                }
                // more setters
                public ImmutablePerson build() {
                        return new ImmutablePerson(this);
                }
        }
        public static Builder newBuilder() {
                return new Builder();
        }
}
```

The downside is that we've got a whole lot of code for such a basic task. Passing around aggregate data is one of the most basic things we do as programmers, so languages should give us a better way to do it. Thankfully, both Scala and Clojure do. Let's take a look, starting with Scala.

In Scala

We'll take a look at three different ways of representing immutable data in Scala: immutable classes, case classes, and tuples. Immutable classes are plain classes that only contain immutable attributes; case classes are a special kind of class intended to work with Scala's pattern matching; and tuples are immutable data structures that let us group data together without defining a new class.

Immutable Classes

Let's start by looking at the Scala way to produce immutable objects. All we need to do is define a class that defines some vals as constructor arguments, which will cause the passed-in values to be assigned to public vals. Here's the code for this solution:

ScalaExamples/src/main/scala/com/mblinn/mbfpp/oo/javabean/Person.scala
```scala
class Person(
    val firstName: String,
    val middleName: String,
    val lastName: String)
```

Now we can create a Person using the constructor parameters positionally:

```scala
scala> val p1 = new Person("John", "Quincy", "Adams")
p1: Person = Person@83d2eb1
```

Or we can use them as named parameters:

```scala
scala> val p2 = new Person(firstName="John", middleName="Quincy", lastName="Adams")
p2: Person = Person@33d6798
```

We can add a default value for parameters, which lets us omit them when using the named parameter form. Here we're adding a default empty middle name:

ScalaExamples/src/main/scala/com/mblinn/mbfpp/oo/javabean/Person.scala
```scala
class PersonWithDefault(
    val firstName: String,
    val middleName: String = "",
    val lastName: String)
```

This lets us handle people who may not have a middle name:

```scala
scala> val p3 = new PersonWithDefault(firstName="John", lastName="Adams")
p3: PersonWithDefault = PersonWithDefault@6d0984e0
```

This gives us a simple way of creating immutable objects in Scala, but it does have a few shortcomings. If we want object equality, hash codes, or a nice representation when printed, we need to implement it ourselves. Case classes give us all this out of the box and are designed to participate in Scala's pattern matching. They can't, however, be extended, so they're not suitable for all purposes.

Case Classes

A case class is defined using case class, as shown below:

ScalaExamples/src/main/scala/com/mblinn/mbfpp/oo/javabean/Person.scala
```scala
case class PersonCaseClass(
    firstName: String,
    middleName: String = "",
    lastName: String)
```

Now we can create a PersonCaseClass in the same ways we'd create a normal class, except we don't have to use the new operator. Here we create one using named parameters and by omitting the middle name:

```scala
scala> val p = PersonCaseClass(firstName="John", lastName="Adams")
p: PersonCaseClass = PersonCaseClass(John,,Adams)
```

Notice how the case class prints as PersonCaseClass(John,,Adams), and we didn't have to implement a toString(). We also get equals() and hashCode() for free with case classes. Here, we test-drive equality:

```
scala> val p2 = PersonCaseClass(firstName="John", lastName="Adams")
p2: PersonCaseClass = PersonCaseClass(John,,Adams)

scala> p.equals(p2)
res1: Boolean = true

scala> val p3 = PersonCaseClass(
       firstName="John",
       middleName="Quincy",
       lastName="Adams")
p3: PersonCaseClass = PersonCaseClass(John,Quincy,Adams)

scala> p2.equals(p3)
res2: Boolean = false
```

Case classes are immutable, so we can't modify them, but we can get the same effect by using the copy() method to create a new case class based on an existing one, as we do in the following REPL session:

```
scala> val p2 = p.copy(middleName="Quincy")
p2: com.mblinn.mbfpp.oo.javabean.PersonCaseClass =
       PersonCaseClass(John,Quincy,Adams)
```

Finally, case classes can be used with Scala's pattern matching. Here we use a pattern match to pick apart the sixth American president:

```
scala> p3 match {
    | case PersonCaseClass(firstName, middleName, lastName) => {
    |     "First: %s - Middle: %s - Last: %s".format(
                                firstName, middleName, lastName)
    | }}
res0: String = First: John - Middle: Quincy - Last: Adams
```

There's one final common way to represent data in Scala: tuples. Tuples let us represent a fixed-size record, but they don't create a new type as classes and case classes do. They're handy for explorative development; you can use them to model your data during early phases when you're not sure what it looks like and then switch to classes or case classes later. Let's take a look at how they work.

Tuples

To create a tuple, you enclose the values that it contains inside of parentheses, like so:

```
scala> def p = ("John", "Adams")
p: (java.lang.String, java.lang.String)
```

To get values back out, reference them by position, as we do below:

```
scala> p._1
res0: java.lang.String = John

scala> p._2
res1: java.lang.String = Adams
```

Finally, tuples can be easily used in pattern matching, just like case classes:

```
scala> p match {
     | case (firstName, lastName) => {
     |     println("First name is: " + firstName)
     |     println("Last name is: " + lastName)
     | }}
First name is: John
Last name is: Adams
```

That covers the three main ways of working with immutable data in Scala.

Plain old immutable classes are handy when you've got more attributes than the twenty-two that a case class can handle, though this might suggest that it's time to refine your data model or that your data objects need to have some methods on them.

Case classes are useful when you want their built-in equals(), hashCode(), and toString, or when you need to work with pattern matching. Finally, tuples are great for explorative development; you can use them to simply model your data before switching to classes or case classes.

In Clojure

We'll take a look at two ways to represent immutable data in Clojure. The first is simply storing it in a map, and the second uses a record. Maps are the humble data structure that we all know and love; records are a bit different. They allow us to define a data type and constrain the attributes that they contain, but they still give us a map-like interface.

Maps

Let's start by taking a look at the simpler of the two options: using an immutable map. All we need to do is create a map with keywords for keys and our data as values, as we do below:

ClojureExamples/src/mbfpp/oo/javabean/person.clj
```
(def p
  {:first-name "John"
   :middle-name "Quincy"
   :last-name "Adams"})
```

We can get at attributes as we would with any map:

```
=> (p :first-name)
"John"
=> (get p :first-name)
"John"
```

One benefit that may not be so obvious is that we can use the full set of operations that maps support, including the ones that treat maps as sequences. For instance, if we wanted to uppercase all the parts of a name, we could do it with the following code:

```
=> (into {} (for [[k, v] p] [k (.toUpperCase v)]))
{:middle-name "QUINCY", :last-name "ADAMS", :first-name "JOHN"}
```

In order to do something similar with objects and getters, we'd need to call all the appropriate getters. That means we've taken a solution to a general problem, the problem of capitalizing all the attributes in a data structure full of strings, and reduced its generality to only capitalize the attributes of a particular type, which in turn means we need to reimplement that solution for every type of object.

Using immutable maps as one of the primary ways to carry data around has a few other advantages. Creating them uses simple syntax, so you have no constraints on the attributes you can add to them. This makes them great for exploratory programming.

This flexibility has some downsides. Clojure maps aren't as efficient as simple Java classes, and once you've got your data model more fleshed out, it may help to constrain the attributes you're dealing with.

Most importantly, however, using plain maps makes it awkward for maps to be used with polymorphism, because using a map doesn't define a new type. Let's take a look at another Clojure feature that solves these problems but still presents a map-like interface.

Records

To demonstrate records, let's borrow an old object-oriented example: creating cats and dogs. To create our Cat and Dog types, we use the code below:

ClojureExamples/src/mbfpp/oo/javabean/catsanddogslivingtogether.clj
```
(defrecord Cat [color name])

(defrecord Dog [color name])
```

We can treat them as maps so that we get the full power mentioned above:

Awkward, Not Impossible

Earlier I said it was awkward to use maps when you want type-based polymorphism. This is true, but Clojure is flexible enough that it's merely awkward, not impossible. We could encode the type in the map itself and use Clojure multimethods, as the code below shows:

ClojureExamples/src/mbfpp/oo/javabean/sidebar.clj
```
(def cat {:type :cat
          :color "Calico"
          :name "Fuzzy McBootings"})

(def dog {:type :dog
          :color "Brown"
          :name "Brown Dog"})

(defmulti make-noise (fn [animal] (:type animal)))
(defmethod make-noise :cat [cat] (println (str (:name cat)) "meows!"))
(defmethod make-noise :dog [dog] (println (str (:name dog)) "barks!"))
```

In general, if you want polymorphism on types, it's best to just use a protocol and save multimethods for fancier polymorphism, when you need the full power that comes with being able to define your own dispatch function.

```
=> (def cat (Cat. "Calico" "Fuzzy McBootings"))
#'mbfpp.oo.javabean.catsanddogslivingtogether/cat
=> (def dog (Dog. "Brown" "Brown Dog"))
#'mbfpp.oo.javabean.catsanddogslivingtogether/dog
=> (:name cat)
"Fuzzy McBootings"
=> (:name dog)
"Brown Dog"
```

And they can easily participate in polymorphism using Clojure's protocols. Here we define a protocol that has a single function, make-noise, and we create a NoisyCat and NoisyDog to take advantage of it:

ClojureExamples/src/mbfpp/oo/javabean/catsanddogslivingtogether.clj
```
(defprotocol NoiseMaker
  (make-noise [this]))

(defrecord NoisyCat [color name]
  NoiseMaker
  (make-noise [this] (str (:name this) " meows!")))

(defrecord NoisyDog [color name]
  NoiseMaker
  (make-noise [this] (str (:name this) " barks!")))

=> (def noisy-cat (NoisyCat. "Calico" "Fuzzy McBootings"))
#'mbfpp.oo.javabean.catsanddogslivingtogether/noisy-cat
```

```
=> (def noisy-dog (NoisyDog. "Brown" "Brown Dog"))
#'mbfpp.oo.javabean.catsanddogslivingtogether/noisy-dog
=> (make-noise noisy-cat)
"Fuzzy McBootingsmeows!"
=> (make-noise noisy-dog)
"Brown Dogbarks!"
```

Those are the two main ways to carry data around in Clojure. The first, plain old maps, is a good place to start. Once you've got your data model more nailed down, or if you want to take advantage of Clojure's protocol polymorphism, you can switch over to a record.

Discussion

There's a basic tension between locking down your data structures and keeping them flexible. Keeping them flexible helps during development time, while your data model is in flux, but locking them down can help to bring bugs to the surface earlier, which is important once your code is in production. This is mirrored somewhat in the wider technical world with some of the debate surrounding traditional relational databases, which impose a strict schema, and some of the newer nonrelational ones, which have no schemas or have more relaxed schemas, with both sides claiming their approach is better.

In reality, both approaches are useful, depending on the situation. Clojure and Scala give us the best of both worlds here by letting us keep our data structures flexible in the beginning (using maps in Clojure and tuples in Scala) and letting us lock them down as we understand our data better (using records in Clojure and classes or case classes in Scala).

For Further Reading

Effective Java [Blo08]—Item 2: Consider a Builder When Faced with Many Constructor Parameters

Effective Java [Blo08]—Item 15: Minimize Mutability

Related Patterns

Pattern 19, *Focused Mutability*, on page 196

Pattern 5

Replacing Iterator

Intent

To iterate through the elements of a sequence in order, without having to index into it

Overview

An iterator is an object that allows us to iterate over all the objects in a sequence. It does so by maintaining an internal bit of state that keeps track of where in the sequence the iterator is currently. At its simplest, an implementation of Iterator just requires a method that returns the next item in the sequence, with some sentinel value returned when there are no more items.

Most implementations have a separate method to check to see if the iterator has any more items, rather than using a sentinel to check. Some implementations of Iterator allow the underlying collection to be modified by removing the current item.

Also Known As

Cursor
Enumerator

Functional Replacement

In this section, we'll focus on replacing an iterator with a combination of higher-order functions and sequence comprehensions. A sequence comprehension is a clever technique that lets us take one sequence and transform it into another in some sophisticated ways. They're a bit like the map function on steroids.

Many basic uses of Iterator can be replaced by simple higher-order functions. For instance, summing a sequence can be done in Clojure using the reduce higher-order function.

Other, more complex uses can be handled with sequence comprehensions. Sequence comprehensions provide a concise way to create a new sequence from an old one, including the ability to filter out unwanted values.

In this section we'll stick with the uses of Iterator that can be expressed using a Java foreach loop. Other, less common uses can be replaced by the functional patterns Pattern 12, *Tail Recursion*, on page 138, and Pattern 13, *Mutual Recursion*, on page 146.

Sample Code: Higher-Order Functions

Let's start by looking at a grab bag of simple uses of Iterator that can be replaced with higher-order functions. First we'll look at identifying the vowels in a string, then we'll take a look at prepending a list of names with "Hello, ", and finally we'll sum up a sequence.

We'll look at these examples first in an imperative style written in Java, and then we'll collapse them into a more declarative style in Scala and Clojure.

Classic Java

To identify the set of vowels in a word, we iterate through the characters and check each character against the set of all vowels. If it's in the set of all vowels, we add it to vowelsInWord and return it. The code below, which assumes an isVowel() helper method, illustrates this solution:

JavaExamples/src/main/java/com/mblinn/oo/iterator/HigherOrderFunctions.java

```java
public static Set<Character> vowelsInWord(String word) {

    Set<Character> vowelsInWord = new HashSet<Character>();

    for (Character character : word.toLowerCase().toCharArray()) {
        if (isVowel(character)) {
            vowelsInWord.add(character);
        }
    }

    return vowelsInWord;
}
```

There's a higher-level pattern here: we're filtering some type of element out of a sequence. Here it's vowels in a string, but it could be odd numbers, people named "Michael" or anything else. We'll exploit this higher-order pattern in our functional replacement, which uses the filter function.

Next up, let's discuss prepending a list of names with the "Hello, " string. Here we take in a list of names, iterate through them, prepend "Hello, " to each name, and add it to a new list. Finally we return that list.

The code below demonstrates this approach:

```
JavaExamples/src/main/java/com/mblinn/oo/iterator/HigherOrderFunctions.java
public static List<String> prependHello(List<String> names) {
        List<String> prepended = new ArrayList<String>();
        for (String name : names) {
                prepended.add("Hello, " + name);
        }
        return prepended;
}
```

Again, there's a higher-level pattern hiding here. We're mapping an operation onto each item in a sequence, here prepending a word with the "Hello, " string. We'll see how we can use the higher-order map function to do so.

Let's examine one final problem: summing up a sequence of numbers. In classic Java, we'd compute a sum by iterating through a list and adding each number to a sum variable, as in the code below:

```
JavaExamples/src/main/java/com/mblinn/oo/iterator/HigherOrderFunctions.java
public static Integer sumSequence(List<Integer> sequence) {
        Integer sum = 0;
        for (Integer num : sequence) {
                sum += num;
        }
        return sum;
}
```

This type of iteration is an example of another pattern, performing an operation on a sequence to reduce it to a single value. We'll take advantage of that pattern in our functional replacement using the reduce function and a closely related function known as fold.

In Scala

Let's take a look at the first of our examples, returning the set of vowels in a word. In the functional world, this can be done in two steps: first we use filter() to filter all the vowels out of a word, and then we take that sequence and turn it into a set to remove any duplicates. To do our filtering, we can take advantage of the fact that Scala sets can be called as predicate functions. If the set contains the passed-in argument, it returns true; otherwise it returns false, as the code below shows:

```
scala>   val isVowel = Set('a', 'e', 'i', 'o', 'u')
isVowel: scala.collection.immutable.Set[Char] = Set(e, u, a, i, o)

scala> isVowel('a')
res0: Boolean = true

scala> isVowel('z')
res1: Boolean = false
```

Now we can use the isVowel() from above, along with filter() and toSet(), to get a set of vowels out of a string:

ScalaExamples/src/main/scala/com/mblinn/mbfpp/oo/iterator/HigherOrderFunctions.scala
```
val isVowel = Set('a', 'e', 'i', 'o', 'u')
def vowelsInWord(word: String) = word.filter(isVowel).toSet
```

Here we can see it in action, filtering vowels out of a string:

```
scala> vowelsInWord("onomotopeia")
res4: scala.collection.immutable.Set[Char] = Set(o, e, i, a)

scala> vowelsInWord("yak")
res5: scala.collection.immutable.Set[Char] = Set(a)
```

Our next example—prepending a list of names with "Hello, "—can be written by mapping a function that does the prepending over a sequence of strings. Here, mapping just means that the function is applied to each element in a sequence and that a new sequence is returned with the result. Here we map a function that prepends the string "Hello, " to each name in a sequence:

ScalaExamples/src/main/scala/com/mblinn/mbfpp/oo/iterator/HigherOrderFunctions.scala
```
def prependHello(names : Seq[String]) =
  names.map((name) => "Hello, " + name)
```

This does the job, as the code below shows. The Scala REPL inserts commas between elements in a sequence, so it's putting an additional comma between each of our greetings.

```
scala> prependHello(Vector("Mike", "John", "Joe"))
res0: Seq[java.lang.String] = Vector(Hello, Mike, Hello, John, Hello, Joe)
```

Finally, our last example—summing a sequence. We're using an operation, in this case, addition, to take a sequence and reduce it to a single value. In Scala, the simplest way to do this is to use the aptly named reduce method, which takes a single argument, a reducing function.

Here we create a reducing function that adds its arguments together, and we use it to sum a sequence:

ScalaExamples/src/main/scala/com/mblinn/mbfpp/oo/iterator/HigherOrderFunctions.scala
```
def sumSequence(sequence : Seq[Int]) =
  if(sequence.isEmpty) 0 else sequence.reduce((acc, curr) => acc + curr)
```

Let's take a look at it in action:

```
scala> sumSequence(Vector(1, 2, 3, 4, 5))
res0: Int = 15
```

That's it—no iterating, no mutation, just a simple higher-order function!

In Clojure

Our first example takes advantage of the same trick we used in Scala, where a set can be used as a predicate function. If the passed-in element is in the set, it's returned (remember, anything but false and nil is treated as true in Clojure); otherwise nil is returned.

Here we take advantage of that property of Clojure sets to define a vowel? predicate, which we can then use with filter to filter the vowels out of a sequence. We then use Clojure's set function to construct a new set from an existing sequence. The code below puts it all together:

ClojureExamples/src/mbfpp/oo/iterator/higher_order_functions.clj
```
(def vowel? #{\a \e \i \o \u})
(defn vowels-in-word [word]
  (set (filter vowel? word)))
```

Now we can use it to filter out sets of vowels from a word:

```
=> (vowels-in-word "onomotopeia")
#{\a \e \i \o}
=> (vowels-in-word "yak")
#{\a}
```

Next up is our friendly little hello prepender, prepend-hello. Just like the Scala example, we simply use map to map a function that prepends "Hello, " to each name in a sequence of names. Here's the code:

ClojureExamples/src/mbfpp/oo/iterator/higher_order_functions.clj
```
(defn prepend-hello [names]
  (map (fn [name] (str "Hello, " name)) names))
```

We can use this to generate a set of greetings:

```
=> (prepend-hello ["Mike" "John" "Joe"])
("Hello, Mike" "Hello, John" "Hello, Joe")
```

Finally, let's look at how we'd sum a sequence in Clojure. Just like Scala, we can use the reduce function, though we don't have to create our own function to add integers together as we did in Scala: we can just use Clojure's + function. Here's the code:

ClojureExamples/src/mbfpp/oo/iterator/higher_order_functions.clj
```
(defn sum-sequence [s]
  {:pre [(not (empty? s))]}
  (reduce + s))
```

And here we are using it to sum a sequence:

```
=> (sum-sequence [1 2 3 4 5])
15
```

Those unfamiliar with Clojure might find it a bit odd that the + is just another function that we can pass into reduce, but this is one of the strengths of Clojure and Lisps in general. Many things that would be special operators in other languages are just functions in Clojure, which lets us use them as arguments to higher-order functions like reduce.

One note on reduce in Clojure and Scala: While we were able to use them the same way here, they're actually somewhat different. Scala's reduce() operates over a sequence of some type, and it returns a single item of that type. For instance, reducing a List of Int will return a single Int.

Clojure, on the other hand, allows you to return anything at all from its reduce function, including another collection of some sort! This is more general (and often very handy), and Scala supports this more general idea of reduction under a different name, foldLeft().

It's usually easier and clearer in Scala to use reduce() when you truly are reducing a sequence of some type to a single instance of that type, and to use foldLeft() otherwise.

Sample Code: Sequence Comprehensions

Both Scala and Clojure support a very handy feature called a sequence comprehension. Sequence comprehensions give us a handy syntax that lets us do a few different things together. Much like the map function, sequence comprehensions let us transform one sequence into another. Sequence comprehensions also let us include a filtering step, and they provide a handy way to get at pieces of aggregate data, known as destructuring.

Let's take a look at how we'd use sequence comprehensions to solve a delicious little problem. We've got a list of people who asked to be notified when our new restaurant, The Lambda Bar and Grille, opens, and we'd like to send them an invitation to a grand-opening party.

We've got names and addresses, and we figure that people who live closest to the Lambda will be more likely to come, so we'd like to send invitations to them first. Finally, we'd like to filter out people who live so far away that we're entirely sure they won't come.

We decide to solve the problem like so: we'll put our customers into groups based on zip codes, and we'll send invitations to the groups of people in zip codes closest to our restaurant first. Additionally, we'll constrain ourselves to a small group of close zip codes.

Let's see how to solve this problem. We'll start, as always, with the iterative solution in Java, and then we'll move onto functional ones using sequence comprehensions in Scala and Clojure.

Classic Java

In Java, we create a Person and an Address in the customary JavaBean format, and we create a method, peopleByZip(), that takes in a list of people, filters out the ones who don't live close enough, and returns a map keyed off zip codes that contains lists of people in each zip code.

To do this we use a standard iterative solution with a couple of helper methods. The first, addPerson(), adds a person to a list, creating the list if it doesn't already exist, so we can handle the case where we come across the first person in a zip code.

The second, isCloseZip(), returns true if the zip is close enough to the Lambda Bar and Grille to get an invite to the party, and false otherwise. To keep the example small, we've hard-coded just a couple of zip codes in there, but since we've factored that check out into its own method, it would be easy to change it to pull from some dynamic data source of zip codes we care about.

To solve the problem, we just iterate through the list of people. For each person, we check to see if he or she has a close zip code, and if yes we add them to a map of lists of people keyed off of zip codes called closePeople. When we're all done with our iteration, we just return the map. This solution is outlined below:

JavaExamples/src/main/java/com/mblinn/oo/iterator/TheLambdaBarAndGrille.java
```java
public class TheLambdaBarAndGrille {

    public Map<Integer, List<String>> peopleByZip(List<Person> people) {
        Map<Integer, List<String>> closePeople =
                new HashMap<Integer, List<String>>();

        for (Person person : people) {
            Integer zipCode = person.getAddress().getZipCode();
            if (isCloseZip(zipCode)){
                List<String> peopleForZip =
                        closePeople.get(zipCode);
                closePeople.put(zipCode,
                        addPerson(peopleForZip, person));
            }
        }

        return closePeople;
    }
```

```
      private List<String> addPerson(List<String> people, Person person) {
             if (null == people)
                    people = new ArrayList<String>();
             people.add(person.getName());
             return people;
      }
      private Boolean isCloseZip(Integer zipCode) {
             return zipCode == 19123 || zipCode == 19103;
      }
}
```

This is a fairly simple data transformation, but it takes quite a bit of doing in an imperative style since we need to muck about with adding elements to the new list, and we don't have a first-class way of filtering elements from the existing one. The more declarative sequence comprehensions help us bump up the level of abstraction here. Now let's take a look at Scala's version.

In Scala

In Scala, we can use Scala's syntax for sequence comprehensions, the for comprehension, to generate our greetings in a cleaner way. We'll use case classes for our Person and Address, and we'll write a for comprehension that takes in a sequence of Person and produces a sequence of greetings.

For comprehensions are handy for this for a few reasons. The first is that we can use Scala's pattern-matching syntax inside of them, which gives us a concise way to pick apart a Person into a name and an address.

Second, for comprehensions let us include a filter directly in the comprehension itself, known as a guard, so we don't need a separate if statement to filter out people with the wrong zip codes. Finally, for comprehensions are intended to create new sequences, so there's no need to have a temporary list to accumulate new values into; we simply return the value of the comprehension.

With a for comprehension, we'll still use a helper isCloseZip() method, but we'll use it as part of a guard in the for comprehension itself, and we'll do away with the mutable list of greetings from the Java solution entirely, since the result we want is just the value of the for comprehension itself.

The code for the entire solution is below:

ScalaExamples/src/main/scala/com/mblinn/mbfpp/oo/iterator/TheLambdaBarAndGrille.scala
```
case class Person(name: String, address: Address)
case class Address(zip: Int)
def generateGreetings(people: Seq[Person]) =
  for (Person(name, address) <- people if isCloseZip(address.zip))
    yield "Hello, %s, and welcome to the Lambda Bar And Grille!".format(name)
def isCloseZip(zipCode: Int) = zipCode == 19123 || zipCode == 19103
```

One thing that may not be obvious when using for comprehensions is how to deal with situations when we absolutely need side effects. Since we're programming in the functional style this should be fairly rare. As we saw above, we don't need a mutable list to generate our list of greetings. One simple use of side effects that we still need in the functional world is printing to the console.

Here we've rewritten the example to just print the greetings to the console, rather than gathering them up into a sequence:

ScalaExamples/src/main/scala/com/mblinn/mbfpp/oo/iterator/TheLambdaBarAndGrille.scala
```
def printGreetings(people: Seq[Person]) =
  for (Person(name, address) <- people if isCloseZip(address.zip))
    println("Hello, %s, and welcome to the Lambda Bar And Grille!".format(name))
```

We've only touched on the basics of Scala's for comprehensions here; they're very powerful beasts. They can be used with multiple sequences and multiple guards at the same time, among several other features, but the ones that we've covered here let us handle the most common cases where we'd use the Iterator pattern.

In Clojure

Clojure also has built-in sequence comprehensions using the for macro. Just as in Scala, the primary point of a Clojure sequence comprehension is to take one sequence and transform it into another with built-in filtering. Clojure's sequence comprehensions also provide a handy way of pulling apart aggregate data with destructuring.

Since Clojure and Scala's sequence comprehensions are similar, at least for this basic usage, the structure of the solution looks pretty much the same. We've got a close-zip? function that takes advantage of Clojure's handy set-as-function feature, and a generate-greetings function that consists of a single for statement.

The for statement uses close-zip? to filter out people outside of the zips we care about, and then it generates a greeting to the people who are left. The code is below:

ClojureExamples/src/mbfpp/oo/iterator/lambda_bar_and_grille.clj
```
(def close-zip? #{19123 19103})

(defn generate-greetings [people]
  (for [{:keys [name address]} people :when (close-zip? (address :zip-code))]
    (str "Hello, " name ", and welcome to the Lambda Bar And Grille!")))
```

Clojure also has a way to use a sequence comprehension-like syntax for side effects, though Clojure separates it out into a doseq macro. Here we use doseq to print our list of greetings rather than gather them up:

ClojureExamples/src/mbfpp/oo/iterator/lambda_bar_and_grille.clj
```
(defn print-greetings [people]
  (doseq [{:keys [name address]} people :when (close-zip? (address :zip-code))]
    (println (str "Hello, " name ", and welcome to the Lambda Bar And Grille!"))))
```

Scala and Clojure's sequence comprehensions are similar in some respects, though not all. Scala's for statement is generally used more pervasively, and often in ways that seem surprising to the uninitiated. For instance, the for statement can be used in conjunction with Scala's option type to provide an elegant solution to problems that would require lots of null checks in Java, as we cover in Pattern 8, *Replacing Null Object*, on page 99.

Also, while Scala's pattern matching and Clojure's destructuring have some similarity, both allow us to pick apart aggregate data structures; pattern matching in Scala is less flexible than Clojure's destructuring. Destructuring lets us pick apart arbitrary maps and vectors, while Scala's pattern matching is confined to case classes and a few other constructs that are statically defined at compile time.

Discussion

One nonobvious difference between Iterator and the solutions we covered in this chapter is that Iterator is fundamentally imperative because it relies on mutable state. Every iterator has a bit of state inside it that keeps track of where the iterator is currently. This can get you in trouble if you start passing iterators around and part of your program unexpectedly advances the iterator, affecting another part.

In contrast, the solutions we've gone over in this chapter rely on transforming one immutable sequence into another. In fact, the sequence comprehensions we went over are both examples of a technique popularized by the highly functional language Haskell that is known as *monadic transformations*, which rely on a concept from category theory known as monads.

Explaining monads is a bit of a cottage industry among functional programmers and has inspired many a blog post attempting to explain monads by analogy to, among other things, burritos, elephants, writing desks, and Muppets. We won't put you through another such explanation here; it's not necessary to understand monads to use sequence comprehensions, and neither Scala nor Clojure particularly emphasize the monadic nature of their respective comprehensions.

At a very high level though, one of the things monads do is provide a way to program in a very functional style by transforming immutable data in a pipeline rather than relying on mutable state. Readers curious about monads should check out the excellent *Learn You a Haskell for Great Good! A Beginner's Guide [Lip11]*.

For Further Reading

Design Patterns: Elements of Reusable Object-Oriented Software [GHJV95]—Iterator

Java Standard Library[3]

Related Patterns

Pattern 12, *Tail Recursion*, on page 138

Pattern 13, *Mutual Recursion*, on page 146

Pattern 14, *Filter-Map-Reduce*, on page 155

---

3. http://docs.oracle.com/javase/7/docs/api/java/util/Iterator.html

Pattern 6

Replacing Template Method

Intent

To specify the outline of an algorithm, letting callers plug in some of the specifics

Overview

The Template Method pattern consists of an abstract class that defines some operation, or set of operations, in terms of abstract suboperations. Users of Template Method implement the abstract template class to provide implementation of the substeps. A template class looks like this code snippet:

```
public abstract class TemplateExample{

  public void anOperation(){
    subOperationOne();
    subOperationTwo();
  }

  protected abstract void subOperationOne();

  protected abstract void subOperationTwo();
}
```

To use it, extend the TemplateExample and implement the abstract suboperations.

For instance, to use Template Method for board games, create a Game template that defines the abstract set of steps it takes to play a board game (setUpBoard(), makeMove(), declareWinner(), and so on). To implement any particular board game, extend the abstract Game class and implement the substeps as appropriate for a particular game.

Functional Replacement

Our functional replacement for Template Method will satisfy its intent, which is to create a skeleton for some algorithm and let callers plug in the details. Instead of using classes to implement our suboperations, we'll use higher-order functions; and instead of relying on subclassing, we'll rely on function composition. We'll do so by passing the suboperations into a *Function Builder* and having it return a new function that does the full operation.

An outline of this approach in Scala looks like so:

```scala
def makeAnOperation(
  subOperationOne: () => Unit,
  subOperationTwo: () => Unit) =
  () => {
    subOperationOne()
    subOperationTwo()
  }
```

This lets us program more directly, since we no longer need to define suboperations and subclasses.

Sample Code: Grade Reporter

As an example, let's take a look at a template method that prints grade reports. It does this in two steps. The first takes a list of grades in numeric form and translates them into letter form, and the second formats and prints the report.

Since those two steps can be done in many different ways, we'll just specify the skeleton required to create a grade report, translate the grades first, and then format and print the report, and we'll leave it up to individual implementations to specify exactly how the grades are translated and the report is printed.

We'll also go over two such implementations. The first translates to the full letter grades A, B, C, D, and F and prints a simple histogram. The second adds plus and minus grades to some of the letters and prints a full list of grades.

Classic Java

A sketch of using Template Method to solve this problem in classic Java uses the following: a GradeReporterTemplate that has a single fully implemented method, reportGrades(), and two abstract methods, numToLetter() and printGradeReport().

The numToLetter() method specifies how to convert a single numeric grade into a letter grade, and printGradeReport() specifies how to format and print a grade report. Both methods must be implemented by users of the template. The class diagram provides an outline:

To get template implementations with different behaviors, the user of the Template class creates different subclasses with different implementations of numToLetter() and printGradeReport().

In Scala

Instead of relying on inheritance, the Scala replacement for Template Method uses *Function Builder* to compose together suboperations.

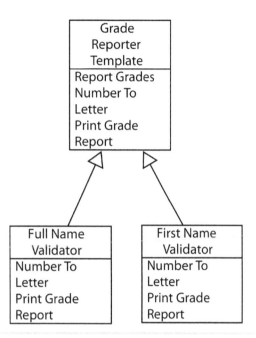

Figure 5—Grade Reporter Template. Using Template Method to report grades

The core of the solution is the function makeGradeReporter(), which takes a numToLetter() function to translate numeric grades to letter grades and a print-GradeReport() to print the report. The makeGradeReporter() function returns a new function that composes its input functions together.

We'll also need a couple of different implementations of the numToLetter() and printGradeReport() functions so we can see this solution in action.

Let's start by looking at makeGradeReporter(). It takes numToLetter() and printGradeReport() as arguments and produces a new function that takes a Seq[Double] to represent a list of grades. It then uses map() to convert each grade to a letter grade and passes the new list into printGradeReport(). Here's the code:

```scala
def makeGradeReporter(
  numToLetter: (Double) => String,
  printGradeReport: (Seq[String]) => Unit) = (grades: Seq[Double]) => {
    printGradeReport(grades.map(numToLetter))
}
```
ScalaExamples/src/main/scala/com/mblinn/mbfpp/oo/tm/GradeReporter.scala

Now let's take a look at the functions we'll need to convert to full letter grades and to print a histogram. The first, fullGradeConverter(), just uses a big if-else statement to do the grade conversion:

ScalaExamples/src/main/scala/com/mblinn/mbfpp/oo/tm/GradeReporter.scala
```scala
def fullGradeConverter(grade: Double) =
  if(grade <= 5.0 && grade > 4.0) "A"
  else if(grade <= 4.0 && grade > 3.0) "B"
  else if(grade <= 3.0 && grade > 2.0) "C"
  else if(grade <= 2.0 && grade > 0.0) "D"
  else if(grade == 0.0) "F"
  else "N/A"
```

The next, printHistogram(), is a bit more involved. It uses a method named groupBy() to group grades together into a Map, which it then turns into a list of tuples of counts using the map() method. Finally, it uses a for comprehension to print the histogram, as the code below shows:

ScalaExamples/src/main/scala/com/mblinn/mbfpp/oo/tm/GradeReporter.scala
```scala
def printHistogram(grades: Seq[String]) = {
  val grouped = grades.groupBy(identity)
  val counts = grouped.map((kv) => (kv._1, kv._2.size)).toSeq.sorted
  for(count <- counts) {
    val stars = "*" * count._2
    println("%s: %s".format(count._1, stars))
  }
}
```

Let's take a look at this sample line by line, starting with the first line of printHistogram()'s body:

```scala
val grouped = grades.groupBy(identity)
```

The groupBy() method takes in a function and uses it to group together all the elements of a sequence for which the function returns the same value. Here we pass in the identity function, which just returns whatever was passed in so we can group together all grades that are the same. The REPL output below shows us using this snippet to group together a vector of grades:

```scala
scala> val grades = Vector("A", "B", "A", "B", "B")
grades: scala.collection.immutable.Vector[java.lang.String] = Vector(A, B, A, B, B)

scala> val grouped = grades.groupBy(identity)
grouped: scala.collection.immutable.Map[...] =
      Map(A -> Vector(A, A), B -> Vector(B, B, B))
```

Next we take the map of grouped grades and use map() and toSeq() to turn it into a sequence of tuples, where the first element is the grade and the second element is the grade count. Then we sort that sequence. By default, Scala sorts sequences of tuples by their first element, so this gives us a sorted sequence of grade counts.

```scala
val counts = grouped.map((kv) => (kv._1, kv._2.size)).toSeq.sorted
```

The REPL output below shows us using this code snippet to get our sequence of grade counts:

```scala
scala> val counts = grouped.map((kv) => (kv._1, kv._2.size)).toSeq.sorted
counts: Seq[(java.lang.String, Int)] = ArrayBuffer((A,2), (B,3))
```

Finally we use a for comprehension over the sequence of tuples to print up a histogram of grades, as the snippet below shows:

```scala
for(count <- counts) {
  val stars = "*" * count._2

  println("%s: %s".format(count._1, stars))
}
```

This highlights an interesting use of Scala's * operator. It can be used to repeat a string, as the following REPL output demonstrates:

```scala
scala> "*" * 5
res0: String = *****
```

Now we just need to use makeGradeReporter() to compose our two functions together to create fullGradeReporter(), as the following code does:

ScalaExamples/src/main/scala/com/mblinn/mbfpp/oo/tm/GradeReporter.scala
```scala
val fullGradeReporter = makeGradeReporter(fullGradeConverter, printHistogram)
```

Then we can define some sample data and run fullGradeReporter() to print a histogram:

ScalaExamples/src/main/scala/com/mblinn/mbfpp/oo/tm/GradeReporter.scala
```scala
val sampleGrades = Vector(5.0, 4.0, 4.4, 2.2, 3.3, 3.5)
```

```scala
scala> fullGradeReporter(sampleGrades)
A: **
B: ***
C: *
```

Now if we want to change the way we do our grade conversion and report printing, we only need to create additional conversion and reporting functions. We can use makeGradeReporter() to compose them together.

Let's see how to rewrite the Template Method example that converts to plus/minus grades and prints up a full list of them. As before, we'll need two functions. The first is plusMinusGradeConverter(), for our grade conversions. The second is the printAllGrades() method, which just prints a simple list of converted grades.

Here's the code for our plusMinusGradeConverter() function:

ScalaExamples/src/main/scala/com/mblinn/mbfpp/oo/tm/GradeReporter.scala
```scala
def plusMinusGradeConverter(grade: Double) =
  if(grade <= 5.0 && grade > 4.7) "A"
    else if(grade <= 4.7 && grade > 4.3) "A-"
        else if(grade <= 4.3 && grade > 4.0) "B+"
        else if(grade <= 4.0 && grade > 3.7) "B"
        else if(grade <= 3.7 && grade > 3.3) "B-"
        else if(grade <= 3.3 && grade > 3.0) "C+"
        else if(grade <= 3.0 && grade > 2.7) "C"
        else if(grade <= 2.7 && grade > 2.3) "C-"
        else if(grade <= 2.3 && grade > 0.0) "D"
        else if(grade == 0.0) "F"
        else "N/A"
```

And here's the code for printAllGrades():

ScalaExamples/src/main/scala/com/mblinn/mbfpp/oo/tm/GradeReporter.scala
```scala
def printAllGrades(grades: Seq[String]) =
  for(grade <- grades) println("Grade is: " + grade)
```

Now we just need to compose them together using makeGradeReporter(), and we can use it to create a full grade report, as the code below shows:

ScalaExamples/src/main/scala/com/mblinn/mbfpp/oo/tm/GradeReporter.scala
```scala
val plusMinusGradeReporter =
  makeGradeReporter(plusMinusGradeConverter, printAllGrades)
```

```scala
scala> plusMinusGradeReporter(sampleGrades)
Grade is: A
Grade is: B
Grade is: A-
Grade is: D
Grade is: C+
Grade is: B-
```

That wraps up our replacement for Template Method in Scala. Next up, let's take a look at how things look in Clojure.

In Clojure

The Clojure replacement for Template Method is similar to the Scala one. Just as in Scala, we'll use Pattern 16, *Function Builder*, on page 167, named make-grade-reporter, to compose together a function that converts numeric grades to letter grades and a function that prints a report. The make-grade-reporter returns a function that maps num-to-letter over a sequence of numeric grades. Let's take a look at the code for it first:

ClojureExamples/src/mbfpp/oo/tm/grade_reporter.clj
```clojure
(defn make-grade-reporter [num-to-letter print-grade-report]
  (fn [grades]
    (print-grade-report (map num-to-letter grades))))
```

Converting a numeric grade to a full letter grade is just a matter of a simple cond expression, as we can see below:

ClojureExamples/src/mbfpp/oo/tm/grade_reporter.clj
```clojure
(defn full-grade-converter [grade]
  (cond
    (and (<= grade 5.0) (> grade 4.0)) "A"
    (and (<= grade 4.0) (> grade 3.0)) "B"
    (and (<= grade 3.0) (> grade 2.0)) "C"
    (and (<= grade 2.0) (> grade 0)) "D"
    (= grade 0) "F"
    :else "N/A"))
```

Printing a histogram can be done much the way we did it in Scala, using group-by to group grades together, mapping a function over the grouped grades to get counts, and then using a sequence comprehension to print the final histogram. Here's the code to print a histogram:

ClojureExamples/src/mbfpp/oo/tm/grade_reporter.clj
```clojure
(defn print-histogram [grades]
  (let [grouped (group-by identity grades)
        counts (sort (map
                       (fn [[grade grades]] [grade (count grades)])
                       grouped))]
    (doseq [[grade num] counts]
      (println (str grade ":" (apply str (repeat num "*")))))))
```

Now we can use make-grade-reporter to combine full-grade-converter and print-histogram into a new function, full-grade-reporter. The code to do so is below:

ClojureExamples/src/mbfpp/oo/tm/grade_reporter.clj
```clojure
(def full-grade-reporter (make-grade-reporter full-grade-converter print-histogram))
```

Here we're running it on some sample data:

ClojureExamples/src/mbfpp/oo/tm/grade_reporter.clj
```clojure
(def sample-grades [5.0 4.0 4.4 2.2 3.3 3.5])

=> (full-grade-reporter sample-grades)
A:**
B:***
C:*
```

To change the way we convert grades and print the report, we just create new functions to compose with make-grade-reporter. Let's create plus-minus-grade-converter and print-all-grades functions and then compose them together into a plus-minus-grade-reporter.

The plus-minus-grade-reporter function is straightforward; it's just a simple cond expression:

ClojureExamples/src/mbfpp/oo/tm/grade_reporter.clj

```clojure
(defn plus-minus-grade-converter [grade]
  (cond
    (and (<= grade 5.0) (> grade 4.7)) "A"
    (and (<= grade 4.7) (> grade 4.3)) "A-"
    (and (<= grade 4.3) (> grade 4.0)) "B+"
    (and (<= grade 4.0) (> grade 3.7)) "B"
    (and (<= grade 3.7) (> grade 3.3)) "B-"
    (and (<= grade 3.3) (> grade 3.0)) "C+"
    (and (<= grade 3.0) (> grade 2.7)) "C"
    (and (<= grade 2.7) (> grade 2.3)) "C"
    (and (<= grade 2.3) (> grade 0)) "D"
    (= grade 0) "F"
    :else "N/A"))
```

The print-all-grades function simply uses a sequence comprehension to print each grade:

ClojureExamples/src/mbfpp/oo/tm/grade_reporter.clj

```clojure
(defn print-all-grades [grades]
  (doseq [grade grades]
    (println "Grade is:" grade)))
```

Now we can compose them together with make-grade-reporter and run them on our sample data to print a grade report:

ClojureExamples/src/mbfpp/oo/tm/grade_reporter.clj

```clojure
(def plus-minus-grade-reporter
  (make-grade-reporter plus-minus-grade-converter print-all-grades))

=> (plus-minus-grade-reporter sample-grades)
Grade is: A
Grade is: B
Grade is: A-
Grade is: D
Grade is: C+
Grade is: B-
```

That's it for our Clojure version of Template Method replacement. Let's wrap up with some discussion on how the Template Method compares to its functional replacement.

Discussion

Our functional replacement for Template Method fulfills the same intent but operates quite differently. Instead of using subtypes to implement specific suboperations, we use functional composition and higher-order functions.

This mirrors the old object-oriented preference of composition over inheritance. Even in the object-oriented world, I prefer to use the pattern described in

Replacing Dependency Injection to inject suboperations into a class, rather than using Template Method and subclassing.

The biggest reason for this is that it helps to prevent code duplication. For instance, in the example we used in this chapter, if we wanted a class that printed a histogram of plus/minus grades, we would have to either create a deeper inheritance hierarchy or cut and paste code from the existing implementations. In a real system, this can get fragile very quickly.

Composition also does a better job of making an API explicit. The Template Method class may expose protected helper methods that are used by framework code but shouldn't be used by a client. The only way to indicate this is with comments in the API documentation.

For Further Reading

Design Patterns: Elements of Reusable Object-Oriented Software [GHJV95] –Template Method

Related Patterns

Pattern 1, *Replacing Functional Interface*, on page 40

Pattern 7, *Replacing Strategy*, on page 92

Pattern 16, *Function Builder*, on page 167

Replacing Strategy

Intent

To define an algorithm in abstract terms so it can be implemented in several different ways, and to allow it to be injected into clients so it can be used across several different clients

Overview

Strategy has a few parts. The first is an interface that represents some algorithm, such as a bit of validation logic or a sorting routine. The second is one or more implementations of that interface; these are the strategy classes themselves. Finally, one or more clients use the strategy objects.

For instance, we may have several different ways we want to validate a set of data input from a form on a website, and we may want to use that validation code in several places. We could create a Validator interface with a validate() method to serve as our strategy object, along with several implementations that could be injected into our code at the appropriate spots.

Also Known As

Policy

Functional Replacement

Strategy is closely related to Pattern 1, *Replacing Functional Interface*, on page 40, in that the strategy objects themselves are generally a simple functional interface, but the Strategy pattern contains more moving parts than just a Functional Interface. Still, this suggests a straightforward replacement for Strategy in the functional world.

To replace the strategy classes, we use higher-order functions that implement the needed algorithms. This avoids the need to create and apply interfaces for different strategy implementations. From there, it's straightforward to pass our strategy functions around and use them where needed.

Sample Code: Person Validation

One common use of Strategy is to create different algorithms that can be used to validate the same set of data. Let's take a look at an example of using Strategy to do just that.

We'll implement two different validation strategies for a person that contain a first, middle, and last name. The first strategy will consider the person valid if he or she has a first name, the second will only consider the person valid if all three names are set. On top of that, we'll look at some simple client code that collects valid people together.

In Java

In Java, we need a PersonValidator interface, which our two validation strategies, FirstNameValidator and FullNameValidator, will implement. The validators themselves are straightforward; they return true if they consider the person valid and false otherwise.

The validators can then be composed in the PersonCollector class, which will collect People objects that pass validation. The class diagram below outlines this solution:

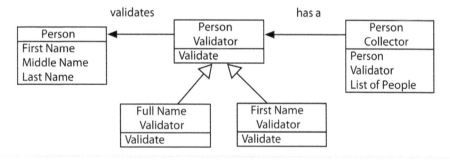

Figure 6—Person Validator Strategy. Using Strategy to validate a person

This works fine, but it involves spreading our logic across several classes for no particularly good reason. Let's see how we can simplify Strategy using functional techniques.

In Scala

In Scala, there's no need for the PersonValidator interface we saw in the Java examples. Instead, we'll just use plain old functions to do our validation. To carry a person around, we'll rely on a case class with attributes for each part of a person's name. Finally, instead of using a full-on class for the person collector, we'll use a higher-order function that itself returns another function that's responsible for collecting people.

Let's start with the Person case class. This is a pretty standard case class, but notice how we're using Option[String] to represent the names instead of just String, since this case class represents a person that may have parts of the name missing:

ScalaExamples/src/main/scala/com/mblinn/mbfpp/oo/strategy/PeopleExample.scala
```scala
case class Person(
    firstName: Option[String],
    middleName: Option[String],
    lastName: Option[String])
```

Now let's take a look at our first name validator, a function called isFirst-NameValid(). As the code below shows, we use the isDefined() method on Scala's Option, which returns true if the Option contains Some and returns false otherwise to see whether the person has a first name:

ScalaExamples/src/main/scala/com/mblinn/mbfpp/oo/strategy/PeopleExample.scala
```scala
def isFirstNameValid(person: Person) = person.firstName.isDefined
```

Our full name validator is a function, isFullNameValid(). Here, we use a Scala match statement to pick apart a Person, and then we ensure that each name is there using isDefined(). The code is below:

ScalaExamples/src/main/scala/com/mblinn/mbfpp/oo/strategy/PeopleExample.scala
```scala
def isFullNameValid(person: Person) = person match {
  case Person(firstName, middleName, lastName) =>
    firstName.isDefined && middleName.isDefined && lastName.isDefined
}
```

Finally, our person collector, a function aptly named personCollector(), takes in a validation function and produces another function that's responsible for collecting valid people. It does so by running a passed-in person through the validation function. It then appends it to an immutable vector and stores a reference to the new vector in the validPeople var if it passes validation. Finally it returns validPeople, as the code below shows:

ScalaExamples/src/main/scala/com/mblinn/mbfpp/oo/strategy/PeopleExample.scala
```scala
def personCollector(isValid: (Person) => Boolean) = {
  var validPeople = Vector[Person]()
  (person: Person) => {
    if(isValid(person)) validPeople = validPeople :+ person
    validPeople
  }
}
```

Let's take a look at our validators and person-collector at work, starting with creating a person-collector that considers single names valid and one that only considers full names valid:

```scala
scala> val singleNameValidCollector = personCollector(isFirstNameValid)
singleNameValidCollector: ...

scala> val fullNameValidCollector = personCollector(isFullNameValid)
fullNameValidCollector: ...
```

We can now define a few test names:

```scala
scala> val p1 = Person(Some("John"), Some("Quincy"), Some("Adams"))
p1: com.mblinn.mbfpp.oo.strategy.PeopleExample.Person = ...

scala> val p2 = Person(Some("Mike"), None, Some("Linn"))
p2: com.mblinn.mbfpp.oo.strategy.PeopleExample.Person = ...

scala> val p3 = Person(None, None, None)
p3: com.mblinn.mbfpp.oo.strategy.PeopleExample.Person = ...
```

Then we run through our two person-collectors, starting with singleNameValidCollector():

```scala
scala> singleNameValidCollector(p1)
res0: scala.collection.immutable.Vector[...] =
        Vector(Person(Some(John),Some(Quincy),Some(Adams)))

scala> singleNameValidCollector(p2)
res1: scala.collection.immutable.Vector[...] =
        Vector(
                Person(Some(John),Some(Quincy),Some(Adams)),
                Person(Some(Mike),None,Some(Linn)))

scala> singleNameValidCollector(p3)
res2: scala.collection.immutable.Vector[...] =
        Vector(
                Person(Some(John),Some(Quincy),Some(Adams)),
                Person(Some(Mike),None,Some(Linn)))
```

And we'll finish up with fullNameValidCollector():

```scala
scala> fullNameValidCollector(p1)
res3: scala.collection.immutable.Vector[...] =
        Vector(Person(Some(John),Some(Quincy),Some(Adams)))

scala> fullNameValidCollector(p2)
res4: scala.collection.immutable.Vector[...] =
        Vector(Person(Some(John),Some(Quincy),Some(Adams)))

scala> fullNameValidCollector(p3)
res5: scala.collection.immutable.Vector[...] =
        Vector(Person(Some(John),Some(Quincy),Some(Adams)))
```

As we can see, the two collectors work as they should, delegating to the validation functions that were passed in when they were created.

In Clojure

In Clojure, we'll solve our person-collecting problem in a similar way to Scala, using functions for the validators and a higher-order function that takes in a validator and produces a person-collecting function. To represent the people, we'll use good old Clojure maps. Since Clojure is a dynamic language and doesn't have Scala's Option typing, we'll use nil to represent the lack of a name.

Let's start by looking at first-name-valid?. It checks to see if the :first-name of the person is not nil and returns true if so; otherwise it returns false.

ClojureExamples/src/mbfpp/oo/strategy/people_example.clj
```
(defn first-name-valid? [person]
  (not (nil? (:first-name person))))
```

The full-name-valid? function pulls out all three names and returns true only if they're all not nil:

ClojureExamples/src/mbfpp/oo/strategy/people_example.clj
```
(defn full-name-valid? [person]
  (and
    (not (nil? (:first-name person)))
    (not (nil? (:middle-name person)))
    (not (nil? (:last-name person)))))
```

Finally, let's take a look at our person-collector, which takes in a validation function and produces a collector function. This works almost exactly like the Scala version, the main difference being that we need to use an atom to store a reference to our immutable vector in an atom.

ClojureExamples/src/mbfpp/oo/strategy/people_example.clj
```
(defn person-collector [valid?]
  (let [valid-people (atom [])]
    (fn [person]
      (if (valid? person)
        (swap! valid-people conj person))
      @valid-people)))
```

Before we wrap up, let's see our Clojure person collection in action, starting by defining the collector functions as we do below:

```
=> (def first-name-valid-collector (person-collector first-name-valid?))
#'mbfpp.oo.strategy.people-example/first-name-valid-collector
=> (def full-name-valid-collector (person-collector full-name-valid?))
#'mbfpp.oo.strategy.people-example/full-name-valid-collector
```

Now we need some test data:

```
=> (def p1 {:first-name "john" :middle-name "quincy" :last-name "adams"})
#'mbfpp.oo.strategy.people-example/p1
=> (def p2 {:first-name "mike" :middle-name nil :last-name "adams"})
#'mbfpp.oo.strategy.people-example/p2
=> (def p3 {:first-name nil :middle-name nil :last-name nil})
#'mbfpp.oo.strategy.people-example/p3
```

And we can run it through our collectors, starting with the collector that only requires a first name for the person to be valid:

```
=> (first-name-valid-collector p1)
[{:middle-name "quincy", :last-name "adams", :first-name "john"}]
=> (first-name-valid-collector p2)
[{:middle-name "quincy", :last-name "adams", :first-name "john"}
{:middle-name nil, :last-name "adams", :first-name "mike"}]
=> (first-name-valid-collector p3)
[{:middle-name "quincy", :last-name "adams", :first-name "john"}
{:middle-name nil, :last-name "adams", :first-name "mike"}]
```

Then we finish up with the collector that requires the full name for the person to be valid:

```
=> (full-name-valid-collector p1)
[{:middle-name "quincy", :last-name "adams", :first-name "john"}]
=> (full-name-valid-collector p2)
[{:middle-name "quincy", :last-name "adams", :first-name "john"}]
=> (full-name-valid-collector p3)
[{:middle-name "quincy", :last-name "adams", :first-name "john"}]
```

Both work as expected, validating the passed-in name before storing it if valid and then returning the full set of valid names.

Discussion

Strategy and Template Method serve similar ends. Both are ways to inject some bit of custom code into a larger framework or algorithm. Strategy does so using composition, and Template Method does so using inheritance. We replaced both patterns with ones based on functional composition.

Though both Clojure and Scala have language features that allow us to build hierarchies, we've replaced both Template Method and Strategy with patterns based on functional composition. This leads to simpler solutions to common problems, mirroring the old object-oriented preference to favor composition over inheritance.

For Further Reading

Design Patterns: Elements of Reusable Object-Oriented Software [GHJV95]
—Strategy

Related Patterns

Pattern 1, *Replacing Functional Interface*, on page 40

Pattern 6, *Replacing Template Method*, on page 83

Pattern 8

Replacing Null Object

Intent

To avoid scattering null checks throughout our code by encapsulating the action taken for null references into a surrogate null object

Overview

A common way to represent the lack of a value in Java is to use a null reference. This leads to a lot of code that looks like so:

```
if(null == someObject){
  // default null handling behavior
}else{
  someObject.someMethod()
}
```

This style leads to scattering null handling logic throughout our code, often repeating it. If we forget to check for null it may lead to a program crashing NullPointerException, even if there is a reasonable default behavior that can handle the lack of a value.

A common solution to this is to create a singleton null object that has the same interface as our real objects but implements our default behavior. We can then use this object in place of null references.

The two main benefits here are these:

1. We can avoid scattering null checks throughout our code, which keeps our code clean and easier to read.

2. We can centralize logic that deals with handling the absence of a value.

Using Null Object has its trade-offs, however. Pervasive use of the pattern means that your program probably won't fail fast. You may generate a null object due to a bug and not know until much later in the program's execution, which makes it much harder to track down the source of the bug.

In Java, I generally use Null Object judiciously when I know that there's a good reason why I may not have a value for something and use null checks elsewhere. The difference between these two situations can be subtle.

For instance, let's imagine we're writing part of a system that looks up a person by a generated, unique ID. If the IDs are closely related to the system we're writing and we know that every lookup should succeed and return a person, I'd stick with using null references. This way, if something goes wrong and we don't have a person, we fail fast and don't pass the problem on.

However, if the IDs aren't closely related to our program, I'd probably use Null Object. Say, for instance, that the IDs are generated by some other system and imported into ours via a batch process, which means that there's some latency between when the ID is created and when it becomes available to our system. In this case, handling a missing ID would be part of our program's normal operation, and I'd use Null Object to keep the code clean and avoid extraneous null checks.

The functional replacements we examine will explore these tradeoffs.

Functional Replacement

We'll examine a few different approaches here. In Scala, we'll take advantage of static typing and Option typing to replace null object references. In Clojure, we'll primarily focus on Clojure's treatment of nil, but we'll also touch on Clojure's optional static typing system, which provides us with an Option much like Scala's.

In Scala

We have null references in Scala just as we do in Java; however, it's not common to use them. Instead we can take advantage of the type system to replace both null references and Null Object. We'll look at two container types, Option and Either. The first, Option, lets us indicate that we may not have a value in a type-safe manner. The second, Either, lets us provide a value when we've got one and a default or error value when we don't.

Let's take a closer look at Option first. Option types are containers, much like a Map or a Vector, except they can only hold one element at most. Option has two important subtypes: Some, which carries a value, and the singleton object None, which does not. In the following code, we create a Some[String] that carries the value "foo" and a reference to None:

```
scala> def aSome = Some("foo")
aSome: Some[java.lang.String]

scala> def aNone = None
aNone: None.type
```

Now we can work with our Option instances in a variety of ways. Perhaps the simplest is the getOrElse() method. The getOrElse() method is called with a single argument, a default value. When called on an instance of Some, the carried value is returned; when called on None the default value is returned. The following code demonstrates this:

```
scala> aSome.getOrElse("default value")
res0: java.lang.String = foo

scala> aNone.getOrElse("default value")
res1: java.lang.String = default value
```

When working with Option, it's cleanest to treat a value as another container type. For example, if we need to do something to a value inside an Option, we can use our old friend map(), as in the following code:

```
scala> aSome.map((s) => s.toUpperCase)
res2: Option[java.lang.String] = Some(FOO)
```

We'll examine some more-sophisticated ways of working with Option in the code samples.

One final note on Option: In its simplest form, it can be used much as we'd use a null check in Java, though there are more powerful ways to use it. However, even in this simplest form, there's one major difference.

Option is part of the type system, so if we use it consistently we know exactly in which parts of our code we may have to deal with the lack of a value or a default value. Everywhere else we can write code safe in the knowledge that we'll have a value.

In Clojure

In Clojure, we don't have the Option typing that Scala's static type system provides us. Instead, we've got nil, which is equivalent to Java's null at the bytecode level. However, Clojure provides several convenient features that make it much cleaner to deal with the lack of a value using nil and that give us many of the same benefits we get with Null Object.

First up, nil is treated the same as false in Clojure. Combined with a pervasive use of expressions, this makes it much simpler to do a nil check in Clojure than it is to check for null in Java, as the following code demonstrates:

```
=> (if nil "default value" "real value")
"real value"
```

Second, the functions that we use to get values of our Clojure's composite data structures provide a way to get a default value if the element we're trying to retrieve isn't present. Here we use the get method to try to retrieve the value for :foo from an empty map, and we get back our passed-in default value instead:

```
=> (get {} :foo "default value")
"default value"
```

The lack of a value for a key is distinct from a key that has the value of nil, as this code demonstrates:

```
=> (get {:foo nil} :foo "default value")
nil
```

Let's dig into some code samples!

Sample Code: Default Values

We'll start by looking at how we'd use Null Object as a default when we don't get back a value from a map lookup. In this example, we'll have a map full of people keyed off of an ID. If we don't find a person for a given ID, we need to return a default person with the name "John Doe."

Classic Java

In classic Java, we'll create a Person interface with two subclasses, RealPerson and NullPerson. The first, RealPerson, allows us to set a first and last name, while NullPerson has them hardcoded to "John" and "Doe".

If we get a null back when we try to get a person by ID, we return an instance of NullPerson; otherwise we use the RealPerson we got out of the map. The following code sketches out this approach:

JavaExamples/src/main/java/com/mblinn/oo/nullobject/PersonExample.java

```java
public class PersonExample {
        private Map<Integer, Person> people;

        public PersonExample() {
                people = new HashMap<Integer, Person>();
        }

        public Person fetchPerson(Integer id) {
                Person person = people.get(id);
                if (null != person)
                        return person;
                else
                        return new NullPerson();
        }
        // Code to add/remove people

        public Person buildPerson(String firstName, String lastName){
```

```
            if(null != firstName && null != lastName)
                    return new RealPerson(firstName, lastName);
        else
                    return new NullPerson();
    }
}
```

Let's see how we can use Scala's Option to eliminate the explicit null check we need to do in Java.

In Scala

In Scala, the get() on Map doesn't return a value directly. If the key exists, the value is returned wrapped in a Some, otherwise a None is returned.

For instance, in the following code we create a map with two integer keys, 1 and 2, and String greetings as values. When we try to fetch either of them using get(), we get back a String wrapped in a Some. For any other key, we get back a None.

```
scala> def aMap = Map(1->"Hello", 2->"Aloha")
aMap: scala.collection.immutable.Map[Int,java.lang.String]

scala> aMap.get(1)
res0: Option[java.lang.String] = Some(Hello)

scala> aMap.get(3)
res1: Option[java.lang.String] = None
```

We could work with the Option type directly, but Scala provides a nice short-hand that lets us get back a default value directly from a map, getOrElse(). In the following REPL output, we use it to attempt to fetch the value for the key 3 from the map. Since it's not there, we get back our default value instead.

```
scala> aMap.getOrElse(3, "Default Greeting")
res3: java.lang.String = Default Greeting
```

Now let's see how we can use this handy feature to implement our person-fetching example. Here we're using a trait as the base type for our people, and we're using case classes for the RealPerson and NullPerson. We can then use an instance of NullPerson as the default value in our lookup. The following code demonstrates this approach:

ScalaExamples/src/main/scala/com/mblinn/mbfpp/oo/nullobject/Examples.scala
```
case class Person(firstName: String="John", lastName: String="Doe")
val nullPerson = Person()

def fetchPerson(people: Map[Int, Person], id: Int) =
  people.getOrElse(id, nullPerson)
```

Let's define some test data so we can see this approach at work:

ScalaExamples/src/main/scala/com/mblinn/mbfpp/oo/nullobject/Examples.scala
```scala
val joe = Person("Joe", "Smith")
val jack = Person("Jack", "Brown")
val somePeople = Map(1 -> joe, 2 -> jack)
```

Now if we use fetchPerson() on a key that exists, it's returned; otherwise our default person is returned:

```scala
scala> fetchPerson(somePeople, 1)
res0: com.mblinn.mbfpp.oo.nullobject.Examples.Person = Person(Joe,Smith)

scala> fetchPerson(somePeople, 3)
res1: com.mblinn.mbfpp.oo.nullobject.Examples.Person = Person(John,Doe)
```

Now let's take a look at how we can accomplish this in Clojure.

In Clojure

When we try to look up a nonexistent key from a map in Clojure, nil is returned.

```clojure
=> ({} :foo)
nil
```

Clojure provides another way to look up keys from a map, the get function, which lets us provide an optional default value. The following REPL snippet shows a simple example of get in action.

```clojure
=> (get :foo {} "default")
"default"
```

To write our person lookup example in Clojure, all we need to do is define a default null-person. We then pass it into get as a default value when we try to do our lookup, as the following code and REPL output demonstrates:

ClojureExamples/src/mbfpp/oo/nullobject/examples.clj
```clojure
(def null-person {:first-name "John" :last-name "Doe"})
(defn fetch-person [people id]
  (get id people null-person))

=> (def people {42 {:first-name "Jack" :last-name "Bauer"}})
#'mbfpp.oo.nullobject.examples/people
=> (fetch-person 42 people)
{:last-name "Bauer", :first-name "Jack"}
=> (fetch-person 4 people)
{:last-name "Doe", :first-name "John"}
```

The code in this example deals with a basic use of Null Object as a default value at lookup time. Next up, let's take a look at how we'd handle working with Null Object and its replacements when the time comes to modify them.

Sample Code: Something from Nothing

Let's take a look at our person example from a different angle. This time, instead of looking up a person that may not exist, we want to create a person only if we've got a valid first and last name. Otherwise, we want to use a default.

Classic Java

In Java, we'll use the same null object we saw in *Classic Java*, on page 102. If we have both a first and last name available to use, we'll use a RealPerson; otherwise we'll use a NullPerson.

To do this, we write a buildPerson() that takes a firstName and a lastName. If either is null, we return a NullPerson; otherwise we return a RealPerson built with the passed-in names. The following code outlines this solution:

```
JavaExamples/src/main/java/com/mblinn/oo/nullobject/PersonExample.java
public Person buildPerson(String firstName, String lastName){
        if(null != firstName && null != lastName)
                return new RealPerson(firstName, lastName);
        else
                return new NullPerson();
}
```

This approach allows us to minimize the surface area of our code where we need to deal with null, which helps cut down on surprise null pointers. Now let's see how we can accomplish the same in Scala without needing to introduce an extraneous null object.

In Scala

Our Scala approach to this problem will take advantage of Option instead of creating a special Null Object type. The firstName and lastName we pass into buildPerson() are Option[String]s, and we return an Option[Person].

If both firstName and lastName are Some[String], then we return a Some[Person]; otherwise we return a None. The right way to do this in Scala is to treat the Options as we would treat any other container, such as a Map or a Vector.

Earlier we saw a simple example of using the map() method on an instance of Some. Let's look at how we'd use Scala's most powerful sequence manipulation tool, the sequence comprehensions we introduced in *Sample Code: Sequence Comprehensions*, on page 77, to manipulate Option types.

First, let's get some test data into our REPL. In the following snippet, we define a simple vector and a few option types:

ScalaExamples/src/main/scala/com/mblinn/mbfpp/oo/nullobject/Examples.scala
```
def vecFoo = Vector("foo")
def someFoo = Some("foo")
def someBar = Some("bar")
def aNone = None
```

As we can see in the following code, manipulating a Some looks much like manipulating a Vector with a single value in it:

```
scala> for(theFoo <- vecFoo) yield theFoo
res0: scala.collection.immutable.Vector[java.lang.String] = Vector(foo)
scala> for(theFoo <- someFoo) yield theFoo
res1: Option[java.lang.String] = Some(foo)
```

The real power of using a for comprehension to work with Option comes in when we're working with multiple Options at a time. We can use multiple generators, one for each option, to get at the values in each. In the following code, we use this technique to pull the strings out of someFoo and someBar and put them into a tuple, which we then yield:

```
scala> for(theFoo <- someFoo; theBar <- someBar) yield (theFoo, theBar)
res2: Option[(java.lang.String, java.lang.String)] = Some((foo,bar))
```

When working with options in this fashion, if any of the generators produces a None, then the value of the entire expression is a None. This gives us a clean syntax for working with Some and None:

```
scala> for(theFoo <- someFoo; theNone <- aNone) yield (theFoo, theNone)
res3: Option[(java.lang.String, Nothing)] = None
```

We can now apply this to our person-building example pretty simply. We use two generators in our for comprehensions, one for the firstName and one for the lastName. We then yield a Person. The for comprehension wraps that up inside of an Option, and we use getOrElse() to get at it or use a default. The following code demonstrates this approach:

ScalaExamples/src/main/scala/com/mblinn/mbfpp/oo/nullobject/Examples.scala
```
def buildPerson(firstNameOption: Option[String], lastNameOption: Option[String]) =
  (for(
      firstName <- firstNameOption;
      lastName <- lastNameOption)
   yield Person(firstName, lastName)).getOrElse(Person("John", "Doe"))
```

Here we can see it in action:

```
scala> buildPerson(Some("Mike"), Some("Linn"))
res4: com.mblinn.mbfpp.oo.nullobject.Examples.Person = Person(Mike,Linn)

scala> buildPerson(Some("Mike"), None)
res5: com.mblinn.mbfpp.oo.nullobject.Examples.Person = Person(John,Doe)
```

Let's finish up the example by seeing how to handle person-building in Clojure.

In Clojure

In Clojure, our person-building example boils down to a simple nil check. We pass first-name and last-name into our build-person function. If they're both not-nil, we use them to create a person; otherwise we create a default person.

Clojure's treatment of nil as a "falsey" value makes this convenient to do, but otherwise it's very similar to our Java approach. The code follows:

ClojureExamples/src/mbfpp/oo/nullobject/examples.clj
```clojure
(defn build-person [first-name last-name]
  (if (and first-name last-name)
    {:first-name first-name :last-name last-name}
    {:first-name "John" :last-name "Doe"}))
```

Here it produces a real person and a default person:

```clojure
=> (build-person "Mike" "Linn")
{:first-name "Mike", :last-name "Linn"}
=> (build-person "Mike" nil)
{:first-name "John", :last-name "Doe"}
```

Discussion

The idiomatic approach to handling the lack of a value in Clojure versus Scala is very different. The difference comes down to Scala's static type system and Clojure's dynamic one. Scala's static type system and type parameters make the Option type possible.

The tradeoffs that Scala and Clojure make here mirror the general tradeoffs between static and dynamic typing. With Scala's approach, the compiler helps to ensure that we're properly handling nothing at compile time, though we have to be careful not to let Java's null creep into our Scala code.

With Clojure's approach, we've got the possibility for null pointers just about anywhere, just as in Java. We need to be more careful that we're handling them appropriately, or we risk runtime errors.

My preference is to take care of all my nothing handling at the outermost layer of my code, whether I'm using Scala's Option typing or the null/nil that Java and Clojure share. For instance, if I'm querying a database for a person who may or may not exist, I prefer to check for his/her existence only once: when we attempt to pull it back from the database. Then I use the techniques outlined in this pattern to create a default person if necessary. This allows the rest of my code to avoid doing null checks or to deal with Option typing. I've found that Scala's approach to Option typing makes it much easier to write programs in this style, because it forces us to explicitly deal with the lack of a value whenever we might not have one and to assume that we'll have a value everywhere else.

For Further Reading

Pattern Languages of Program Design 3 [MRB97]—Null Object

Refactoring: Improving the Design of Existing Code [FBBO99]—Introduce Null Object

Pattern 9

Replacing Decorator

Intent

To add behavior to an individual object rather than to an entire class of objects—this allows us to change the behavior of an existing class.

Overview

Decorator is useful when we've got an existing class that we need to add some behavior to but we can't change the existing class. We may want to introduce a breaking change, but we can't change every other part of the system where the class is used. Or the class may be part of a library that we can't, or don't want to, modify.

Decorator uses a combination of inheritance and composition. It starts with an interface with at least one concrete implementation. This implementation is the class that we can't or don't want to change.

We then implement the interface with an abstract decorator class, which gets an instance of our existing, concrete class composed into it. Our abstract decorator class can itself have several implementations, which tweak the behavior of the existing class using composition, as shown in this figure:

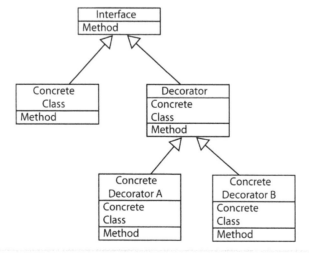

Figure 7—Decorator Diagram. A class diagram for the Decorator pattern

This gives us some ability to add or modify behavior on existing classes, but we're mostly limited to small tweaks since we rely on the base behavior of the composed class.

Also Known As

Wrapper

Functional Replacement

The essence of Decorator is wrapping an existing class with a new one so that the new class can tweak the behavior of the existing one. In the functional world, one simple replacement is to create a higher-order function that takes in the existing function and returns a new, wrapped function.

The wrapped function does its job and then delegates to the existing function. For instance, we could create a wrapWithLogger() function that wraps up an existing function with a bit of logging, returning a new function.

Sample Code: Logging Calculator

Let's take a look at using Decorator with a basic four-function calculator. The calculator has four operations, add(), subtract(), multiply(), and divide(). To demonstrate Decorator, we'll take a basic calculator and decorate it so that it logs out the calculation it's performing to the console.

Classic Java

In Java, our solution consists of an interface and two concrete classes. The Calculator interface is implemented by both CalculatorImpl and LoggingCalculator. The LoggingCalculator class serves as our decorator and needs a CalculatorImpl composed into it to do its job. An outline of this approach can be found in the following image:

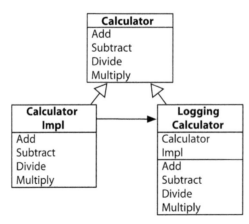

The LoggingCalculator class delegates to the composed CalculatorImpl and then logs the calculation to the console.

In Scala

In Scala, our calculator is just a collection of four functions. To keep things simple, we'll constrain ourselves to integer operations, since implementing generic numeric functions in Scala is a bit involved. The code for our Scala calculator follows:

ScalaExamples/src/main/scala/com/mblinn/mbfpp/oo/decorator/Examples.scala
```scala
def add(a: Int, b: Int) = a + b
def subtract(a: Int, b: Int) = a - b
def multiply(a: Int, b: Int) = a * b
def divide(a: Int, b: Int) = a / b
```

To wrap our calculator functions in logging code, we use makeLogger(). This is a higher-order function that takes in a calculator function and returns a new function that runs the original calculator function and prints the result to the console before returning it.

ScalaExamples/src/main/scala/com/mblinn/mbfpp/oo/decorator/Examples.scala
```scala
def makeLogger(calcFn: (Int, Int) => Int) =
  (a: Int, b: Int) => {
    val result = calcFn(a, b)
    println("Result is: " + result)
    result
  }
```

To use makeLogger(), we run our original calculator functions through it and assign the results into new vals, as the following code shows:

ScalaExamples/src/main/scala/com/mblinn/mbfpp/oo/decorator/Examples.scala
```scala
val loggingAdd = makeLogger(add)
val loggingSubtract = makeLogger(subtract)
val loggingMultiply = makeLogger(multiply)
val loggingDivide = makeLogger(divide)
```

Now we can use our printing calculator function to do some arithmetic and print the results:

```
scala> loggingAdd(2, 3)
Result is: 5
res0: Int = 5

scala> loggingSubtract(2, 3)
Result is: -1
res1: Int = -1
```

Let's take a look at our calculator solution in Clojure.

In Clojure

The structure of our Clojure solution is similar to the Scala one, the main difference being that our Clojure solution isn't constrained to integers since Clojure is dynamically typed. The following code defines our calculator functions:

ClojureExamples/src/mbfpp/oo/decorator/examples.clj

```
(defn add [a b] (+ a b))
(defn subtract [a b] (- a b))
(defn multiply [a b] (* a b))
(defn divide [a b] (/ a b))
```

Next we need a make-logger higher-order function to wrap our calculator functions up with logging code:

ClojureExamples/src/mbfpp/oo/decorator/examples.clj

```
(defn make-logger [calc-fn]
  (fn [a b]
    (let [result (calc-fn a b)]
      (println (str "Result is: " result))
      result)))
```

Finally, we can create some logging calculator functions and use them to do some logging math:

ClojureExamples/src/mbfpp/oo/decorator/examples.clj

```
(def logging-add (make-logger add))
(def logging-subtract (make-logger subtract))
(def logging-multiply (make-logger multiply))
(def logging-divide (make-logger divide))

=> (logging-add 2 3)
Result is: 5
5
=> (logging-subtract 2 3)
Result is: -1
-1
```

It's no accident that the Scala and Clojure solutions to the calculator problem are so similar: they both rely only on basic higher-order functions, which are similar across both languages.

For Further Reading

Design Patterns: Elements of Reusable Object-Oriented Software [GHJV95] —Decorator

Related Patterns

Pattern 7, *Replacing Strategy*, on page 92

Pattern 16, *Function Builder*, on page 167

Pattern 10

Replacing Visitor

Intent

To encapsulate an action to be performed on a data structure in a way that allows the addition of new operations to the data structure without having to modify it.

Overview

A common sticking point in large, long-lived programs is how to extend a data type. We want to extend along two dimensions. First, we may want to add new operations to existing implementations of the data type. Second, we may want to add new implementations of the data type.

We'd like to be able to do this without recompiling the original source, indeed, possibly without even having access to it. This is a problem that's as old as programming itself, and it's now known as the *expression problem*.

For example, consider Java's Collection as a sample data type. The Collection interface defines many methods, or operations, and has many implementations. In a perfect world, we'd be able to easily add both new operations to Collection as well as new implementations of Collection.

In object-oriented languages, however, it's only easy to do the latter. We can create a new implementation of Collection by implementing the interface. If we want to add new operations to Collection that work with all the existing Collection implementation, we're out of luck.

In Java, we often get around this by creating a class full of static utility methods, rather than by adding the operations directly to the data type. One such library for Collection is the Apache foundation's CollectionUtils.

Visitor is another partial solution to this sort of problem. It allows us to add new operations to an existing data type and is often used with tree-structured data. Visitor allows us to fairly easily add new operations to an existing data type, but it makes adding new implementations of the data type difficult.

Visitor Pattern

The Visitor class diagram (shown in the following figure) shows the main pieces of the Visitor pattern. Our data type here is the DataElement class, which has two implementations. Instead of implementing operations directly on the subclasses of DataElement, we create an accept() method that takes a Visitor and calls visit(), passing itself in.

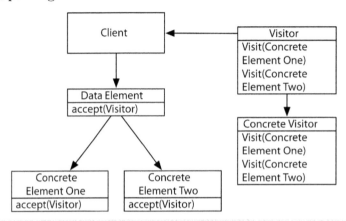

Figure 8—Visitor Classes. A sketch of the Visitor pattern

This inverts the normal object-oriented constraint that it's easy to add new implementations of a data type but difficult to add new operations. If we want to add a new operation, we just need to create a new visitor and write code such that it knows how to visit each existing concrete element.

However, it's hard to add new implementations of DataElement. To do so, we'd need to modify all of the existing visitors to know how to visit the new DataElement implementation. If those Visitor classes are outside of our control, it may be impossible!

Functional Replacement

The Visitor pattern makes it possible to add new operations to an object-oriented data type but difficult, or impossible, to add new implementations of the type. In the functional world, this is the norm. It's easy to add a new operation on some data type by writing a new function that operates on it, but it's difficult to add new data types to an existing operation.

In our replacements, we'll examine a few different ways to deal with this extensibility problem in Scala and Clojure. The solutions are quite different in the two languages. In part, this is because Scala is statically typed while

Clojure is dynamically typed. This means that Scala has a harder problem to solve in that it attempts to perform its extensions while preserving static type safety.

The other difference is that Scala's take on polymorphism is an extension of the traditional object-oriented model, which uses a hierarchy of subclasses. Clojure takes a novel view and provides polymorphism in a more ad hoc manner. Since polymorphism is intimately bound up with extensibility, this affects the overall shape of the solutions.

In Scala

Since Scala is a hybrid language, extending existing code requires us to dip into its object-oriented features, especially its type system.

First we'll look at a method of extending the operations in an existing library that uses Scala's *implicit conversion* system. This allows us to add new operations to existing libraries.

Second we'll look at a solution that takes advantage of Scala's mix-in inheritance and traits, which allows us to easily add both new operations and new implementations to a data type.

In Clojure

In Clojure we'll take a look at the language's unique take on polymorphism. First we'll look at Clojure's datatypes and protocols. These allow us to specify data types and the operations performed on them independently and to extend datatypes with both new implementations and new operations while taking advantage of the JVMs highly optimized method dispatch.

Next we'll look at Clojure's multimethods. These allow us to provide our own dispatch function, which lets us dispatch a method call however we please. They're more flexible than protocols but slower, since they require an additional function call to the user-provided dispatch function.

The Scala and Clojure solutions we examine aren't exactly equivalent, but they both provide flexible ways to extend existing code.

Sample Code: Extensible Persons

In this example, we'll look at a Person type and see how we can extend it to have both new implementations and operations. This doesn't replace the full Visitor pattern, but it's a simpler example of the sorts of problems that Visitor touches on.

In Java

The code that we'll look at here is a basic example of extending an existing library without wrapping the original objects. In Java, it would be easy to create new implementations of a Person type, assuming the original libraries' authors defined an interface for it.

More difficult would be adding new operations to Person. We can't just create a subinterface of Person with new methods, as that could no longer be used in place of a plain Person. Wrapping Person in a new class is also out for the same reason.

Java doesn't have a good story for extending an existing type to have new operations, so we often end up faking it by creating classes full of static utility methods that operate on the type. Scala and Clojure give us more flexibility to extend along both dimensions.

In Scala

In Scala, our Person is defined by a trait. The trait specifies methods to get a person's first name, last name, house number, and street. In addition, there's a method to get the person's full name, as the following code shows:

ScalaExamples/src/main/scala/com/mblinn/mbfpp/oo/visitor/Examples.scala
```
trait Person {
  def fullName: String
  def firstName: String
  def lastName: String
  def houseNum: Int
  def street: String
}
```

Now let's create an implementation of our Person type, SimplePerson. We'll take advantage of the fact that Scala will automatically create methods that expose the attributes passed into a constructor. The only method we need to implement by hand is fullName(), as the following code snippet shows:

ScalaExamples/src/main/scala/com/mblinn/mbfpp/oo/visitor/Examples.scala
```
class SimplePerson(val firstName: String, val lastName: String,
                   val houseNum: Int, val street: String) extends Person {
  def fullName = firstName + " " + lastName
}
```

Now we can create a SimplePerson and call the fullName() method:

```
scala> val simplePerson = new SimplePerson("Mike", "Linn", 123, "Fake. St.")
simplePerson: com.mblinn.mbfpp.oo.visitor.Examples.SimplePerson = ...
scala> simplePerson.fullName
res0: String = Mike Linn
```

What if we want to extend the Person type to have another operation, fullAddress()? One way to do so would be to simply create a new subtype with the new operation, but then we couldn't use that new type where a Person is needed.

In Scala a better way is to define an *implicit conversion* that converts from a Person to a new class with the fullAddress() method. An implicit conversion changes from one type to another depending on context.

Most languages have a certain set of explicit conversions, or casts, built in. For instance, if you use the + operator on an int and a String in Java, the int will be converted to a String and the two will be concatenated.

Scala lets programmers define their own implicit conversions. One way to do so is by using an *implicit class*. An implicit class exposes its constructor as a candidate for implicit conversions. The following code snippet creates an implicit class that converts from a Person to an ExtendedPerson with a fullAddress():

ScalaExamples/src/main/scala/com/mblinn/mbfpp/oo/visitor/Examples.scala
```
implicit class ExtendedPerson(person: Person) {
  def fullAddress = person.houseNum + " " + person.street
}
```

Now when we try to call fullAddress() on a Person, the Scala compiler will realize that the Person type has no such method. It will then search for an implicit conversion from a Person to a type that does and find it in the ExtendedPerson class.

The compiler will then construct an ExtendedPerson by passing the Person into its primary constructor and call fullAddress() on it, as the following REPL output demonstrates:

```
scala> simplePerson.fullAddress
res1: String = 123 Fake. St.
```

Now that we've seen the trick that allows us to simulate adding new methods to an existing type, the hard part is done. Adding a new implementation of the type is as simple as creating a new implementation of the original Person trait.

Let's take a look at a Person implementation called ComplexPerson that uses separate objects for its name and its address:

ScalaExamples/src/main/scala/com/mblinn/mbfpp/oo/visitor/Examples.scala
```
class ComplexPerson(name: Name, address: Address) extends Person {
  def fullName = name.firstName + " " + name.lastName

  def firstName = name.firstName
  def lastName = name.lastName
```

```
    def houseNum = address.houseNum
    def street = address.street
}
class Address(val houseNum: Int, val street: String)
class Name(val firstName: String, val lastName: String)
```

Now we create a new ComplexPerson:

```
scala> val name = new Name("Mike", "Linn")
name: com.mblinn.mbfpp.oo.visitor.Examples.Name = ..

scala> val address = new Address(123, "Fake St.")
address: com.mblinn.mbfpp.oo.visitor.Examples.Address = ..

scala> val complexPerson = new ComplexPerson(name, address)
complexPerson: com.mblinn.mbfpp.oo.visitor.Examples.ComplexPerson = ...
```

Our existing implicit conversion will still work!

```
scala> complexPerson.fullName
res2: String = Mike Linn

scala> complexPerson.fullAddress
res3: String = 123 Fake St.
```

This means we were able to extend a data type with both a new operation and a new implementation.

In Clojure

Let's take a look at our extensible persons example in Clojure. We'll start by defining a protocol with a single operation in it, extract-name. This operation is intended to extract a full name out of a person and is defined in the following code snippet:

ClojureExamples/src/mbfpp/oo/visitor/examples.clj
```
(defprotocol NameExtractor
  (extract-name [this] "Extracts a name from a person."))
```

Now we can create a Clojure record, SimplePerson, using defrecord. This creates a data type with several fields on it:

ClojureExamples/src/mbfpp/oo/visitor/examples.clj
```
(defrecord SimplePerson [first-name last-name house-num street])
```

We can create a new instance of a SimplePerson using the ->SimplePerson factory function, as we do in the following snippet:

```
=> (def simple-person (->SimplePerson "Mike" "Linn" 123 "Fake St."))
#'mbfpp.oo.visitor.examples/simple-person
```

Once created, we can get at fields in the data type as if it were a map with keywords for keys. In the following snippet, we get the first name out of our simple person instance:

```
=> (:first-name simple-person)
"Mike"
```

Notice how we defined our data type and the set of operations independently? To hook the two together, we can use extend-type to have our SimplePerson implement the NameExtractor protocol, as we do in the following snippet:

ClojureExamples/src/mbfpp/oo/visitor/examples.clj
```
(extend-type SimplePerson
  NameExtractor
  (extract-name [this]
    (str (:first-name this) " " (:last-name this))))
```

Now we can call extract-name on a SimplePerson and have it extract the person's full name:

```
=> (extract-name simple-person)
"Mike Linn"
```

Now let's see how to create a new type, ComplexPerson, which represents its name and address as an embedded map. We'll use a version of defrecord that allows us to extend the type to a protocol at the same time we create it. This is just a convenience; the record and protocol that we've created are still their own entities:

ClojureExamples/src/mbfpp/oo/visitor/examples.clj
```
(defrecord ComplexPerson [name address]
  NameExtractor
  (extract-name [this]
    (str (-> this :name :first) " " (-> this :name :last))))
```

Now we can create a ComplexPerson and extract its full name:

```
=> (def complex-person (->ComplexPerson {:first "Mike" :last "Linn"}
                                        {:house-num 123 :street "Fake St."}))
#'mbfpp.oo.visitor.examples/complex-person
=> (extract-name complex-person)
"Mike Linn"
```

To add a new operation or set of operations to our existing types, we only need to create a new protocol and extend the types. In the following snippet, we create a protocol that allows us to extract an address from a person:

ClojureExamples/src/mbfpp/oo/visitor/examples.clj
```
(defprotocol
  AddressExtractor
  (extract-address [this] "Extracts and address from a person."))
```

Now we can extend our existing types to conform to the new protocol, as we do in the following code:

ClojureExamples/src/mbfpp/oo/visitor/examples.clj
```
(extend-type SimplePerson
  AddressExtractor
  (extract-address [this]
                   (str (:house-num this) " " (:street this))))

(extend-type ComplexPerson
  AddressExtractor
  (extract-address [this]
                   (str (-> this :address :house-num)
                        " "
                        (-> this :address :street))))
```

As we can see from the following REPL output, both of our datatypes now conform to the new protocol:

```
=> (extract-address complex-person)
"123 Fake St."
=> (extract-address simple-person)
"123 Fake St."
```

While we've used Scala's implicit conversions and Clojure protocols to achieve a similar end here, they're not the same. In Scala, the operations we saw were methods defined on classes, which are part of a type. Scala's implicit conversion technique allows us to implicitly convert from one type to another, which makes it look as if we can add operations to an existing type.

Clojure's protocols, on the other hand, define sets of operations and types completely independently via protocols and records. We can then extend any record with any number of protocols, which allows us to easily extend an existing solution both with new operations and new types.

Sample Code: Extensible Geometry

Let's take a look at a more involved example. We'll start off by defining two shapes, a circle and a rectangle, and an operation that calculates their perimeters.

Then we'll show how we can independently add new shapes that work with the existing perimeter operation and new operations that work with our existing shapes. Finally, we'll show how to combine both types of extensions.

In Java

In Java, this is a problem that's impossible to solve well. Extending the shape type to have additional implementations is easy. We create a Shape interface with multiple implementations.

If we want to extend Shape so that it has new methods, it's a bit more difficult, but we can use Visitor as demonstrated in the Visitor Classes diagram.

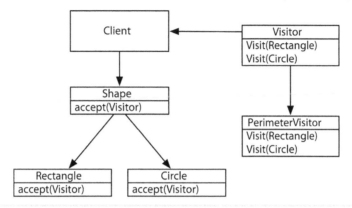

Figure 9—Shape Visitor. The Visitor pattern implemented

However, if we go this route, it's now difficult to have new implementations because we'd have to modify all of the existing Visitors. If the Visitors are implemented by third-party code, it can be impossible to extend in this dimension without introducing backwards-incompatible changes.

In Java, we need to decide at the outset whether we want to add new operations over our Shape or whether we want new implementations of it.

In Scala

In Scala, we use a simplified version of a technique introduced in a paper written by Scala's designer, Martin Odersky.

We'll create a trait, Shape, to serve as the base for all of our shapes. We'll start off with a single method, perimeter(), and two implementations, Circle and Rectangle.

To perform our extension magic, we'll use some advanced features of Scala's type system. First, we'll take advantage of the fact that we can use Scala's traits as modules. At each step, we'll package our code in a top-level trait separate from the one we're using to represent Shape.

This allows us to bundle sets of data types and operations together and to extend those bundles later on using Scala's mix-in inheritance. Then we can have a new type extend many different traits, an ability we take advantage of to combine independent extensions.

Let's dig into the code, starting with our initial Shape trait and the first two implementations:

ScalaExamples/src/main/scala/com/mblinn/mbfpp/oo/visitor/Shapes.scala
```scala
trait PerimeterShapes {
  trait Shape {
    def perimeter: Double
  }

  class Circle(radius: Double) extends Shape {
    def perimeter = 2 * Math.PI * radius
  }

  class Rectangle(width: Double, height: Double) extends Shape {
    def perimeter = 2 * width + 2 * height
  }
}
```

Outside of the top-level PerimeterShapes trait, this is a pretty straightforward declaration of a Shape trait and a couple of implementations. To use our shape code we can extend an object with the top-level trait.

This adds our Shape trait and its implementations to the object. We can now use them directly or easily import them into the REPL, as we do in the following code:

ScalaExamples/src/main/scala/com/mblinn/mbfpp/oo/visitor/Shapes.scala
```scala
object FirstShapeExample extends PerimeterShapes {
  val aCircle = new Circle(4);
  val aRectangle = new Rectangle(2, 2);
}
```

Now we can import our shapes into the REPL and try them out, like in the following snippet:

```scala
import com.mblinn.mbfpp.oo.visitor.FirstShapeExample._

scala> aCircle.perimeter
res1: Double = 25.132741228718345

scala> aRectangle.perimeter
res2: Double = 8.0
```

Extending our Shape with new operations is what's difficult in most purely object-oriented languages, so let's tackle that first. To extend our initial set of shapes, we create a new top-level trait called AreaShapes, which extends PerimeterShapes.

Inside of AreaShapes we extend our initial Shape class to have an area() method, and we create a new Circle and a new Rectangle, which implement area(). The code for our extensions follows:

ScalaExamples/src/main/scala/com/mblinn/mbfpp/oo/visitor/Shapes.scala
```scala
trait AreaShapes extends PerimeterShapes {
  trait Shape extends super.Shape {
    def area: Double
  }

  class Circle(radius: Double) extends super.Circle(radius) with Shape {
    def area = Math.PI * radius * radius
  }

  class Rectangle(width: Double, height: Double)
      extends super.Rectangle(width, height) with Shape {
    def area = width * height
  }
}
```

Let's take a look at this in greater detail. First we create our top-level trait AreaShapes, which extends PerimeterShapes. This lets us easily refer to and extend the classes and trait inside of AreaShapes:

```scala
trait AreaShapes extends PerimeterShapes {
    «area-shapes»
}
```

Next we create a new Shape trait inside of AreaShapes and have it extend the old one inside of PerimeterShapes:

```scala
trait Shape extends super.Shape {
    def area: Double
}
```

We need to refer to the Shape class in PerimeterShapes as super.Shape to differentiate it from the one we just created in AreaShapes.

Now we're ready to implement our area(). To so we first extend our old Circle and Rectangle classes, and then we mix in our new Shape trait, which has area() on it.

Finally, we implement the area() on our new Circle and Rectangle, as shown in the following snippet:

```scala
class Circle(radius: Double) extends super.Circle(radius) with Shape {
    def area = Math.PI * radius * radius
}
```

```
class Rectangle(width: Double, height: Double)
              extends super.Rectangle(width, height) with Shape {
      def area = width * height
}
```

Now we can create some sample shapes and see both perimeter() and area() in action:

ScalaExamples/src/main/scala/com/mblinn/mbfpp/oo/visitor/Shapes.scala
```
object SecondShapeExample extends AreaShapes {
    val someShapes = Vector(new Circle(4), new Rectangle(2, 2));
}
```

```
scala> for(shape <- someShapes) yield shape.perimeter
res0: scala.collection.immutable.Vector[Double] = Vector(25.132741228718345, 8.0)
```

```
scala> for(shape <- someShapes) yield shape.area
res1: scala.collection.immutable.Vector[Double] = Vector(50.26548245743669, 4.0)
```

That covers the hard part, extending Shape with a new operation. Now let's take a look at the easier part. We'll extend Shape to have a new implementation by creating a Square class.

In the first piece of our extension we create the MorePerimeterShapes top-level trait, which extends the original PerimeterShapes. Inside, we create a new Square implementation of our original trait class. The first piece of our extension is in the following code:

ScalaExamples/src/main/scala/com/mblinn/mbfpp/oo/visitor/Shapes.scala
```
trait MorePerimeterShapes extends PerimeterShapes {
  class Square(side: Double) extends Shape {
    def perimeter = 4 * side;
  }
}
```

Now we can create another new top-level trait, MoreAreaShapes, that extends our original AreaShapes and mixes in the MorePerimeterShapes trait we just created. Inside this trait, we extend the Square we just created to also have an area() method:

ScalaExamples/src/main/scala/com/mblinn/mbfpp/oo/visitor/Shapes.scala
```
trait MoreAreaShapes extends AreaShapes with MorePerimeterShapes {
  class Square(side: Double) extends super.Square(side) with Shape {
    def area = side * side
  }
}
```

Now we can add a Square to our test shapes and see the full set of shapes and operations in action, as we do in the following code:

```
ScalaExamples/src/main/scala/com/mblinn/mbfpp/oo/visitor/Shapes.scala
object ThirdShapeExample extends MoreAreaShapes {
    val someMoreShapes = Vector(new Circle(4), new Rectangle(2, 2), new Square(4));
}

scala> for(shape <- someMoreShapes) yield shape.perimeter
res2: scala.collection.immutable.Vector[Double] =
        Vector(25.132741228718345, 8.0, 16.0)

scala> for(shape <- someMoreShapes) yield shape.area
res3: scala.collection.immutable.Vector[Double] =
        Vector(50.26548245743669, 4.0, 16.0)
```

Now we've successfully added both new implementations of Shape and new operations over it, and we've done so in a typesafe manner!

In Clojure

Our Clojure solution relies on multimethods, which let us specify an arbitrary dispatch function. Let's take a look at a simple example.

First, we create the multimethod using defmulti. This doesn't specify any implementations of the method; rather, it contains a dispatch function. In the following snippet we create a multimethod named test-multimethod. The dispatch function is a function of one argument, and it returns that argument untouched. However, it can be an arbitrary piece of code:

```
ClojureExamples/src/mbfpp/oo/visitor/examples.clj
(defmulti test-multimethod (fn [keyword] keyword))
```

The multimethod is implemented using defmethod. Method definitions look much like function definitions, except that they also contain a dispatching value, which corresponds to the values returned from the dispatch function.

In the following snippet, we define two implementations of test-multimethod. The first expects a dispatch value of :foo, and the second, :bar.

```
ClojureExamples/src/mbfpp/oo/visitor/examples.clj
(defmethod test-multimethod :foo [a-map]
  "foo-method was called")

(defmethod test-multimethod :bar [a-map]
  "bar-method was called")
```

When the multimethod is called, the dispatch function is first called, and then Clojure dispatches the call to the method with the matching dispatch value. Since our dispatch function returns its input, we call it with the desired dispatch values. The following REPL output demonstrates this:

```
=> (test-multimethod :foo)
"foo-method was called"
=> (test-multimethod :bar)
"bar-method was called"
```

Now that we've seen a basic example of multimethods in action, let's dig a bit deeper in. We'll define our perimeter operation as a multimethod. The dispatch function expects a map that represents our shape. One of the keys in the map is :shape-name, which the dispatch function extracts as our dispatch value.

Our perimeter multimethod is defined below, along with implementations for the circle and the rectangle:

ClojureExamples/src/mbfpp/oo/visitor/examples.clj
```
(defmulti perimeter (fn [shape] (:shape-name shape)))
(defmethod perimeter :circle [circle]
  (* 2 Math/PI (:radius circle)))
(defmethod perimeter :rectangle [rectangle]
  (+ (* 2 (:width rectangle)) (* 2 (:height rectangle))))
```

Now we can define a few test shapes:

ClojureExamples/src/mbfpp/oo/visitor/examples.clj
```
(def some-shapes [{:shape-name :circle :radius 4}
                  {:shape-name :rectangle :width 2 :height 2}])
```

Then we can run our perimeter method over them:

```
=> (for [shape some-shapes] (perimeter shape))
(25.132741228718345 8)
```

To add new operations, we create a new multimethod that handles the existing dispatch values. In the following snippet, we add support for an area operation:

ClojureExamples/src/mbfpp/oo/visitor/examples.clj
```
(defmulti area (fn [shape] (:shape-name shape)))
(defmethod area :circle [circle]
  (* Math/PI (:radius circle) (:radius circle)))
(defmethod area :rectangle [rectangle]
  (* (:width rectangle) (:height rectangle)))
```

Now we can calculate an area for our shapes as well:

```
=> (for [shape some-shapes] (area shape))
(50.26548245743669 4)
```

To add a new shape into the set of shapes we can handle across both the perimeter and area operations, we add new implementations of our multimethods that handle the appropriate dispatch values. In the following code, we add support for squares:

ClojureExamples/src/mbfpp/oo/visitor/examples.clj
```
(defmethod perimeter :square [square]
  (* 4 (:side square)))
(defmethod area :square [square]
  (* (:side square) (:side square)))
```

Let's add a square to our vector of test shapes:

ClojureExamples/src/mbfpp/oo/visitor/examples.clj
```
(def more-shapes (conj some-shapes
                       {:shape-name :square :side 4}))
```

And we can verify that our operations work on squares as well:

```
=> (for [shape more-shapes] (perimeter shape))
(25.132741228718345 8 16)
=> (for [shape more-shapes] (area shape))
(50.26548245743669 4 16)
```

We've only scratched the surface of what multimethods can do. Since we can specify an arbitrary dispatch function, we can dispatch on just about anything. Clojure also provides a way to make multimethods work with user-defined hierarchies, much like class hierarchies in object-oriented languages. However, even the simple usage of multimethods we just saw is enough to replace the interesting aspects of the Visitor pattern.

Discussion

Scala has a much harder problem to solve here, since it maintains static type safety while allowing for extensions both to implementations of a data type and the operations performed on it. Since Clojure is dynamically typed, it has no such requirement.

Our Visitor replacements are a great example of the tradeoffs between an expressive statically typed language like Scala and a dynamically typed language like Clojure. We had to expend more effort in Scala, and our solutions aren't quite as straightforward as the Clojure solutions. However, if we try to perform some operation on a type that can't handle it in Clojure, it's a runtime rather than a compile-time problem.

For Further Reading

Design Patterns: Elements of Reusable Object-Oriented Software [GHJV95]—Visitor

Related Patterns

Pattern 9, *Replacing Decorator*, on page 109

Pattern 11

Replacing Dependency Injection

Intent

To compose objects together using an external configuration or code, rather than having an object instantiate its own dependencies—this allows us to easily inject different dependency implementations into an object and provides a centralized place to understand what dependencies a given object has.

Overview

Objects are the primary unit of composition in the object-oriented world. Dependency Injection is about composing graphs of objects together. In its simplest form, all that's involved in Dependency Injection is to inject an object's dependencies through a constructor or setter.

For instance, the following class outlines a movie service that's capable of returning a user's favorite movies. It depends on a favorites service to pull back a list of favorite movies and a movie DAO to fetch details about individual movies:

JavaExamples/src/main/java/com/mblinn/mbfpp/oo/di/MovieService.java
```java
package com.mblinn.mbfpp.oo.di;
public class MovieService {

        private MovieDao movieDao;
        private FavoritesService favoritesService;
        public MovieService(MovieDao movieDao, FavoritesService favoritesService){
                this.movieDao = movieDao;
                this.favoritesService = favoritesService;
        }
}
```

Here we're using classic, constructor-based Dependency Injection. When it's constructed, the MovieService class needs to have its dependencies passed in. This can be done manually, but it's generally done using a dependency-injection framework.

Dependency Injection has several benefits. It makes it easy to change the implementation for a given dependency, which is especially handy for swapping out a real dependency with a stub in a unit test.

With appropriate container support, dependency injection can also make it easier to declaratively specify the overall shape of a system, as each component has its dependencies injected into it in a configuration file or in a bit of configuration code.

Functional Replacement

There's less of a need for a Dependency Injection–like pattern when programming in a more functional style. Functional programming naturally involves composing functions, as we've seen in patterns like Pattern 16, *Function Builder*, on page 167. Since this involves composing functions much as Dependency Injection composes classes, we get some of the benefits for free just from functional composition.

However, simple functional composition doesn't solve all of the problems Dependency Injection does. This is especially true in Scala because it's a hybrid language, and larger bodies of code are generally organized into objects.

In Scala

Classic Dependency Injection can be used in Scala. We can even use familiar Java frameworks like Spring or Guice. However, we can achieve many of the same goals without the need for any framework.

We'll take a look at a Scala pattern called the Cake pattern. This pattern uses Scala traits and self-type annotations to accomplish the same sort of composition and structure that we get with Dependency Injection without the need for a container.

In Clojure

The unit of injection in Clojure is the function, since Clojure is not object oriented. For the most part, this means that the problems we solve with Dependency Injection in an object-oriented language don't exist in Clojure, as we can naturally compose functions together.

However, one use for Dependency Injection does need a bit of special treatment in Clojure. To stub out functions for testing purposes, we can use a macro named with-redefs, which allows us to temporarily replace a function with a stub.

Sample Code: Favorite Videos

Let's take a closer look at the sketch of a problem we saw in the *Overview*, on page 128. There we created a movie service that allows us to do several movie-related actions. Each video is associated with a movie and needs to be decorated with details related to that movie, such as the movie's title.

To accomplish this, we've got a top-level movie service that depends on a movie DAO to get movie details and on a favorites service to fetch favorites for a given user.

Classic Java

In Java, our top-level MovieService is sketched out in the following class. We use Dependency Injection to inject a FavoritesService and a MovieDao via a constructor:

```
JavaExamples/src/main/java/com/mblinn/mbfpp/oo/di/MovieService.java
package com.mblinn.mbfpp.oo.di;
public class MovieService {

    private MovieDao movieDao;
    private FavoritesService favoritesService;
    public MovieService(MovieDao movieDao, FavoritesService favoritesService){
        this.movieDao = movieDao;
        this.favoritesService = favoritesService;
    }
}
```

In a full program, we'd then use a framework to wire up MovieService's dependencies. We have quite a few ways to do this, ranging from XML configuration files to Java configuration classes to annotations that automatically wire dependencies in.

All of these share one common trait: they need an external framework to be effective. Here we'll examine Scala and Clojure options that have no such limitation.

In Scala

Now we'll take a look at an example of Scala's Cake pattern. The rough idea is that we'll encapsulate the dependencies we want to inject inside of top-level traits, which represent our injectable components. Instead of instantiating dependencies directly inside of the trait, we create abstract vals that will hold references to them when we wire everything up.

We'll then use Scala's self-type annotation and mixin inheritance to specify wiring in a typesafe manner. Finally, we use a simple Scala object as a component registry. We mix all of our dependencies into the container object and instantiate them, holding references to them in the abstract vals mentioned previously.

This approach has a few nice properties. As we mentioned before, it doesn't require an outside container to use. In addition, wiring things up maintains static type safety.

Let's start off with a look at the data we'll be operating over. We've got three case classes, a Movie, a Video, and a DecoratedMovie, which represents a movie decorated with a video about it.

```scala
ScalaExamples/src/main/scala/com/mblinn/mbfpp/oo/di/ex1/Services.scala
case class Movie(movieId: String, title: String)
case class Video(movieId: String)
case class DecoratedMovie(movie: Movie, video: Video)
```

Now let's define some traits as interfaces for our dependencies, FavoritesService and MovieDao. We'll nest these traits inside of another set of traits that represent the injectable components. We'll see why this is necessary later in the example.

```scala
ScalaExamples/src/main/scala/com/mblinn/mbfpp/oo/di/ex1/Services.scala
trait MovieDaoComponent {
  trait MovieDao {
    def getMovie(id: String): Movie
  }
}

trait FavoritesServiceComponent {
  trait FavoritesService {
    def getFavoriteVideos(id: String): Vector[Video]
  }
}
```

Next up, we've got our implementations of the components introduced previously. Here we'll stub out the MovieDao and FavoritesService to return static responses by implementing the interfaces. Note that we need to extend the component traits we've wrapped them in as well.

```scala
ScalaExamples/src/main/scala/com/mblinn/mbfpp/oo/di/ex1/Services.scala
trait MovieDaoComponentImpl extends MovieDaoComponent {
  class MovieDaoImpl extends MovieDao {
    def getMovie(id: String): Movie = new Movie("42", "A Movie")
  }
}

trait FavoritesServiceComponentImpl extends FavoritesServiceComponent {
  class FavoritesServiceImpl extends FavoritesService {
    def getFavoriteVideos(id: String): Vector[Video] = Vector(new Video("1"))
  }
}
```

Now let's take a look at MovieServiceImpl, which depends on the FavoritesService and MovieDao defined previously. This class implements a single method, getFavoriteDecoratedMovies(), which takes a user ID and returns that user's favorite movies decorated by a video of that movie.

The full code for MovieServiceImpl, wrapped up in a top-level MovieServiceComponentImpl trait, follows:

```
ScalaExamples/src/main/scala/com/mblinn/mbfpp/oo/di/ex1/Services.scala
trait MovieServiceComponentImpl {
  this: MovieDaoComponent with FavoritesServiceComponent =>

  val favoritesService: FavoritesService
  val movieDao: MovieDao

  class MovieServiceImpl {
    def getFavoriteDecoratedMovies(userId: String): Vector[DecoratedMovie] =
      for (
        favoriteVideo <- favoritesService.getFavoriteVideos(userId);
        val movie = movieDao.getMovie(favoriteVideo.movieId)
      ) yield DecoratedMovie(movie, favoriteVideo)
  }
}
```

Let's take a closer look at this bit by bit. First we've got the self-type annotation on the top-level MovieServiceComponentImpl trait. This is part of the Scala magic that makes the Cake pattern typesafe.

```
this: MovieDaoComponent with FavoritesServiceComponent =>
```

The self-type annotation ensures that whenever MovieServiceComponentImpl is mixed into an object or a class, this reference of that object has the type MovieDaoComponent with FavoritesServiceComponent. Put another way, it ensures that when the MovieServiceComponentImpl is mixed into something, MovieDaoComponent and FavoritesServiceComponent or one of their subtypes are as well.

Next up are the explicit vals that we'll store references to our dependencies in:

```
val favoritesService: FavoritesService
val movieDao: MovieDao
```

These ensure that when we mix MovieServiceComponentImpl into our container object, we'll need to assign to the abstract vals.

Finally, we've got the object that serves as our component registry, ComponentRegistry. The registry extends implementations of all of our dependencies and instantiates them, storing references to them in the abstract vals we previously defined:

ScalaExamples/src/main/scala/com/mblinn/mbfpp/oo/di/ex1/Services.scala

```
object ComponentRegistry extends MovieServiceComponentImpl
  with FavoritesServiceComponentImpl with MovieDaoComponentImpl {
  val favoritesService = new FavoritesServiceImpl
  val movieDao = new MovieDaoImpl

  val movieService = new MovieServiceImpl
}
```

Now we can pull a full wired-up MovieService out of the registry when needed:

```
scala> val movieService = ComponentRegistry.movieService
movieService: ...
```

Earlier I claimed that this wiring preserves static type safety. Let's explore what this means in greater detail. First, let's take a look at what happens if we only extend MovieServiceComponentImpl itself in our object registry, as in the following code outline:

```
object BrokenComponentRegistry extends MovieServiceComponentImpl {

}
```

This causes a compiler error, something like the following:

> illegal inheritance; self-type com.mblinn.mbfpp.oo.di.ex1.Example.
> BrokenComponentRegistry.type *does not conform to com.mblinn.mbf-
> pp.oo.di.ex1.Example.MovieServiceComponentImpl's selftype...*

Here, the compiler is telling us that BrokenComponentRegistry doesn't conform to the self-type we declared for MovieServiceComponentImpl, as we're not also mixing in MovieDaoComponent and FavoritesServiceComponent.

We can fix that error by extending FavoritesServiceComponentImpl and MovieDaoComponentImpl, as we do in the following code:

```
object BrokenComponentRegistry extends MovieServiceComponentImpl
       with FavoritesServiceComponentImpl with MovieDaoComponentImpl {

}
```

However, this will get us another compiler error, which starts as follows:

> object creation impossible, since: it has 2 unimplemented members...

This error is saying we haven't implemented the favoritesService and movieDao members that MovieServiceComponentImpl requires us to.

In Clojure

Clojure doesn't have a direct analog to Dependency Injection. Instead, we pass functions directly into other functions as needed. For instance, here we declare our get-movie and get-favorite-videos functions:

ClojureExamples/src/mbfpp/functional/di/examples.clj

```
(defn get-movie [movie-id]
  {:id "42" :title "A Movie"})

(defn get-favorite-videos [user-id]
  [{:id "1"}])
```

Here we pass them into get-favorite-decorated-videos where they're used:

ClojureExamples/src/mbfpp/functional/di/examples.clj

```
(defn get-favorite-decorated-videos [user-id get-movie get-favorite-videos]
  (for [video (get-favorite-videos user-id)]
    {:movie (get-movie (:id video))
     :video video}))
```

Another possibility is to use Pattern 16, *Function Builder*, on page 167, to package up the dependent functions in a closure.

However, in Clojure, we generally only do this sort of direct injection when we want the user of the function to have control over the passed-in dependencies. We tend not to need it to define the overall shape of our programs.

Instead, programs in Clojure and other Lisps are generally organized as a series of layered, domain-specific languages. We'll see an example of such in Pattern 21, *Domain-Specific Language*, on page 218.

Sample Code: Test Stubs

While Dependency Injection is largely concerned with the organization of programs as a whole, one specific area in which it's especially helpful is injecting stubbed-out dependencies into tests.

Classic Java

In Java, we can just take our MovieService and manually inject stubs or mocks into it using constructor injection. Another option is to use the dependency injection container to instantiate a set of test dependencies.

The best approach depends on what sort of tests we're currently writing. For unit tests, it's generally simpler to just manually inject individual mocks. For larger integration-style tests, I prefer to go with the full-container approach.

In Scala

With Scala's Cake pattern, we can easily created mocked out versions of our dependencies. We do so in the following code snippet:

```
ScalaExamples/src/main/scala/com/mblinn/mbfpp/oo/di/ex1/Services.scala
trait MovieDaoComponentTestImpl extends MovieDaoComponent {
  class MovieDaoTestImpl extends MovieDao {
    def getMovie(id: String): Movie = new Movie("43", "A Test Movie")
  }
}

trait FavoritesServiceComponentTestImpl extends FavoritesServiceComponent {
  class FavoritesServiceTestImpl extends FavoritesService {
    def getFavoriteVideos(id: String): Vector[Video] = Vector(new Video("2"))
  }
}
```

Now we only need to mix in and instantiate the stubbed components rather than the real ones, and then our test movie service is ready to use:

```
ScalaExamples/src/main/scala/com/mblinn/mbfpp/oo/di/ex1/Services.scala
object TestComponentRegistery extends MovieServiceComponentImpl
  with FavoritesServiceComponentTestImpl with MovieDaoComponentTestImpl {
  val favoritesService = new FavoritesServiceTestImpl
  val movieDao = new MovieDaoTestImpl

  val movieService = new MovieServiceImpl
}
```

In Clojure

With our example Clojure code written as it is in the previous example, we only need to create test versions of our dependent functions and pass them into get-favorite-decorated-videos. We demonstrate this in the following code snippet:

```
ClojureExamples/src/mbfpp/functional/di/examples.clj
(defn get-test-movie [movie-id]
  {:id "43" :title "A Test Movie"})

(defn get-test-favorite-videos [user-id]
  [{:id "2"}])

=> (get-favorite-decorated-videos "2" get-test-movie get-test-favorite-videos)
({:movie {:title "A Test Movie", :id "43"}, :video {:id "2"}})
```

However, since we don't always structure whole Clojure programs by passing in every dependency as a higher-order function, we often need an alternative method for stubbing out test dependencies. Let's take a look at another version of get-favorite-decorated-videos that relies on its dependencies directly, rather than on having them passed in:

ClojureExamples/src/mbfpp/functional/di/examples.clj
```
(defn get-favorite-decorated-videos-2 [user-id]
  (for [video (get-favorite-videos user-id)]
    {:movie (get-movie (:id video))
     :video video}))
```

If we call get-favorite-decorated-videos-2, it'll use its hard-coded dependencies:

```
=> (get-favorite-decorated-videos-2 "1")
({:movie {:title "A Movie", :id "42"}, :video {:id "1"}})
```

We can use with-redefs to temporarily redefine those dependencies, as we demonstrate below:

```
=> (with-redefs
     [get-favorite-videos get-test-favorite-videos
      get-movie get-test-movie]
     (doall (get-favorite-decorated-videos-2 "2")))
({:movie {:title "A Test Movie", :id "43"}, :video {:id "2"}})
```

Note that we wrapped our call to get-favorite-decorated-videos-2 in a call to doall. The doall form forces the lazy sequence produced by get-favorite-decorated-videos-2 to be realized.

We need to use it here because laziness and with-redefs have a subtle interaction that can be confusing. Without forcing the sequence to be realized, it won't be fully realized until the REPL attempts to print it. By that time, the rebound function bindings will have reverted to their original bindings.

Clojure's with-redefs is a blunt instrument. As you might guess, replacing function definitions on the fly can be quite dangerous, so this is best saved only for test code.

Related Patterns

Pattern 16, *Function Builder*, on page 167

Pattern 21, *Domain-Specific Language*, on page 218

CHAPTER 4

Functional Patterns

4.1 Introduction

Functional programming has its own set of patterns that have evolved out of the functional style.

These patterns rely heavily on immutability. For instance, Pattern 12, *Tail Recursion*, on page 138, shows a general purpose replacement for iteration that doesn't rely on a mutable counter, while Pattern 15, *Chain of Operations*, on page 159, shows how to work with immutable data by chaining transformations on an immutable data structure.

Another theme in these patterns is the use of higher-order functions as a primary unit of composition. This dovetails nicely with the first theme, immutability and transformation of immutable data. By using higher-order functions we can easily do these transformations, as we demonstrate in Pattern 14, *Filter-Map-Reduce*, on page 155.

One final theme we'll explore is the ability of functional languages to be adapted to create little languages that solve particular problems. This type of programming has spread well outside the functional style, but it started with the Lisp tradition that Clojure carries on. We'll see it in Pattern 12, *Tail Recursion*, on page 138, and Pattern 21, *Domain-Specific Language*, on page 218.

Let's take a look at our first pattern, Tail Recursion.

Pattern 12

Tail Recursion

Intent

To repeat a computation without using mutable state and without overflowing the stack

Overview

Iteration is an imperative technique that requires mutable state. For example, let's examine a trivial problem, writing a function that will calculate the sum from one up to an arbitrary number, inclusive. The code below does just that, but it requires both i and sum to be mutable:

JavaExamples/src/main/java/com/mblinn/functional/tailrecursion/Sum.java
```java
public static int sum(int upTo) {
        int sum = 0;
        for (int i = 0; i <= upTo; i++)
                sum += i;
        return sum;
}
```

Since the functional world emphasizes immutability, iteration is out. In its place, we can use recursion, which does not require immutability. Recursion has its own problems, though; in particular, each recursive call will lead to another frame on the program's call stack.

To get around that, we can use a particular form of recursion called *tail recursion*, which can be optimized to use a single frame on the stack, a process known as *tail call optimization* or *TCO*.

Let's think about how we'd write the sum() as a recursive function, sumRecursive(). First, we need to decide when our recursion should stop and start. Since we're summing together all numbers stopping at some arbitrary number, it makes sense to work down from that number and stop at zero. This stopping point is known as our *base case*.

Next we need to figure out what to do to perform the actual computation. In this case, we take the number we're currently working on and add it to the results of calling tailRecursive() with that number minus one. Eventually, we get down to our base case of zero, at which point the stack unwinds, returning partial sums as it goes, until it reaches the top and returns the final sum. The code below demonstrates this solution:

```
JavaExamples/src/main/java/com/mblinn/functional/tailrecursion/Sum.java
public static int sumRecursive(int upTo) {
        if (upTo == 0)
                return 0;
        else
                return upTo + sumRecursive(upTo - 1);
}
```

There's a problem with this, though. Each recursive call adds a frame to the stack, which means this solution takes memory proportional to the size of the sequence we're summing, as shown in the following figure.

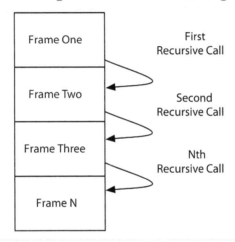

Figure 10—Simple Stack. An illustration of the stack during normal recursive calls—each recursive call adds a call to the stack; these frames represent memory that cannot be reclaimed until after the recursion is done.

Clearly this isn't practical, but we can do better. The ultimate cause for exploding stack use is that each time we make a recursive call, we need the result of that call to finish the computation we're doing in the current call. This means that the runtime has no choice but to store the intermediate results on the stack.

If we were to make sure that the recursive call was the last thing that happens in each branch of the function, known as the tail position, this would no longer be the case. Doing so requires us to take the intermediate values that were formerly stored on the stack and pass them through the call chain. The code below illustrates this:

JavaExamples/src/main/java/com/mblinn/functional/tailrecursion/Sum.java
```
public static int sumTailRecursive(int upTo, int currentSum) {
        if (upTo == 0)
                return currentSum;
        else
                return sumTailRecursive(upTo - 1, currentSum + upTo);
}
```

Once we rewrite the function to be tail recursive, it's possible to use TCO to run it in only a single stack frame, as shown in this figure.

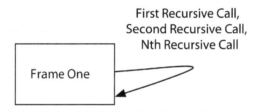

Figure 11—Stack with TCO. With TCO, recursive calls in the tail position don't generate a new stack frame. Instead, each call uses the existing stack frame, removing whatever data was there from the previous call.

Unfortunately, the JVM doesn't support TCO directly, so Scala and Clojure need to use some tricks to compile their tail recursive calls down to the same bytecode used for iteration. In Clojure's case, this is done by providing two special forms, loop and recur, instead of using general purpose function calls.

In Scala's case, the Scala compiler will attempt to translate tail recursive calls into iteration behind the scenes, and Scala provides an annotation, @tailrec, that can be placed on functions that are meant to be used in a tail recursive manner. If the function is called recursively without being in the tail position, the compiler will generate an error.

Code Sample: Recursive People

Let's take a look at a recursive solution to a simple problem. We've got a sequence of first names and a sequence of last names, and we want to put them together to make people. To solve this, we need to go through both sequences in lock step. We'll assume that some other part of the program has verified that the two sequences are of the same size.

At each step in the recursion, we'll take the first element in both sequences and put them together to form a full name. We'll then pass the rest of each sequence onto the next recursive call along with a sequence of the people we've formed so far. Let's see how it looks in Scala.

In Scala

The first thing we'll need is a Scala case class to represent our people. Here we've got one with a first and a last name:

ScalaExamples/src/main/scala/com/mblinn/mbfpp/functional/tr/Names.scala
```scala
case class Person(firstNames: String, lastNames: String)
```

Next up is our recursive function itself. This is actually split into two functions. The first is a function named makePeople, which takes in two sequences, firstNames and lastNames. The second is a helper function nested inside of makePeople, which adds an additional argument used to pass the list of people through recursive calls. Let's take a look at the whole function before we break it down into smaller parts:

ScalaExamples/src/main/scala/com/mblinn/mbfpp/functional/tr/Names.scala
```scala
def makePeople(firstNames: Seq[String], lastNames: Seq[String]) = {
  @tailrec
  def helper(firstNames: Seq[String], lastNames: Seq[String],
                     people: Vector[Person]): Seq[Person] =
    if (firstNames.isEmpty)
      people
    else {
      val newPerson = Person(firstNames.head, lastNames.head)
      helper(firstNames.tail, lastNames.tail, people :+ newPerson)
    }
  helper(firstNames, lastNames, Vector[Person]())
}
```

First, let's examine the function signature of makePeople:

```scala
def makePeople(firstNames: Seq[String], lastNames: Seq[String]) = {
      «function-body»
}
```

This just says that makePeople takes two Seqs of String. Since we don't specify a return type, the compiler will infer it from the function body.

Next up, let's look at the signature of the helper function. This function is responsible for the actual tail recursive calls. The helper function is annotated with a @tailrec annotation, which makes the compiler generate an error if it's called recursively but not tail recursively. The function signature simply adds an additional argument, the people vector, which will accumulate results through recursive calls.

Notice that we specified a return type here, though we generally omit it in our Scala examples. This is because the compiler can't infer types for recursively called functions.

```scala
def helper(firstNames: Seq[String], lastNames: Seq[String],
                  people: Vector[Person]): Seq[Person] =
              «function-body»
```

Now the body for helper. If the firstNames sequence is empty, we return the list of people we've built up. Otherwise, we pick the first first name and the first last name off of their respective sequences, create a Person out of them, and call the helper function again with the tail of the two sequences and the new person appended to the list of people:

```scala
if (firstNames.isEmpty)
      people
else {
      val newPerson = Person(firstNames.head, lastNames.head)
      helper(firstNames.tail, lastNames.tail, people :+ newPerson)
}
```

Finally, we simply call helper with the sequences of names and an empty Vector to hold our people:

```scala
helper(firstNames, lastNames, Vector[Person]())
```

One closing note on the syntax: using some of Scala's object-oriented features, namely methods, would let us cut out some of the verbosity that comes along with a recursive function definition. The method signatures would look like this:

```scala
def makePeopleMethod(firstNames: Seq[String], lastNames: Seq[String]) = {
      @tailrec
      def helper(firstNames: Seq[String], lastNames: Seq[String],
                  people: Vector[Person]): Seq[Person] =
              «method-body»
      }
}
```

Since we're sticking mainly to the functional bits of Scala in this book, we're using functions for most of the examples rather than methods. Methods can often be used as higher-order functions in Scala, but it can sometimes be awkward to do so.

In Clojure

In Clojure, tail recursive calls are never optimized, so even a tail recursive call will end up consuming a stack frame. Instead of providing TCO, Clojure gives us two forms, loop and recur. The loop form defines a recursion point, and the keyword recur jumps back to it, passing it new values.

In practice, this looks almost exactly like defining a private helper function does, so the form of our solution is very similar to the Scala solution, though we'll use a simple map to store our people, as is standard in Clojure. Let's take a look at the code:

```
ClojureExamples/src/mbfpp/functional/tr/names.clj
(defn make-people [first-names last-names]
  (loop [first-names first-names last-names last-names people []]
    (if (seq first-names)
      (recur
        (rest first-names)
        (rest last-names)
        (conj
          people
          {:first (first first-names) :last (first last-names)}))
      people)))
```

The first interesting bit of code here is the loop declaration. Here, we define our recursion point and the values we'll start our recursion at: the passed-in sequences of first and last names and an empty vector we'll use to accumulate people as we recur.

```
(loop [first-names first-names last-names last-names people []]
      «loop-body»
)
```

The code snippet first-names first-names last-names last-names people [] might look a little funny, but all it's doing is initializing the first-names and last-names that we're defining in the loop to be the values that were passed into the function and the people to an empty vector.

The bulk of the example is in the if expression. If the sequence of first names still has items in it, then we take the first item from each sequence, create a map to represent the person, and conj it onto our people accumulator.

Once we've conjed the new person onto the people vector, we use recur to jump back to the recursion point we defined with loop. This is analogous to the recursive call that we made in the Scala example.

If we don't jump back, we know that we've gone through the sequences of names, and we return the people we've constructed.

```
(if (seq first-names)
      (recur
            (rest first-names)
            (rest last-names)
            (conj
                  people
                  {:first (first first-names) :last (first last-names)}))
      people)
```

It may not be immediately apparent why the test in the if expression above works. It's because the seq of an empty collection is nil, which evaluates to false, while the seq of any other collection yields a nonempty sequence. The snippet below demonstrates this:

```
=> (seq [])
nil
=> (seq [:hi])
(:hi)
```

Using nil as the base case for a recursion when you're dealing with sequences is common in Clojure.

Discussion

Tail recursion is equivalent to iteration. In fact, the Scala and Clojure compilers will compile their respective ways of handling tail recursion down to the same sort of bytecode that iteration in Java would. The main advantage of tail recursion over iteration is simply that it eliminates a source of mutability in the language, which is why it's so popular in the functional world.

I personally prefer tail recursion over iteration for a couple of other minor reasons. The first is that it eliminates an extra index variable. The second is that it makes it explicit exactly what data structures are being operated on and what data structures are being generated, because they're both passed as arguments through the call chain.

In an iterative solution, if we were trying to operate on two sequences in lock step and generate another data structure, they would all just be mixed in with the body of a function that may be doing other things. I've found that using tail recursion over iteration acts as a nice forcing factor to structure our functions well, since all of the data we're operating on must be passed through the call chain, and it's hard to do that if you've got more than a few pieces of data.

Since tail recursion is equivalent to iteration, it's really a fairly low-level operation. There's generally some higher-level, more-declarative way to solve a problem than using tail recursion. For instance, here's a shorter version of the solution to our person-making example that takes advantage of some higher-order functions in Clojure:

ClojureExamples/src/mbfpp/functional/tr/names.clj
```
(defn shorter-make-people [first-names last-names]
  (for [[first last] (partition 2 (interleave first-names last-names))]
    {:first first :last last}))
```

Which solution to use is a matter of preference, but experienced functional programmers tend to prefer the shorter, more-declarative solutions. They're easier for the experienced functional programmer to read at a glance. The downside to these solutions is that they're harder for the novice to grok, since they may require knowledge of many higher-order library functions.

Whenever I'm about to write a solution that requires tail recursion, I like to comb the API docs for higher-order functions, or a combination of higher-order functions, that do what I want. If I can't find a higher-order function that works, or if the solution I come up with involves many higher-order functions combined in Byzantine ways, then I fall back to tail recursion.

Related Patterns

Pattern 5, *Replacing Iterator*, on page 72

Pattern 13, *Mutual Recursion*, on page 146

Pattern 14, *Filter-Map-Reduce*, on page 155

Pattern 13

Mutual Recursion

Intent

To use mutually recursive functions to express certain algorithms, such as walking tree-like data structures, recursive descent parsing, and state machine manipulations

Overview

In Pattern 12, *Tail Recursion*, on page 138, we looked at using tail recursion to walk over sequences of data and the tricks that Clojure and Scala use to avoid consuming stack frames while doing so, since the JVM doesn't directly support tail recursion.

For the majority of cases, the simple tail recursion we looked at in Pattern 12, *Tail Recursion*, on page 138, where the only recursive calls are *self-recursive*, is all we need. However, some of the more complex problems require solutions where functions can call each other recursively.

For instance, *finite state machines* are a great way of modeling many classes of problems, and mutual recursion is a great way to program them. Network protocols, many physical systems like vending machines and elevators, and parsing semistructured text can all be done with state machines.

In this pattern, we'll look at some problems that can be solved cleanly using mutual recursion. Since the JVM doesn't support tail recursive optimization, Scala and Clojure have to use a neat trick to support practical mutual recursion, just as they did with normal tail recursion, to avoid running out of stack space.

For mutual recursion, this trick is called a trampoline. Instead of making mutually recursive calls directly, we return a function that *would* make the desired call, and we let the compiler or runtime take care of the rest.

Scala's support for trampolining hides a lot of the details of this and provides us with both a tailcall() method to make mutually recursive calls and a done() method to call when we're done with the recursion.

That might sound bizarre, but it's deceptively simple. To prove it, let's take a quick look at the "Hello, World" for mutual recursion, a mathematically pretty but horribly inefficient way of telling if a number is even or odd, before we get into more real-world examples.

Here's how it works: we need two functions, isEven() and isOdd(). Each function takes a single Long n. The isEven() function checks to see if n is zero and, if so, it returns true. Otherwise it decrements n and calls isOdd. The isOdd() method checks to see if n is zero and if so returns false. Otherwise it decrements n and calls isEven.

This is clearest in code, so here it is:

ScalaExamples/src/main/scala/com/mblinn/mbfpp/functional/mr/EvenOdd.scala
```
def isOdd(n: Long): Boolean = if (n == 0) false else isEven(n - 1)

def isEven(n: Long): Boolean = if (n == 0) true else isOdd(n - 1)

scala> isEven(0)
res0: Boolean = true

scala> isOdd(1)
res1: Boolean = true

scala> isEven(1000)
res2: Boolean = true

scala> isOdd(1001)
res3: Boolean = true
```

That works fine for small numbers, but what if we try it with a larger one?

```
scala> isOdd(100001)
java.lang.StackOverflowError
...
```

As we can see, each mutually recursive call consumes a stack frame, so this causes our stack to overflow! Let's see how to fix that using Scala's trampoline.

Support for trampolining in Scala lives in scala.util.control.TailCalls, and it comes in two parts. The first is a done() function, which is used to return the final result from the recursive calls. The second is a tailcall() function, which is used to make the recursive calls.

In addition, the results returned by the tail recursive functions are wrapped in a TailRec type rather than being returned directly. To get them out at the end, we can call result() on the final TailRec instance.

Here's our even/odd code, rewritten to take advantage of Scala's trampolining:

ScalaExamples/src/main/scala/com/mblinn/mbfpp/functional/mr/EvenOdd.scala
```scala
def isOddTrampoline(n: Long): TailRec[Boolean] =
  if (n == 0) done(false) else tailcall(isEvenTrampoline(n - 1))

def isEvenTrampoline(n: Long): TailRec[Boolean] =
  if (n == 0) done(true) else tailcall(isOddTrampoline(n - 1))
```

```scala
scala> isEvenTrampoline(0).result
res0: Boolean = true

scala> isEvenTrampoline(1).result
res1: Boolean = false

scala> isEvenTrampoline(1000).result
res2: Boolean = true

scala> isEvenTrampoline(1001).result
res3: Boolean = false
```

Let's try running it:

```scala
scala> isOddTrampoline(100001).result
res4: Boolean = true
```

This time, there's no stack overflow with big numbers, though if you try with a big enough number, you should expect to wait a very long time, since this algorithm's runtime is linearly proportional to the size of the number!

Also Known As

Indirect Recursion

Example Code: Phases of Matter

In this example, we'll use Mutual Recursion to build a simple state machine that takes a sequence of transitions between the different phases of matter—liquid, solid, vapor, and plasma—and verifies that the sequence is valid. For instance, it's possible to go from solid to liquid, but not from solid to plasma.

Each state in the machine is represented by a function, and the transitions are represented by a sequence of transition names, like condensation and vaporization. A state function picks the first transition off of the sequence and, if it's valid, calls the function that gets it to where it should transition, passing it the remainder of the transitions. If the transition isn't valid, we stop and return false.

For example, if we're in the solid state and the transition we see is melting, then we call the liquid function. If it's condensation, which isn't a valid transition out of the solid state, then we immediately return false.

Before we jump into the code, let's take a look at a picture of the phases-of-matter state machine.

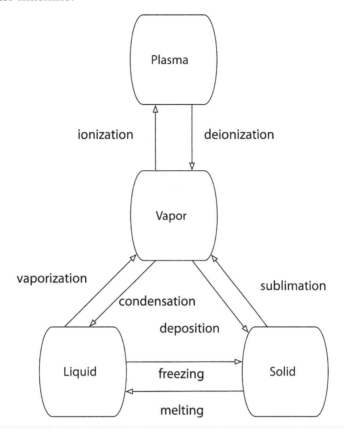

Figure 12—The Phases of Matter. The phases of matter and the transitions between them

The nodes in this graph represent the functions we'll need to model this state machine using Mutual Recursion, and the edges represent the transitions that those functions will operate on. Let's take a look at the code, starting with Scala.

In Scala

Our Scala solution relies on four functions, one for each phase of matter: plasma(), vapor(), liquid(), and solid(). In addition, we'll need a set of case objects to represent the transitions: Ionization, Deinonizaton, Vaporization, and so forth.

Each of the four functions takes a single argument and a List of transitions, and each uses Scala's pattern matching to destructure it. If the list is Nil, then we know we've reached the end successfully and we call done(), passing in true.

Otherwise, we check the first transition in the list to see if it's valid. If so, we transition to the state it indicates and pass the remainder of the transitions. If the first transition isn't valid, we call done, passing in false.

Let's look at the code, starting with the case objects to represent our transitions. They're pretty straightforward; each transition is its own object, and they all inherit from a Transition class.

ScalaExamples/src/main/scala/com/mblinn/mbfpp/functional/mr/Phases.scala
```
class Transition
case object Ionization extends Transition
case object Deionization extends Transition
case object Vaporization extends Transition
case object Condensation extends Transition
case object Freezing extends Transition
case object Melting extends Transition
case object Sublimation extends Transition
case object Deposition extends Transition
```

Now let's take a look at the meat of the example, the functions that represent our phases of matter. As promised, there are four: plasma(), vapor(), liquid(), and solid(). Here's the full set of functions we'll need:

ScalaExamples/src/main/scala/com/mblinn/mbfpp/functional/mr/Phases.scala
```
def plasma(transitions: List[Transition]): TailRec[Boolean] = transitions match {
  case Nil => done(true)
  case Deionization :: restTransitions => tailcall(vapor(restTransitions))
  case _ => done(false)
}
def vapor(transitions: List[Transition]): TailRec[Boolean] = transitions match {
  case Nil => done(true)
  case Condensation :: restTransitions => tailcall(liquid(restTransitions))
  case Deposition :: restTransitions => tailcall(solid(restTransitions))
  case Ionization :: restTransitions => tailcall(plasma(restTransitions))
  case _ => done(false)
}

def liquid(transitions: List[Transition]): TailRec[Boolean] = transitions match {
  case Nil => done(true)
  case Vaporization :: restTransitions => tailcall(vapor(restTransitions))
  case Freezing :: restTransitions => tailcall(solid(restTransitions))
  case _ => done(false)
}

def solid(transitions: List[Transition]): TailRec[Boolean] = transitions match {
  case Nil => done(true)
  case Melting :: restTransitions => tailcall(liquid(restTransitions))
  case Sublimation :: restTransitions => tailcall(vapor(restTransitions))
  case _ => done(false)
}
```

We've already described how they work at a high level, so let's pick apart one of them, vapor(), in detail, starting with its signature:

```
def vapor(transitions: List[Transition]): TailRec[Boolean] = transitions match {
    «function-body»
}
```

As we can see, it just takes in a List of Transitions named transitions and takes pattern matches on it. Instead of returning a Boolean directly, it returns a TailRec of Boolean, so we can take advantage of Scala's support for trampolining.

Moving on to the first case clause in the match expression, we see that it calls done to return true if the list is empty, or Nil. This is the base case of the recursion; if we get here it means we've successfully processed all the transitions originally in the sequence.

```
case Nil => done(true)
```

Next up are the three middle clauses. These use pattern matching to pick off the head of the sequence if it's a valid transition and call the function to transition to the appropriate state, passing the rest of the transitions:

```
case Condensation :: restTransitions => tailcall(liquid(restTransitions))
case Deposition :: restTransitions => tailcall(solid(restTransitions))
case Ionization :: restTransitions => tailcall(plasma(restTransitions))
```

Finally, the last clause, which is a catchall. If we fall through to here, we know we haven't processed all the transitions and the transition we saw wasn't valid, so we call done() and pass in false.

```
case _ => done(false)
```

Let's take a look at it in action, first with a valid list starting from the solid state:

```
scala>   val validSequence = List(Melting, Vaporization, Ionization, Deionization)
validSequence: List[com.mblinn.mbfpp.functional.mr.Phases.Transition] =
        List(Melting, Vaporization, Ionization, Deionization)

scala> solid(validSequence).result
res0: Boolean = true
```

Next we have an invalid list starting from the liquid state:

```
scala>   val invalidSequence = List(Vaporization, Freezing)
invalidSequence: List[com.mblinn.mbfpp.functional.mr.Phases.Transition] =
        List(Vaporization, Freezing)

scala> liquid(invalidSequence).result
res1: Boolean = false
```

This wraps up our first look at Mutual Recursion in Scala. Let's see how it looks in Clojure.

In Clojure

The Clojure code is similar to the Scala code, at least at a high level. We've got plasma, vapor, liquid, and solid functions, each of which takes a sequence of transitions.

We use Clojure's destructuring to pick apart the sequence into the current transition, which we bind to transition and to the rest of the transitions in rest-transitions.

If transition is nil, we know we've reached the end successfully and we return true. Otherwise we check to see if it's a valid transition, and, if so, we transition to the appropriate phase. If not, we return false. Here's the full code:

ClojureExamples/src/mbfpp/functional/mr/phases.clj
```clojure
(declare plasma vapor liquid solid)

(defn plasma [[transition & rest-transitions]]
  #(case transition
     nil true
     :deionization (vapor rest-transitions)
     :false))

(defn vapor [[transition & rest-transitions]]
  #(case transition
     nil true
     :condensation (liquid rest-transitions)
     :deposition (solid rest-transitions)
     :ionization (plasma rest-transitions)
     false))

(defn liquid [[transition & rest-transitions]]
  #(case transition
     nil true
     :vaporization (vapor rest-transitions)
     :freezing (solid rest-transitions)
     false))

(defn solid [[transition & rest-transitions]]
  #(case transition
     nil true
     :melting (liquid rest-transitions)
     :sublimation (vapor rest-transitions)
     false))
```

Notice how there are no calls to done or tailcall like there are in the Scala version? Instead of using tailcall, we just return a function that *will* make the call we want to make. In this case, we're using Clojure's shorthand for anonymous functions to do so.

When we actually want to start the chain of mutually recursive calls, we pass the function we want to call into trampoline, along with its arguments:

```
=> (def valid-sequence [:melting :vaporization :ionization :deionization])
#'mbfpp.functional.mr.phases/valid-sequence
=> (trampoline solid valid-sequence)
true
=> (def invalid-sequence [:vaporization :freezing])
#'mbfpp.functional.mr.phases/invalid-sequence
=> (trampoline liquid invalid-sequence)
false
```

This returns true for the valid sequence and false for the invalid one, just as we'd expect.

Before we leave this example, I'd like to talk a little bit about Nil in Scala and nil in Clojure. The code we wrote looked fairly similar, but there's a subtle difference between the two nils that's worth mentioning.

In Scala, Nil is just a synonym for the empty list, as we can see if we enter it into the Scala REPL:

```
scala> Nil
res0: scala.collection.immutable.Nil.type = List()
```

In Clojure, nil just means "nothing": it means that we don't have a value, and it's distinct from the empty list. Various functional languages have treated nil differently over the years, so whenever you come across a new one it's always worth taking a minute to understand just what the language means by nil.

Discussion

Mutual Recursion can be pretty handy, but usually only in specific circumstances. State machines are one of these circumstances; they're actually very useful little beasts. Unfortunately, most developers just remember them from their undergraduate computer science years, where they had to prove the equivalence between finite state machines and regular expressions, which is interesting but of no use to most developers.

State machines have been a bit more popular in recent years, though. They're a big part of the actor model, a model for concurrent and distributed programming, that's used by Scala's Akka library and by Erlang, another functional language. Ruby has a clever gem for creating them, aptly named state_machine.

Another thing that's worth noting is that the trampoline we saw here, in both Scala and Clojure, is just one way of doing Mutual Recursion. It's only necessary because the JVM doesn't implement tail call optimization directly.

Related Patterns

Pattern 5, *Replacing Iterator*, on page 72

Pattern 14, *Filter-Map-Reduce*, on page 155

Filter-Map-Reduce

Intent

To manipulate a sequence (list, vector, and so on) declaratively using filter, map, and reduce to produce a new one—this is a powerful, high-level way of doing many sequence manipulations that would otherwise be verbose.

Overview

The way we manipulate sequences in a procedural language is more closely related to the way a computer works than to the way humans think. Iteration is a step above the dreaded goto statement, and it's intended to be easily translated into machine code more than it's intended to be easy to use.

Filter-Map-Reduce gives us a more declarative way to do many sequence manipulations. Instead of writing code that reorders or alters the elements in a sequence by working its way iteratively through them, element by element, we can work at a higher level by using a filter function to select the elements we care about: map to transform each element and reduce, sometimes known as fold, to combine the results.

Filter-Map-Reduce replaces many, though not all, iterative algorithms used by object-oriented programmers with declarative code.

The main advantage to Filter-Map-Reduce over iteration is code clarity. A well-written Filter-Map-Reduce takes a fraction of the code that the iterative equivalent takes. It can often be read at a glance, like prose, by an experienced practitioner, while the iterative solution requires parsing at least one loop and a conditional.

One downside is that not all iteration can be replaced with Filter-Map-Reduce. Another is that it may sometimes be difficult or unclear how to create a sequence that lends itself to Filter-Map-Reduce. In these cases, one of the patterns in the list of *Related Patterns*, on page 158, may be a better fit.

Code Sample: Calculate Discount

The implementation of Filter-Map-Reduce combines filter, map, and reduce, though not always in that order. Let's look at an example of calculating a total discount on a sequence of prices, where any price twenty dollars or over is discounted at ten percent, and any under twenty is full price.

In Scala

Filter-Map-Reduce in Scala is very similar to the Clojure implementation. We start with a filter function to select prices greater than twenty dollars:

```
scala> Vector(20.0, 4.5, 50.0, 15.75, 30.0, 3.5) filter (price => price >= 20)
res0: scala.collection.immutable.Vector[Double] = Vector(20.0, 50.0, 30.0)
```

We use map to get ten percent of them:

```
scala> Vector(20.0, 50.0, 30.0) map (price => price * 0.10)
res1: scala.collection.immutable.Vector[Double] = Vector(2.0, 5.0, 3.0)
```

And we sum them together using reduce:

```
scala> Vector(2.0, 5.0, 3.0) reduce ((total, price) => total + price)
res2: Double = 10.0
```

Putting it together gives us calculateDiscount:

ScalaExamples/src/main/scala/com/mblinn/mbfpp/functional/mfr/Discount.scala
```
def calculateDiscount(prices : Seq[Double]) : Double = {
  prices filter(price => price >= 20.0) map
      (price => price * 0.10) reduce
               ((total, price) => total + price)
}
```

```
scala> calculateDiscount(Vector(20.0, 4.5, 50.0, 15.75, 30.0, 3.5))
res1: Double = 10.0
```

You can also use named functions if that's more your style, though I prefer the anonymous function version here:

ScalaExamples/src/main/scala/com/mblinn/mbfpp/functional/mfr/Discount.scala
```
def calculateDiscountNamedFn(prices : Seq[Double]) : Double = {
  def isGreaterThan20(price : Double) = price >= 20.0
  def tenPercent(price : Double) = price * 0.10
  def sumPrices(total: Double, price : Double) = total + price

  prices filter isGreaterThan20 map tenPercent reduce sumPrices
}
```

In Clojure

Let's create a function calculate-discount that uses Filter-Map-Reduce to calculate a total discount. For the sake of example, we'll use a vector of doubles to represent our prices. We need to filter first so that only prices greater than twenty dollars remain, like this:

```
=> (filter (fn [price] (>= price 20)) [20.0 4.5 50.0 15.75 30.0 3.50])
(20.0 50.0 30.0)
```

Then we need to take the filtered prices and multiply them by 0.10 to get ten percent of each, using map:

```
=> (map (fn [price] (* price 0.10)) [20.0 50.0 30.0])
(2.0 5.0 3.0)
```

Finally, we need to combine those results using reduce and addition:

```
=> (reduce + [2.0 5.0 3.0])
10.0
```

Putting this together, we get calculate-discount:

ClojureExamples/src/mbfpp/functional/mfr/discount.clj
```
(defn calculate-discount [prices]
  (reduce +
          (map (fn [price] (* price 0.10))
               (filter (fn [price] (>= price 20.0)) prices))))
```

There's a trick to reading Lisp code that lets experienced Lispers read this at a glance but which frustrates the uninitiated. To read this easily, you need to work from the inside out. Start with the filter function, move on to map, and finally to reduce.

In prose, this would be, "Filter the prices so that only those greater than twenty remain, multiply the remaining prices by a tenth, and add them together." With a little practice, reading this sort of code is not only natural, but since it's at a much higher level and closer to natural language, it's much quicker than the equivalent iterative solution.

We can make a slight modification to the pattern by naming the map and filter functions, as shown in the code below:

ClojureExamples/src/mbfpp/functional/mfr/discount.clj
```
(defn calculate-discount-namedfn [prices]
  (letfn [(twenty-or-greater? [price] (>= price 20.0))
          (ten-percent [price] (* price 0.10))]
    (reduce + 0.0 (map ten-percent (filter twenty-or-greater? prices)))))
```

This makes the pattern read more like prose at the expense of some extra code. When the map and filter functions are one-offs, as they are here, I prefer the original version with anonymous functions, but both styles are common. Which one to use is a matter of taste.

Discussion

The Filter-Map-Reduce pattern relies on declarative data manipulation, which is higher level than iterative solutions and often higher level than explicitly recursive ones. It's much like the difference between using SQL to generate a report from data in a relational database versus iterating over the lines in a flat file with the same data. A well-written SQL version will generally be shorter and clearer, since it's using a language created specifically for manipulating data. Using Map-Reduce-Filter gives us much of that declarative power.

One other thing to note is how we built our solutions from the bottom up, starting by creating our map, reduce, and filter functions in the REPL and then combining them. This bottom-up workflow is extremely common in functional programming. The ability to experiment in the REPL and build up programs through exploration is extremely powerful, and we'll see many more examples of it in functional patterns.

Related Patterns

Pattern 5, *Replacing Iterator*, on page 72

Pattern 12, *Tail Recursion*, on page 138

Pattern 13, *Mutual Recursion*, on page 146

Pattern 15

Chain of Operations

Intent

To chain a sequence of computations together—this allows us to work cleanly with immutable data without storing lots of temporary results.

Overview

Sending some bit of data through a set of operations is a useful technique. This is especially true when working with immutable data. Since we can't mutate a data structure, we need to send an immutable one through a series of transformations if we want to make more than a single change.

Another reason we chain operations is because it leads to succinct code. For instance, the builder we saw in Pattern 4, *Replacing Builder for Immutable Object*, on page 62, chains setting operations to keep our code lean, as the following snippet shows:

```
JavaExamples/src/main/java/com/mblinn/oo/javabean/PersonHarness.java
ImmutablePerson.Builder b = ImmutablePerson.newBuilder();
ImmutablePerson p = b.firstName("Peter").lastName("Jones").build();
```

Other times we chain method invocations to avoid creating noisy temporary values. In the code below we get a String value out of a List and uppercase it in one shot:

```
JavaExamples/src/main/java/com/mblinn/mbfpp/functional/coo/Examples.java
List<String> names = new ArrayList<String>();
names.add("Michael Bevilacqua Linn");
names.get(0).toUpperCase();
```

This style of programming is even more powerful in the functional world, where we have higher-order functions. For example, here we've got a snippet of Scala code that creates initials from a name:

```
ScalaExamples/src/main/scala/com/mblinn/mbfpp/functional/coo/Examples.scala
val name = "michael bevilacqua linn"
val initials = name.split(" ") map (_.toUpperCase) map (_.charAt(0))  mkString
```

It does so by calling split() on the name, turning it into an array, then mapping functions over it that uppercase the strings and pick out the first character in each. Finally, we turn the array back into a string.

This is concise and declarative, so it reads nicely.

Sample Code: Function Call Chaining

Let's take a look at a sample that involves several chained function calls. The objective is to write the code such that when we read it we can easily trace the flow of data from one step to the next.

We'll take a vector of videos that represent a person's video-viewing history, and we'll calculate the total time spent watching cat videos. To do so, we'll need to pick only the cat videos out of the vector, get their length, and finally add them together.

In Scala

For our Scala solution, we'll represent videos as a case class with a title, video type, and length. The code to define this class and populate some test data follows:

ScalaExamples/src/main/scala/com/mblinn/mbfpp/functional/coo/Examples.scala
```scala
case class Video(title: String, video_type: String, length: Int)

val v1 = Video("Pianocat Plays Carnegie Hall", "cat", 300)
val v2 = Video("Paint Drying", "home-improvement", 600)
val v3 = Video("Fuzzy McMittens Live At The Apollo", "cat", 200)

val videos = Vector(v1, v2, v3)
```

To calculate the total time spent watching cat videos, we filter out videos where the video_type is equal to "cat", extract the length field from the remaining videos, and then sum those lengths. The code to do so follows:

ScalaExamples/src/main/scala/com/mblinn/mbfpp/functional/coo/Examples.scala
```scala
def catTime(videos: Vector[Video]) =
  videos.
  filter((video) => video.video_type == "cat").
  map((video) => video.length).
  sum
```

Now we can apply catTime() to our test data to get the total amount of time spent on cat videos:

```scala
scala> catTime(videos)
res0: Int = 500
```

This solution reads nicely from top to bottom, almost like prose. It does so without needing extra variables or any mutation, so it's ideal in the functional world.

In Clojure

Let's take a look at our cat-viewing problem in Clojure. Here, we'll use maps for our videos. The following code snippet creates some test data:

```
ClojureExamples/src/mbfpp/functional/coo/examples.clj
(def v1
  {:title "Pianocat Plays Carnegie Hall"
   :type :cat
   :length 300})

(def v2
  {:title "Paint Drying"
   :type :home-improvement
   :length 600})

(def v3
  {:title "Fuzzy McMittens Live At The Apollo"
   :type :cat
   :length 200})

(def videos [v1 v2 v3])
```

Let's take a shot at writing cat-time in Clojure. As before, we'll filter the vector of videos and extract their lengths. To sum up the sequence of lengths, we'll use apply and the + function. The code for this solution follows:

```
ClojureExamples/src/mbfpp/functional/coo/examples.clj
(defn cat-time [videos]
  (apply +
         (map :length
              (filter (fn [video] (= :cat (:type video))) videos))))
```

To understand this code, start with the filter function, move onto map, and then up to apply. For long sequences this can get tricky. One option would be to name the intermediate results using let to make things easier to understand.

Another option in this situation is to use Clojure's -> and ->> macros. These macros can be used to thread a piece of data through a series of function calls.

The -> macro threads an expression through a series of forms, inserting it as the second item in each form. For instance, in the following snippet we use -> to thread an integer through two subtractions:

```
=> (-> 4 (- 2) (- 2))
0
```

The -> macro first threads 4 into the second position in (- 2), which subtracts 2 from 4 to get 2. Then, that result is threaded into the second slot in the later (- 2) to get a final result of 0.

If we use ->> we get a different result, as the following code snippet shows:

```
=> (->> 4 (- 2) (- 2))
4
```

Here, the ->> threads 4 into the last slot in the first (- 2), so 4 is subtracted from 2 to get a result of -2. That -2 is then threaded into the last slot of the second (-2), which subtracts a -2 from 2 to get a final result of 4.

Now that we've seen the threading operators, we can use ->> to make our original catTime read from top to bottom. We do so in the following snippet:

ClojureExamples/src/mbfpp/functional/coo/examples.clj
```
(defn more-cat-time [videos]
  (->> videos
    (filter (fn [video] (= :cat (:type video))))
    (map :length)
    (apply +)))
```

This works the same as our original:

```
=> (more-cat-time videos)
500
```

One limitation of the threading macros is that if we want to use them to chain function calls, the piece of data we're passing through the chain of function calls must be consistently in the first or last position.

Sample Code: Chaining Using Sequence Comprehensions

A common use for Chain of Operations is that we need to perform multiple operations on values inside of some container type. This is especially common in statically typed languages like Scala.

For instance, we may have a series of Option values that we want to combine into a single value, returning None if any of them are None. There are several ways to do so, but the most concise relies on using a for comprehension to pick out the values and yield a result.

In Scala

We came across sequence comprehensions in *Sample Code: Sequence Comprehensions*, on page 77, as a replacement for Iterator. Here we'll take advantage of the fact that they can operate over more than one sequence at a time, which makes them useful for Chain of Operations.

Let's take a look at a sequence comprehension that operates over two vectors, each with a single integer. We'll use it to add the values in the vectors together. Our test vectors are defined in the following code:

ScalaExamples/src/main/scala/com/mblinn/mbfpp/functional/coo/Examples.scala
```
val vec1 = Vector(42)
val vec2 = Vector(8)
```

Here's the for comprehension we use them with. We pick i1 out of the first vector and i2 out of the second, and we use yield to add them together:

```
scala> for { i1 <- vec1; i2 <- vec2 } yield(i1 + i2)
res0: scala.collection.immutable.Vector[Int] = Vector(50)
```

From there, it's only a short hop to using for with Option. In the following code we define a couple of optional values:

ScalaExamples/src/main/scala/com/mblinn/mbfpp/functional/coo/Examples.scala
```
val o1 = Some(42)
val o2 = Some(8)
```

Now we can add them together as we did with the values out of our vectors.

```
scala> for { v1 <- o1; v2 <- o2 } yield(v1 + v2)
res1: Option[Int] = Some(50)
```

One advantage is that we don't have to call get() or pattern match to pull values out of Option. The power of this approach becomes more apparent when we add a None into the mix:

ScalaExamples/src/main/scala/com/mblinn/mbfpp/functional/coo/Examples.scala
```
val o3: Option[Int] = None
```

```
scala> for { v1 <- o1; v3 <- o3 } yield(v1 + v3)
res2: Option[Int] = None
```

Now our for comprehension yields a None.

A Chain of Operations, each of which might yield a None, is common in Scala. Let's take a look at an example that goes through a series of operations to retrieve a user's list of favorite videos on a movie website.

To get the list of videos, we first need to look up a user by ID, then we need to look up the list of favorite videos by user. Finally, we need to look up the list of videos associated with that movie, such as cast interviews, trailers, and perhaps a full-length video of the movie itself.

We'll start out by creating a couple of classes to represent a User and a Movie:

```scala
case class User(name: String, id: String)
case class Movie(name: String, id: String)
```

Now we'll define a set of methods to fetch a user, a favorite movie, and the
list of videos for that movie. Each function returns None if it can't find a
response for its input. For this simple example we'll do so using hardcoded
values, but in real life this would likely involve a lookup from a database or
service:

```scala
def getUserById(id: String) = id match {
  case "1" => Some(User("Mike", "1"))
  case _ => None
}


def getFavoriteMovieForUser(user: User) = user match {
  case User(_, "1") => Some(Movie("Gigli", "101"))
  case _ => None
}


def getVideosForMovie(movie: Movie) = movie match {
  case Movie(_, "101") =>
    Some(Vector(
        Video("Interview With Cast", "interview", 480),
        Video("Gigli", "feature", 7260)))
  case _ => None
}
```

Now we can write a function to get a user's favorite videos by chaining
together calls to the functions we previously defined inside of a for statement:

```scala
def getFavoriteVideos(userId: String) =
  for {
    user <- getUserById(userId)
    favoriteMovie <- getFavoriteMovieForUser(user)
    favoriteVideos <- getVideosForMovie(favoriteMovie)
  } yield favoriteVideos
```

If we call getFavoriteVideos() with a valid user ID, it'll return the list of favorite
videos.

```scala
scala> getFavoriteVideos("1")
res3: Option[scala.collection.immutable.Vector[...] =
      Some(Vector(Video(Interview With Cast,interview,480),
                      Video(Gigli,feature,7260)))
```

If we call it with a user who doesn't exist, the whole chain will return None
instead:

```scala
scala> getFavoriteVideos("42")
res4: Option[scala.collection.immutable.Vector[...]] = None
```

In Clojure

Since Clojure isn't statically typed, it doesn't have anything like Scala's Option as a core part of the language.

However, Clojure's sequence comprehensions do work much like Scala's for other container types. For instance, we can use for to pick out their contents and add them together, as we did in our Scala example. In the following code snippet, we do just that:

ClojureExamples/src/mbfpp/functional/coo/examples.clj
```clojure
(def v1 [42])
(def v2 [8])

=> (for [i1 v1 i2 v2] (+ i1 i2))
(50)
```

If one of our vectors is the empty vector, then for will result in an empty sequence. The following code demonstrates:

ClojureExamples/src/mbfpp/functional/coo/examples.clj
```clojure
(def v3 [])

=> (for [i1 v1 i3 v3] (+ i1 i3))
()
```

Even though Clojure's sequence comprehension works much the same as Scala's, the lack of static typing and the Option type means that the sort of chaining we saw in Scala isn't idiomatic. Instead we generally rely on chaining together functions with explicit null checks.

The flexibility of Lisp makes it possible to add on even something as fundamental as a static type checker into the language as a library. Just such a library is currently under development in the core.typed library,[1] which provides optional static typing.

As this library gains maturity, the type of chaining we saw in the Scala examples may become more and more common.

Discussion

The examples we saw in *Sample Code: Chaining Using Sequence Comprehensions*, on page 162, are examples of the *sequence* or *list monad*. While we didn't define exactly what a monad is, we did show a basic example of the sort of

---

1.   https://github.com/clojure/core.typed

problems that they can solve. They make it natural to chain together operations on a container type while operating on the data inside of the container.

In the programming world, monads are most commonly known as a way to get IO and other nonpure features into a purely functional language. From the examples we saw above, it may not be immediately apparent what monads have to do with IO in a purely functional language.

Since neither Scala nor Clojure make use of monads in this way, we won't go into it in detail here. The general reason, however, is that the monadic container type can carry along some extra information through the call chain. For instance, a monad to do IO would gather up all of the IO done through the Chain of Operations and then hand it off to a runtime when done. The runtime would then be responsible for performing the IO.

This style of programming was pioneered by Haskell. The curious reader can find an excellent introduction to it in *Learn You a Haskell for Great Good!: A Beginner's Guide [Lip11]*.

For Further Reading

Learn You a Haskell for Great Good!: A Beginner's Guide [Lip11]

Related Patterns

Pattern 4, *Replacing Builder for Immutable Object*, on page 62

Pattern 5, *Replacing Iterator*, on page 72

Pattern 14, *Filter-Map-Reduce*, on page 155

Pattern 16, *Function Builder*, on page 167

Function Builder

Intent

To create a function that itself creates functions, allowing us to synthesize behaviors on the fly

Overview

Sometimes we've got a function that performs a useful action, and we need a function that performs some other, related action. We might have a vowel? predicate that returns true when a vowel is passed in and need a consonant? that does the same for consonants.

Other times, we've got some data that we need to turn into an action. We might have a discount percentage and need a function that can apply that discount to a set of items.

With Function Builder, we write a function that takes our data or function (though, as we've seen, the distinction between functions and data is blurry) and uses it to create a new function.

To use Function Builder, we write a higher-order function that returns a function. The Function Builder implementation encodes some pattern we've discovered.

For example, to create a consonant? predicate from a vowel? predicate, we create a new function that calls vowel? and negates the result. To create odd? from even?, we create a function that calls even? and negates the result. To create dead? from alive?, we create a function that calls dead? and negates the result.

There's an obvious pattern here. We can encode it with a Function Builder implementation named negate. The negate function takes in a function and returns a new one that calls the passed-in function and negates the result.

Another common use for Function Builder is when we've got a piece of static data we need to use as the basis for some action. For instance, we could convert a static percentage to a function that calculates percentages by writing a function that takes in the percentage and returns a function of one argument. This function takes in a number to calculate a percentage of and uses the percentage stored in its closure to do so. We'll see several examples of both flavors of Function Builder a bit later on.

Code Sample: Functions from Static Data

One way to use Function Builder is to create functions out of static data. This lets us take a bit of data—a noun—and turn it into an action—a verb. Let's look at a couple of examples, starting with a function that takes a percentage and creates a function that calculates discounted prices based on those percentages.

Discount Calculator Builder

The Function Builder discount() takes in a percentage between 0 and 100 and returns a function that computes a discounted price based on that percentage. Passing 50 into discount() returns a function that calculates a 50 percent discount, 25 gets us a 25 percent discount, and so on. Let's take a look at the Scala version.

In Scala

Our Scala code defines discount(), which takes a Double, named percent, and checks to ensure that it's between 0 and 100. It then creates a function that uses discountPercentage to calculate a discount. Here's the code:

ScalaExamples/src/main/scala/com/mblinn/mbfpp/functional/fb/DiscountBuilder.scala
```scala
def discount(percent: Double) = {
  if(percent < 0.0 || percent > 100.0)
    throw new IllegalArgumentException("Discounts must be between 0.0 and 100.0.")
  (originalPrice: Double) =>
    originalPrice - (originalPrice * percent * 0.01)
}
```

Let's take a look at how it works. The simplest way to use discountedPrice() is to have it create an anonymous function, which we call directly. Here we use it to calculate a 50 percent discount on a price of 200:

```scala
scala> discount(50)(200)
res0: Double = 100.0
```

And here we use it to calculate a 0 percent discount (full price) and a 100 percent discount (free!), respectively:

```scala
scala> discount(0)(200)
res1: Double = 200.0

scala> discount(100)(200)
res2: Double = 0.0
```

If we need to use the discount function more than once, we can name it. Here we do so and use it to calculate discounted totals on a couple of vectors of items:

```scala
scala> val twentyFivePercentOff = discountedPrice(25)
twentyFivePercentOff: Double => Double = <function1>

scala> Vector(100.0, 25.0, 50.0, 25.0) map twentyFivePercentOff sum
res3: Double = 150.0

scala> Vector(75.0, 25.0) map twentyFivePercentOff sum
res4: Double = 75.0
```

In Clojure

This example works much the same in Clojure. The only interesting difference is that we can use Clojure's preconditions to ensure that the discount is in the valid range. Let's take a look at the code:

ClojureExamples/src/mbfpp/functional/fb/discount_builder.clj
```clojure
(defn discount [percentage]
  {:pre [(and (>= percentage 0) (<= percentage 100))]}
  (fn [price] (- price (* price percentage 0.01))))
```

We can create a discounted price and call it as an anonymous function:

```clojure
=> ((discount 50) 200)
100.0
```

As advertised, trying to create a discount outside the acceptable range throws an exception:

```clojure
=> (discount 101)
AssertionError Assert failed: ...
```

And if we want to name our discount function to use it multiple times, we can do so:

```clojure
=> (def twenty-five-percent-off (discount 25))
=> (apply + (map twenty-five-percent-off [100.0 25.0 50.0 25.0]))
150.0
=> (apply + (map twenty-five-percent-off [75.0, 25.0]))
75.0
```

The discount calculator is a fairly simple example; we'll take a look at one that's a bit more involved in the next section.

Map Key Selector

Let's take a look at a more involved implementation of Function Builder. The problem we're trying to solve is this: we've got a data structure consisting of maps nested inside each other, and we want to create functions that help us pick out values, possibly from deeply nested parts.

In a way, this is writing a very simple declarative language to pick values out of deeply nested maps. This is a lot like how XPath lets us select an arbitrary element from a deeply nested XML structure, or how a CSS selector lets us do the same with HTML.

Our solution starts with creating a function, selector, which takes a path to the data we're looking for. For instance, if we've got a map that represents a person, which contains a name key whose value is another map, which contains a first key whose value is the first name, we want to be able to create a selector for the first name like this: selector('name, 'first). We can see this in the code below:

```scala
scala> val person = Map('name -> Map('first -> "Rob"))
person: ...

scala> val firstName = selector('name, 'first)
firstName: scala.collection.immutable.Map[Symbol,Any] => Option[Any] = <function1>

scala> firstName(person)
res0: Option[Any] = Some(Rob)
```

This sort of structure is extremely handy when working with structured data like XML or JSON. The data can be parsed into a nested structure, and this type of Function Builder can help pick it apart.

In Scala

The Scala version of selector creates functions that can pick values out of deeply nested maps, as described previously. The selectors that it creates will return Some(Any) if it can find the nested value; otherwise it returns None.

To create a selector, we need to pass in several Symbols corresponding to the keys in the path we want to select. Since this is all we need to pass into selector, we can use Scala's support for varargs instead of passing in an explicit list; this means that creating a selector to pick a street name from a person's address looks like this:

```scala
scala> selector('address, 'street, 'name)
res0: scala.collection.immutable.Map[Symbol,Any] => Option[Any] = <function1>
```

Once created, a map is passed into the selector, and it attempts to select a value based on the path it was given when it was created by recursively walking through the map. This is a slightly tricky bit of code, so let's look at the whole thing and then break it down into smaller parts:

ScalaExamples/src/main/scala/com/mblinn/mbfpp/functional/fb/Selector.scala
```scala
def selector(path: Symbol*): (Map[Symbol, Any] => Option[Any]) = {

  if(path.size <= 0) throw new IllegalArgumentException("path must not be empty")

  @tailrec
  def selectorHelper(path: Seq[Symbol], ds: Map[Symbol, Any]): Option[Any] =
    if(path.size == 1) {
      ds.get(path(0))
    }else{
      val currentPiece = ds.get(path.head)
      currentPiece match {
        case Some(currentMap: Map[Symbol, Any]) =>
          selectorHelper(path.tail, currentMap)
        case None => None
        case _ => None
      }
    }

  (ds: Map[Symbol, Any]) => selectorHelper(path.toSeq, ds)
}
```

Let's start by examining the signature of selector:

```scala
def selector(path: Symbol*): (Map[Symbol, Any] => Option[Any]) = {
      «selector-body»
}
```

This says that selector takes a variable number of Symbol arguments and returns a function. The function it returns itself takes a map from Symbol to Any and returns an Option[Any].

The first line simply checks to make sure that the path has at least one element and throws an exception if it doesn't:

```scala
if(path.size <= 0) throw new IllegalArgumentException("path must not be empty")
```

The meat of the function is a nested, recursive helper function. Let's take a look at its type signature:

```scala
@tailrec
def selectorHelper(path: Seq[Symbol], ds: Map[Symbol, Any]): Option[Any] =
      «selector-helper-body»
}
```

This says that selectorHelper takes a sequence of Symbols as a path and a data structure that consists of a map from Symbol to Any. It returns an Option[Any], which represents the final value we're trying to find with the selector. In the above example, this would be the name of a person's street.

Next, we get the base case for our recursion. This happens when we reach the end of the path. We find the value we're looking for and return it. The get() method returns None if the value doesn't exist:

```
if(path.size == 1) {
        ds.get(path(0))
}
```

The largest piece of code contains the tail recursive call. Here, we get the current piece of the data structure. If it exists, then we call the helper function recursively with the remainder of the path and the data structure we just picked out. If it doesn't exist, or if it doesn't have the proper type, we return None:

```
else{
        val currentPiece = ds.get(path.first)
        currentPiece match {
                case Some(currentMap: Map[Symbol, Any]) =>
                        selectorHelper(path.tail, currentMap)
                case None => None
                case _ => None
                }
        }
```

Finally, here is the last line, which just returns a function that calls selectorHelper with the appropriate arguments:

```
(ds: Map[Symbol, Any]) => selectorHelper(path.toSeq, ds)
```

Let's take a closer look at how we can use selector, starting with a very simple example, a map that has a single key-value pair:

```
scala> val simplePerson = Map('name -> "Michael Bevilacqua-Linn")
simplePerson: scala.collection.immutable.Map[Symbol,java.lang.String] =
        Map('name -> Michael Bevilacqua-Linn)

scala> val name = selector('name)
name: scala.collection.immutable.Map[Symbol,Any] => Option[Any] = <function1>

scala> name(simplePerson)
res0: Option[Any] = Some(Michael Bevilacqua-Linn)
```

Of course the real power is only apparent when we start working with nested data structures, like so:

```
scala> val moreComplexPerson =
        Map('name -> Map('first -> "Michael", 'last -> "Bevilacqua-Linn"))
moreComplexPerson: scala.collection.immutable.Map[...] =
        Map('name -> Map('first -> Michael, 'last -> Bevilacqua-Linn))
```

```
scala> val firstName = selector('name, 'first)
firstName: scala.collection.immutable.Map[Symbol,Any] => Option[Any] = <function1>

scala> firstName(moreComplexPerson)
res1: Option[Any] = Some(Michael)
```

If the selector doesn't match anything, a None is returned:

```
scala> val middleName = selector('name, 'middle)
middleName: scala.collection.immutable.Map[Symbol,Any] => Option[Any] = <function1>

scala> middleName(moreComplexPerson)
res2: Option[Any] = None
```

In Clojure

The Clojure version of selector is much simpler than the Scala one. In part, this is because Clojure is dynamically typed, so we don't have to worry about the type system as we did in Scala. In addition, Clojure has a handy function called get-in, which is tailor-made to pick values out of deeply nested maps.

Let's take a quick look at get-in before we dig into the code. The get-in function takes a nested map as its first argument and a sequence that represents the path to the value you're looking for. Here's an example of using it to pick a street name from a nested map:

```
=> (def person {:address {:street {:name "Fake St."}}})
#'mbfpp.functional.fb.selector/person
=> (get-in person [:address :street :name])
"Fake St."
```

Building selector on top of get-in is extremely straightforward. We've just got to add a validator to ensure that the path isn't empty and use varargs for the path. Here's the code:

ClojureExamples/src/mbfpp/functional/fb/selector.clj
```
(defn selector [& path]
  {:pre [(not (empty? path))]}
  (fn [ds] (get-in ds path)))
```

Using it is just as easy as the Scala version. Here we pick out a person name from a flat map:

```
=> (def person {:name "Michael Bevilacqua-Linn"})
#'mbfpp.functional.fb.selector/person
=> (def personName (selector :name))
#'mbfpp.functional.fb.selector/personName
=> (personName person)
"Michael Bevilacqua-Linn"
```

And here we pick out a street name from a more deeply nested one:

```
=> (def person {:address {:street {:name "Fake St."}}})
#'mbfpp.functional.fb.selector/person
=> (def streetName (selector :address :street :name))
#'mbfpp.functional.fb.selector/streetName
=> (streetName person)
"Fake St."
```

Before we move on, here's a quick note on the relative complexity of the Scala and Clojure versions of this example. The fact that Clojure has get-in, which does almost exactly what we want to do, helps make the Clojure version much more concise. The other factor is that Clojure is a dynamically typed language. Since the nested maps can hold values of any type, this takes some type system gymnastics to handle in Scala, which is statically typed.

In Clojure, using maps to hold data like this is very idiomatic. In Scala, it's more common to use classes or case classes. However, for this sort of very dynamic problem, I much prefer just keeping things in a map. Using a map means we can manipulate the data structure with all the built-in tools for manipulation maps and collections.

Functions from Other Functions

Since functions in the functional world are themselves pieces of data that can be manipulated, it's common to use Function Builder to transform one function into another. This can be done very simply by just creating a new function that manipulates the return value of another function. For instance, if we have a function isVowel and we want a function isNotVowel, we can simply have it delegate to isVowel and negate the result. This creates a complementary function, as the Scala code shows:

```
scala> def isNotVowel(c: Char) = !isVowel(c)
isNotVowel: (c: Char)Boolean

scala> isNotVowel('b')
res0: Boolean = true
```

In this example, we'll take a closer look at two other ways to create functions from existing functions: function composition and partial function application. Function composition lets us take multiple functions and chain them together. Partial function application lets us take one function and some of its arguments and create a new function of fewer arguments. These are two of the most generally useful ways of creating functions from functions.

Function Composition

Function composition is a way to chain function invocations together. Composing a list of functions together gives us a new function that invokes the first function, passes its output to the next, which passes it to the next, and so on until a result is returned.

In many ways, function composition is similar to the way that Pattern 9, *Replacing Decorator*, on page 109, is used. With the Decorator pattern, multiple decorators, each of which does one part of some task, are chained together. Here multiple functions are chained together.

It's possible to use function composition by simply chaining together functions by hand, but since this is such a common task, functional languages provide first class support for it. Clojure and Scala are no exception here, so let's take a look at it.

In Scala

In Scala, we can compose functions together with the compose operator. As a simple example, let's define three functions, appendA, appendB, and appendC, which append the strings "a", "b", and "c", respectively, as the code shows:

ScalaExamples/src/main/scala/com/mblinn/mbfpp/functional/fb/CompositionExamples.scala
```
val appendA = (s: String) => s + "a"
val appendB = (s: String) => s + "b"
val appendC = (s: String) => s + "c"
```

Now if we want a function that appends all three letters, we can define it like so using function composition:

ScalaExamples/src/main/scala/com/mblinn/mbfpp/functional/fb/CompositionExamples.scala
```
val appendCBA = appendA compose appendB compose appendC
```

As the name suggests, this appends the letters *c*, *b*, and *a*, in that order. It's equivalent to writing a function that takes an argument, passes it into appendC(), takes the returned value and passes it into appendB(), and finally passes that returned value into appendA():

```
scala> appendCBA("z")
res0: java.lang.String = zcba
```

This is a trivial example, but it illustrates an important thing about function composition, which is the order in which the composed functions are called. The last function in the composition chain is called first, and the first function is called last, which is why *c* is the first letter appended to our string.

Let's take a look at a more involved example. One common situation that comes up in web application frameworks is the need to pass an HTTP request through a series of user-defined chunks of code. J2EE's servlet filters,[2] which pass a request through a chain of filters before it is handled, are a common example of such a filter chain.

Filter chains allow application code to do anything that needs to be done before request handling, like decrypting and decompressing the request, checking authentication credentials, logging to a request log, and so forth. Let's sketch out how we'd do this using function composition. First, we'll need a way to represent HTTP requests. For the purpose of this example, we'll keep it simple and stick to a map of request headers and a string request body:

ScalaExamples/src/main/scala/com/mblinn/mbfpp/functional/fb/CompositionExamples.scala
```scala
case class HttpRequest(
    headers: Map[String, String],
    payload: String,
    principal: Option[String] = None)
```

Next, let's define some filters. Each filter is a function that takes in an HttpRequest, does something, and returns an HttpRequest. For this simple example, we're returning the same HttpRequest; but if the filter needed to modify or add something to the request, it could do so by creating a new HttpRequest with its modifications.

Here are a couple of example filters—the first mimics checking an Authorization header and adding a user principal to the request if it's valid, and the second mimics logging out a request fingerprint for troubleshooting:

ScalaExamples/src/main/scala/com/mblinn/mbfpp/functional/fb/CompositionExamples.scala
```scala
def checkAuthorization(request: HttpRequest) = {
  val authHeader = request.headers.get("Authorization")
  val mockPrincipal = authHeader match {
    case Some(headerValue) => Some("AUser")
    case _ => None
  }
  request.copy(principal = mockPrincipal)
}
def logFingerprint(request: HttpRequest) = {
  val fingerprint = request.headers.getOrElse("X-RequestFingerprint", "")
  println("FINGERPRINT=" + fingerprint)
  request
}
```

Finally, we need a function that takes a sequence of filters and composes them together. We can do this by simply reducing the composition function over the sequence:

---

2. http://www.oracle.com/technetwork/java/filters-137243.html

```
ScalaExamples/src/main/scala/com/mblinn/mbfpp/functional/fb/CompositionExamples.scala
def composeFilters(filters: Seq[Function1[HttpRequest, HttpRequest]]) =
  filters.reduce {
    (allFilters, currentFilter) => allFilters compose currentFilter
  }
```

Let's watch it work by composing the sample filters into a single filter chain and running a test HttpRequest through it:

```
scala> val filters = Vector(checkAuthorization, logFingerprint)
filters: ...

scala> val filterChain = composeFilters(filters)
filterChain: ...

scala> val requestHeaders =
        Map("Authorization" -> "Auth", "X-RequestFingerprint" -> "fingerprint")
requestHeaders: ...

scala> val request = HttpRequest(requestHeaders, "body")
request: ...

scala> filterChain(request)
FINGERPRINT=fingerprint
res0: com.mblinn.mbfpp.functional.fb.ScalaExamples.HttpRequest =
        HttpRequest(
                Map(Authorization -> Auth, X-RequestFingerprint -> fingerprint),
                body,
                Some(AUser))
```

As we can see, the filter chain properly runs the HttpRequest through each filter in the chain, which adds a user principal to the request and logs our fingerprint to the console.

In Clojure

The easiest way to do function composition in Clojure is to use comp. Here we are using it to compose together the string appenders:

```
ClojureExamples/src/mbfpp/functional/fb/composition_examples.clj
(defn append-a [s] (str s "a"))
(defn append-b [s] (str s "b"))
(defn append-c [s] (str s "c"))

(def append-cba (comp append-a append-b append-c))
```

This works much like the Scala version:

```
=> (append-cba "z")
"zcba"
```

In Clojure we'll model the HTTP request itself, as well as the headers, as a map. A sample request looks like so:

ClojureExamples/src/mbfpp/functional/fb/composition_examples.clj
```
(def request
  {:headers
   {"Authorization" "auth"
    "X-RequestFingerprint" "fingerprint"}
   :body "body"})
```

Our sample filter functions pick keys out of a map and use nil instead of None to represent missing values. Here they are, along with the function builder, compose-filters, to compose them into a filter chain:

ClojureExamples/src/mbfpp/functional/fb/composition_examples.clj
```
(defn check-authorization [request]
  (let [auth-header (get-in request [:headers "Authorization"])]
    (assoc
      request
      :principal
      (if-not (nil? auth-header)
        "AUser"))))

(defn log-fingerprint [request]
  (let [fingerprint (get-in request [:headers "X-RequestFingerprint"])]
    (println (str "FINGERPRINT=" fingerprint))
    request))

(defn compose-filters [filters]
  (reduce
    (fn [all-filters, current-filter] (comp all-filters current-filter))
    filters))
```

And here's that filter chain in action, running through the filters, performing them, and finally returning the HTTP request:

```
=> (def filter-chain (compose-filters [check-authorization log-fingerprint]))
#'mbfpp.functional.fb.composition-examples/filter-chain
=> (filter-chain request)
FINGERPRINT=fingerprint
{:principal "AUser",
 :headers {"X-RequestFingerprint" "fingerprint", "Authorization" "auth"},
 :body "body"}
```

Function composition is a very general operation, and we've only touched on a few uses of it here. Any time you find yourself calling the same set of functions in the same order multiple times, or you have a dynamically generated list of functions that need to be chained together, function composition is a good place to turn to.

Partially Applied Functions

While function composition takes multiple functions and chains them together, partially applying a function takes one function and a subset of the arguments that that function takes and returns a new function. The new function has fewer arguments than the original and keeps track of the subset that was passed in when the partially applied function was created so it can use them later when it gets the rest of the arguments.

Let's see how it works in Scala.

In Scala

Partial function application is another functional feature that's important enough to warrant first-class support in Scala. The way it works is that you call a function and replace the arguments you don't currently have values for with underscores. For example, if we've got a function that adds two integers together and we want a function that adds 42 to a single integer, we could create it like this:

ScalaExamples/src/main/scala/com/mblinn/mbfpp/functional/fb/PartialExamples.scala
```scala
def addTwoInts(intOne: Int, intTwo: Int) = intOne + intTwo

val addFortyTwo = addTwoInts(42, _: Int)
```

As the code below shows, addFortyTwo is a function of one argument, to which it adds 42.

```scala
scala> addFortyTwo(100)
res0: Int = 142
```

Creating partially applied functions is simple, but spotting when to use them can be a bit tough. Here's one example where they come in handy. Say we've got a function that calculates income tax by state, and we want to create functions that let us calculate the income tax for a particular state. We can use a partially applied function to do it, like so:

ScalaExamples/src/main/scala/com/mblinn/mbfpp/functional/fb/PartialExamples.scala
```scala
def taxForState(amount: Double, state: Symbol) = state match {
  // Simple tax logic, for example only!
  case ('NY) => amount * 0.0645
  case ('PA) => amount * 0.045
  // Rest of states...
}
val nyTax = taxForState(_: Double, 'NY)
val paTax = taxForState(_: Double, 'PA)
```

This correctly calculates taxes for the different states:

```
scala> nyTax(100)
res0: Double = 6.45

scala> paTax(100)
res1: Double = 4.5
```

In Clojure

Partially applying functions in Clojure is similar to how it's done in Scala, but there is one twist. To keep its syntax simple, Clojure only allows for the arguments that the function is being partially applied to, to come at the start of the argument list. For example, we could still write add-forty-two, much as we did in Scala, as this code shows:

ClojureExamples/src/mbfpp/functional/fb/partial_examples.clj
```
(defn add-two-ints [int-one int-two] (+ int-one int-two))

(def add-fourty-two (partial add-two-ints 42))

=> (add-forty-two 100)
142
```

But to write ny-tax and pa-tax, we'd have to swap the arguments to tax-for-state around, like this:

ClojureExamples/src/mbfpp/functional/fb/partial_examples.clj
```
(defn tax-for-state [state amount]
  (cond
    (= :ny state) (* amount 0.0645)
    (= :pa state) (* amount 0.045)))

(def ny-tax (partial tax-for-state :ny))
(def pa-tax (partial tax-for-state :pa))

=> (ny-tax 100)
6.45
=> (pa-tax 100)
4.5
```

Partially applied functions are very simple to use, but I often find it a bit tricky to know when to use them. I usually catch myself calling the same function over and over again, with a subset of the arguments remaining the same. Then a light bulb goes off and I realize I can clean that up a bit by using a partially applied function.

Discussion

In this section, we've covered some of the more general ways to use Function Builder, but these are by no means the only ways. The Clojure and Scala libraries contain many other examples, since this is an extremely common pattern in the functional world.

While most of the Clojure and Scala examples were very similar, the examples in *Map Key Selector*, on page 169, differed drastically. In particular, the Scala version was much more verbose. In part, this is because Clojure has an extremely handy get-in function that does almost exactly what we need; however, a large part of the difference was caused by Scala's type system.

Since Scala is statically typed, we had to specify types for the contents of the maps that we dealt with. Internal nodes were themselves Maps, while leaf nodes could be anything at all. This led to the slight bit of type system gymnastics we had to do in the Scala version.

This is a general trade-off between dynamic and static typing. Even with a powerful type system like Scala's, there's still a cost to static typing in terms of the complexity it can add and in just understanding how the type system works. The trade-off is that we can catch many errors at compile time that would otherwise become runtime errors with a dynamic type system.

Related Patterns

Pattern 1, *Replacing Functional Interface*, on page 40

Pattern 9, *Replacing Decorator*, on page 109

Memoization

Intent

To cache the results of a pure function call to avoid performing the same computation more than once

Overview

Since pure functions always return the same value for given arguments, it's possible to replace a pure function call with cached results.

We can do this manually by writing a function that keeps track of its previous arguments. When it's called, it first checks its cache to see if it has already been called with the passed-in arguments. If it has, it returns the cached value. Otherwise, it performs the computation.

Some languages provide first-class support for Memoization using higher-order functions. Clojure, for instance, has a function called memoize that takes a function and returns a new one that will cache results. Scala doesn't have a built-in memoization function, so we'll use a simple manual implementation.

Sample Code: Simple Caching

One use for Memoization is as a simple cache for expensive or time-consuming functions, especially when the function is called multiple times with the same argument. In this example, we'll simulate the time-consuming operation by having it sleep the thread.

In Scala

Let's get started with a look at our simulated expensive function call. As an example, we're using a lookup by ID from some (presumably slow) datastore. To fake it out here, we sleep the thread for a second before returning a value from a static map. We also print the ID we're looking up to the console to demonstrate when the function is being executed:

ScalaExamples/src/main/scala/com/mblinn/mbfpp/functional/memoization/Examples.scala
```
def expensiveLookup(id: Int) = {
  Thread.sleep(1000)
  println(s"Doing expensive lookup for $id")
  Map(42 -> "foo",  12 -> "bar",  1 -> "baz").get(id)
}
```

Just as we'd expect, the lengthy function is executed each time we call it, as we can see from the console output:

```scala
scala> expensiveLookup(42)
Doing expensive lookup for 42
res0: Option[String] = Some(foo)

scala> expensiveLookup(42)
Doing expensive lookup for 42
res1: Option[String] = Some(foo)
```

Now let's take a look at a simple memoized version of expensiveLookup(). To create it we'll use memoizeExpensiveLookup(), which initializes a cache and returns a new function that wraps calls to memoizeExpensiveFunction().

The new function first checks its cache to see if it has results from a previous function call. If it does, it returns the cached results. Otherwise it calls the expensive lookup and caches the results before returning them.

Finally, we call memoizeExpensiveFunction() and store a reference to the function it returns into a new var. The full solution is in the following code:

```scala
ScalaExamples/src/main/scala/com/mblinn/mbfpp/functional/memoization/Examples.scala
def memoizeExpensiveLookup() = {
  var cache = Map[Int, Option[String]]()
  (id: Int) =>
    cache.get(id) match {
      case Some(result: Option[String]) => result
      case None => {
        val result = expensiveLookup(id)
        cache += id -> result
        result
      }
    }
}
val memoizedExpensiveLookup = memoizeExpensiveLookup
```

As we can see from the following REPL output, the expensive function is only called the first time for a given argument. After that, it returns the cached copy:

```scala
scala> memoizedExpensiveLookup(42)
Doing expensive lookup for 42
res2: Option[String] = Some(foo)

scala> memoizedExpensiveLookup(42)
res3: Option[String] = Some(foo)
```

One quirk with this example is in the last line:

```scala
val memoizedExpensiveLookup = memoizeExpensiveLookup
```

Here, we're having memoizeExpensiveLookup() return a new function, and we're storing a reference to it. This allows us to wrap the cache up in a closure so that only the function has a reference to it. If we needed another cache, we could create it like so:

```scala
scala> val memoizedExpensiveLookup2 = memoizeExpensiveLookup
memoizedExpensiveLookup2: Int => Option[String] = <function1>

scala> memoizedExpensiveLookup2(42)
Doing expensive lookup for 42
res4: Option[String] = Some(foo)
```

Our Scala solution is a bit clumsy since we've done it manually for a single, specific case, but it serves as a good model for how memoization works behind the scenes. Let's take a look at how we can use Clojure's memoize function to solve the same problem.

In Clojure

In Clojure, we'll start with a similar simulated expensive function. However, we won't manually memoize it. Instead, we'll use Clojure's memoize function to automatically return a memoized version of the function, as this code shows:

ClojureExamples/src/mbfpp/functional/memoization/examples.clj
```clojure
(defn expensive-lookup [id]
  (Thread/sleep 1000)
  (println (str "Lookup for " id))
  ({42 "foo" 12 "bar" 1 "baz"} id))

(def memoized-expensive-lookup
  (memoize expensive-lookup))
```

As we can see from the following REPL output, it behaves similarly to the Scala version and only performs the expensive operation once:

```clojure
=> (memoized-expensive-lookup 42)
Lookup for 42
"foo"
=> (memoized-expensive-lookup 42)
"foo"
```

Behind the scenes, the memoize function creates a new function that's much like the manual example we saw in Scala that uses a map as a cache.

Discussion

One use of Memoization we didn't cover here is in solving dynamic programming problems, which is one of its original uses. Dynamic programming problems are problems that can be broken down into simpler subproblems recursively. A classic, easy-to-understand example is computing a Fibonacci number.

The formula for calculating the *n*th Fibonacci number adds together the previous two numbers in the sequence. A simple Clojure function to calculate a Fibonacci number using this definition follows:

ClojureExamples/src/mbfpp/functional/memoization/examples.clj
```
(def slow-fib
  (fn [n]
    (cond
      (<= n 0) 0
      (< n 2) 1
      :else (+ (slow-fib (- n 1)) (slow-fib (- n 2))))))
```

The nice thing about this function is that it mirrors the mathematical definition. However, it needs to recursively compute its subparts repeatedly, so its performance is terrible for even moderately large numbers. If we memoize the function, as we do in the following code, then the subparts are cached and the function can perform reasonably well:

ClojureExamples/src/mbfpp/functional/memoization/examples.clj
```
(def mem-fib
  (memoize
    (fn [n]
      (cond
        (<= n 0) 0
        (< n 2) 1
        :else (+ (mem-fib (- n 1)) (mem-fib (- n 2)))))))
```

Running the two functions shows the drastic difference in performance:

```
=> (time (slow-fib 40))
"Elapsed time: 6689.204 msecs"
102334155
=> (time (mem-fib 40))
"Elapsed time: 0.402 msecs"
102334155
```

Dynamic programming problems are rich and fascinating; however, they only pop up in a limited number of domains. I've generally seen memoization used as a simple, convenient cache for expensive or long-lived operations rather than as a dynamic programming tool.

Pattern 18

Lazy Sequence

Intent

To create a sequence whose members are computed only when needed—this allows us to easily stream results from a computation and to work with infinitely long sequences

Overview

We often deal with elements of a sequence one at a time. Since this is so, we generally don't need to have the entire sequence realized before we start processing it. For instance, we may wish to stream lines of a file off of disk and process them without ever holding the entire file in memory. We could use Pattern 12, *Tail Recursion*, on page 138, to seek through the file, but Lazy Sequence provides a much cleaner abstraction for this sort of streaming computation.

Lazy Sequence does so by only creating an element in a sequence when it's asked for. In the file-reading example, the lines are only read off of disk when asked for, and they can be garbage-collected when we're done processing them, though we need to take a bit of care to ensure that they are.

When we create an element, we call that *realizing* the element. Once realized, elements are put into a cache using Pattern 17, *Memoization*, on page 182, which means we only need to realize each element in the sequence once. This is demonstrated in Figure 13, *Lazy Sequence*, on page 187.

Lazy Sequence also lets us create an extremely useful abstraction: an infinitely long sequence. This may not seem useful at first blush, but since the entire sequence isn't realized at once, we can work with the beginning of the sequence and defer creation of the rest. This allows us to create, say, an infinitely long string of pseudorandom numbers of which we realize only a portion.

Sample Code: Built-In Lazy Sequences

Let's start with a couple of simple examples from the built-in library. In the first example, we'll show how to work with an infinitely long list of integers.

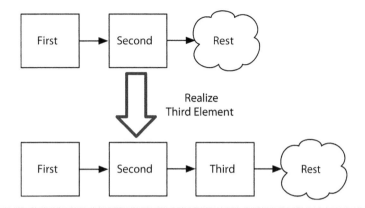

Figure 13—Lazy Sequence. An instance of Lazy Sequence before and after the third element has been realized.

In the second, we'll show how to use Lazy Sequence to generate a series of random test data.

Let's get started with a dive into the Scala code.

In Scala

Scala's has built-in support for Lazy Sequence in its Stream library. Perhaps the simplest thing we can do with a lazy sequence is to create an infinite sequence of all integers. Scala's Stream library has a method that does just that, called from(). According to the ScalaDoc, it will "create an infinite stream starting at start and incrementing by step."

Here, we use from() to create a sequence of all integers, starting at 0:

ScalaExamples/src/main/scala/com/mblinn/mbfpp/functional/ls/LazySequence.scala
```
val integers = Stream.from(0)
```

This may seem a strange thing to do, but we can use another method, take(), to work with the first few numbers in the sequence. Here we're using it to take the first five integers from our infinitely long list and then print them:

```
scala> val someints = integers take 5
someints: scala.collection.immutable.Stream[Int] = Stream(0, ?)

scala> someints foreach println
0
1
2
3
4
```

Let's take a look at a slightly fancier instance of Lazy Sequence that uses another method in Scala's Sequence library. The continually() method creates an infinitely long sequence by repeatedly evaluating the expression passed into here.

Let's use this to create an infinitely long sequence of pseudorandom numbers. To do so, we create a new random number generator in the val generate, and then we pass generate.nextInt in the continually() method, as illustrated in the following code:

```
ScalaExamples/src/main/scala/com/mblinn/mbfpp/functional/ls/LazySequence.scala
val generate = new Random()
val randoms = Stream.continually(generate.nextInt)
```

We can now take a few random numbers from our infinite list:

```
scala> val aFewRandoms = randoms take 5
aFewRandoms: scala.collection.immutable.Stream[Int] = Stream(326862669, ?)

scala> aFewRandoms foreach println
326862669
-473217479
-1619928859
785666088
1642217833
```

If we want a few more random numbers, we can use take() again with a larger number:

```
scala> val aFewMoreRandoms = randoms take 6
aFewMoreRandoms: scala.collection.immutable.Stream[Int] = Stream(326862669, ?)

scala> aFewMoreRandoms foreach println
326862669
-473217479
-1619928859
785666088
1642217833
1819425161
```

Notice how the first five numbers here are repeated. This is because the Stream library relies on Pattern 17, *Memoization*, on page 182, to cache copies it's already seen. The first five values were realized when we originally printed aFewRandoms, the sixth only once we printed aFewMoreRandoms.

In Clojure

Lazy Sequence is built into Clojure as well, but it's not focused in a single library. Rather, most of Clojure's core sequence manipulation functions work in a lazy manner. Clojure's normal range function, for instance, works with Lazy Sequence. The following code generates a list of all the positive integers that fit into an Integer:

ClojureExamples/src/mbfpp/functional/ls/examples.clj
```
(def integers (range Integer/MAX_VALUE))
```

We can then use the take function to take a few integers from the start of our long list:

```
=> (take 5 integers)
(0 1 2 3 4)
```

To generate our list of random integers, we can use Clojure's repeatedly function. This takes a function of one argument and repeats it an infinite number of times, as the following code shows:

ClojureExamples/src/mbfpp/functional/ls/examples.clj
```
(def randoms (repeatedly (fn [] (rand-int Integer/MAX_VALUE))))
```

To take a few, we can use take again:

```
=> (take 5 randoms)
(1416806782 956363594 262805953 1830450442 834342645)
```

If we want some more, we use take with a bigger argument. Again, the first five random integers won't be recomputed, they'll be pulled from a memoized cache:

```
=> (take 6 randoms)
(1416806782 956363594 262805953 1830450442 834342645 1793189704)
```

Scala and Clojure's treatments of Lazy Sequence have a few key differences. Most of Clojure's sequence-handling functions are lazy, but they recognize the sequence in chunks of thirty-two. If we take a single number from a lazy sequence of integers, Clojure will recognize the first thirty-two integers even though we only asked for one.

We can see this if we add a side effect into the lazy sequence generation. Here, we can see that take recognizes thirty-two integers, even though it only returns the first one:

```
=> (defn print-num [num] (print (str num " ")))
#'mbfpp.functional.ls.examples/print-num
=> (take 1 (map print-num (range 100)))
(0 1 2 3 4 5 6 7 8 9 10 11 12 13 14 15 16 17 18
 19 20 21 22 23 24 25 26 27 28 29 30 31 nil)
```

Another, more subtle difference comes into play when using Lazy Sequence in the REPL. When the Scala REPL comes across an instance of Lazy Sequence in the form of a Stream, it does not attempt to realize the whole thing.

This is easiest to see when we've got an obvious side effect. In the following Scala code, we use continually() to print "hello" to the console and store a reference to the produced Stream in printHellos. As we can see, the first "hello" is printed when we call continually, which indicates that the method realizes the first element in the stream:

```scala
scala>    val printHellos = Stream.continually(println("hello"))
hello
printHellos: scala.collection.immutable.Stream[Unit] = Stream((), ?)
```

If we now call take() on printHellos, we don't get any further "hello"s printed to the console, which means the REPL isn't trying to realize the returned Stream.

```scala
scala> printHellos take 5
res0: scala.collection.immutable.Stream[Unit] = Stream((), ?)
```

If we want to force the remainder of our "hello"s to be realized, we can use any method that iterates over Stream, or we can just use the force():

```scala
scala> printHellos take 5 force
hello
hello
hello
hello
res1: scala.collection.immutable.Stream[Unit] = Stream((), (), (), (), ())
```

This isn't something you generally need to do, but it's important to understand when the elements of Lazy Sequence are realized.

In contrast, Clojure's REPL will attempt to realize an instance of Lazy Sequence; however, defining an instance of Lazy Sequence may not realize the first element! Here we define a print-hellos much like the Scala version. Notice how "hello" isn't printed to the console.

```
(def print-hellos (repeatedly (fn [] (println "hello"))))
```

However, if we take five elements, the REPL evaluating the resulting instance of Lazy Sequence will force it to print to the console.

```
=> (take 5 print-hellos)
(hello
hello
nil hello
nil hello
nil hello
nil nil)
```

This reflects the difference in how Scala and Clojure's REPL evaluate Lazy Sequence. It also highlights something to watch out for when using Lazy Sequence. Since you can create infinite sequences, we need to ensure that we don't attempt to realize an entire infinite sequence at once. For instance, if we had forgotten to use take in the Clojure example and had just evaluated (repeatedly (fn [] (println "hello"), we would have attempted to realize an infinitely long sequence of printing "hello"!

Sample Code: Paged Response

In our first example, we looked at a couple of higher-order functions that let us create an instance of Lazy Sequence. Now let's take a look at how we'd make one from scratch.

The example we'll use here is a lazy sequence that lets us go through a set of paged data. In our simple example, we'll simulate the paged data with a local function call, though in a real program this would probably come from an external source such as a web service. Let's get started with a look at the Scala code.

In Scala

Our Scala solution has two parts: the sequence itself, pagedSequence, and a method to generate some sample paged data, getPage().

We need to define the solution to our problem recursively, much as we would in Pattern 12, *Tail Recursion*, on page 138. However, instead of passing our sequence through the call stack, we add to it in each recursive call using the #:: operator.

The following code is the full solution to our paged data problem:

ScalaExamples/src/main/scala/com/mblinn/mbfpp/functional/ls/LazySequence.scala
```scala
def pagedSequence(pageNum: Int): Stream[String] =
  getPage(pageNum) match {
    case Some(page: String) => page #:: pagedSequence(pageNum + 1)
    case None => Stream.Empty
  }

def getPage(page: Int) =
  page match {
    case 1 => Some("Page1")
    case 2 => Some("Page2")
    case 3 => Some("Page3")
    case _ => None
  }
```

Let's dig into pagedSequence a bit more, starting with the #:: operator, which allows us to prepend a value to a Stream. Here we use it to append the strings "foo" and "bar" to a new Stream:

```
scala> val aStream = "foo" #:: "bar" #:: Stream[String]()
aStream: scala.collection.immutable.Stream[String] = Stream(foo, ?)
```

We can get at the head and tail of our Stream, just as we could with other sequences:

```
scala> aStream.head
res0: String = foo

scala> aStream.tail
res1: scala.collection.immutable.Stream[String] = Stream(bar, ?)
```

Let's take a closer look at the heart of our solution in the following code snippet:

```
getPage(pageNum) match {
  case Some(page: String) => page #:: pagedSequence(pageNum + 1)
  case None => Stream.Empty
}
```

We call getPage() and match on the result. If we match a Some, then we know that we got back a valid page. We prepend it to our sequence and then recursively call the method generating the sequence, passing in the next page we're trying to fetch.

If we get a None, we know we've gone through all our pages, and we append the empty stream, Stream.Empty, to our lazy sequence. This signals the end of the sequence.

Now we can work with pagedSequence just like we worked with some of the sequences we saw in the previous example. Here we take two pages from the sequence, starting at the first element:

```
scala> pagedSequence(1) take 2 force
res2: scala.collection.immutable.Stream[String] = Stream(Page1, Page2)
```

Here we force the whole thing to be realized, which is safe since this sequence, while lazy, isn't infinite:

```
scala> pagedSequence(1) force
res3: scala.collection.immutable.Stream[String] = Stream(Page1, Page2, Page3)
```

That wraps up our Scala paged sequence example. Now let's take a look at how to do it in Clojure.

In Clojure

In Clojure, we can construct an instance of Lazy Sequence from scratch using lazy-sequence and add to it with cons, as shown in the following snippet:

```
=> (cons 1 (lazy-seq [2]))
(1 2)
```

We can then use recursive function calls to build up useful sequences. To write our paged sequence example in Clojure, we first define a get-page function to mock up our paged data. The core of our solution is in the paged-sequence function.

The paged-sequence function is called with the start page, and it recursively builds up a lazy sequence by fetching that page, appending it to the sequence, and then calling itself with the number of the next page. The entire solution follows:

ClojureExamples/src/mbfpp/functional/ls/examples.clj
```
(defn get-page [page-num]
  (cond
    (= page-num 1) "Page1"
    (= page-num 2) "Page2"
    (= page-num 3) "Page3"
    :default nil))

(defn paged-sequence [page-num]
  (let [page (get-page page-num)]
    (when page
      (cons page (lazy-seq (paged-sequence (inc page-num)))))))
```

Now we can work with our lazy sequence like any other. If we call paged-sequence in the REPL, we get the entire sequence:

```
=> (paged-sequence 1)
("Page1" "Page2" "Page3")
```

If we use take, we can get a portion of it:

```
=> (take 2 (paged-sequence 1))
("Page1" "Page2")
```

This can give us a very clean way of working with streaming data.

Discussion

One thing to watch out for when using lazy sequences is accidentally holding on to the head of the sequence when you don't mean to, as Figure 14, *Holding on to the Head*, on page 194 demonstrates.

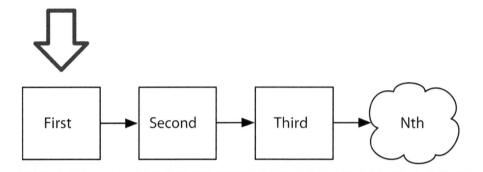

Figure 14—Holding on to the Head. Holding on to the head of a lazy sequence will keep the entire sequence in memory.

In Scala, it's easy to accidentally do this simply by assigning our lazy sequence into a val, as we do in the following code:

ScalaExamples/src/main/scala/com/mblinn/mbfpp/functional/ls/LazySequence.scala
```
val holdsHead = {
  def pagedSequence(pageNum: Int): Stream[String] =
    getPage(pageNum) match {
      case Some(page: String) => {
        println("Realizing " + page)
        page #:: pagedSequence(pageNum + 1)
      }
      case None => Stream.Empty
    }
  pagedSequence(1)
}
```

If we try to force the sequence more than once, we can see that the second time uses the cached copy, as the following REPL output demonstrates:

```
scala> holdsHead force
Realizing Page1
hello
Realizing Page2
Realizing Page3
res0: scala.collection.immutable.Stream[String] = Stream(Page1, Page2, Page3)
scala> holdsHead force
res1: scala.collection.immutable.Stream[String] = Stream(Page1, Page2, Page3)
```

If we don't want to hold on to the head of the sequence, we can use def instead of val, as we do in the following code:

ScalaExamples/src/main/scala/com/mblinn/mbfpp/functional/ls/LazySequence.scala
```
def doesntHoldHead = {
  def pagedSequence(pageNum: Int): Stream[String] =
    getPage(pageNum) match {
```

```
      case Some(page: String) => {
        println("Realizing " + page)
        page #:: pagedSequence(pageNum + 1)
      }
      case None => Stream.Empty
    }
  pagedSequence(1)
}
```

This forces the sequence to be realized fresh each time it's forced and does not hold onto the head:

```
scala> doesntHoldHead force
Realizing Page1
Realizing Page2
Realizing Page3
res2: scala.collection.immutable.Stream[String] = Stream(Page1, Page2, Page3)

scala> doesntHoldHead force
Realizing Page1
Realizing Page2
Realizing Page3
res3: scala.collection.immutable.Stream[String] = Stream(Page1, Page2, Page3)
```

Holding on to the head of a sequence by accident is really no more mysterious than holding on to a reference to any object when you don't mean to, but it can be surprising if you're not watching out for it.

Pattern 19

Focused Mutability

Intent

To use mutable data structures in small, performance-sensitive parts of a program hidden inside of a function while still using immutable data throughout the majority

Overview

Programming with performant, immutable data on machines that are built out of fundamentally mutable components, like main memory and disk, is almost magical. A whole host of technology has contributed to making it possible, especially on the JVM. Growing processor power and memory sizes make it increasingly unnecessary to squeeze every last drop of performance out of a machine.

Small, transient objects are cheap to create and to destroy, thanks to the JVM's excellent generational garbage collector. Both Scala and Clojure use extremely clever data structures that allow immutable collections to share state. This obviates the need to copy the entire collection when one piece of it is changed, which means collections have a reasonable memory footprint and can be modified fairly quickly.

Still, using immutable data has some performance costs. Even the clever data structures Clojure and Scala use may take up more memory than their mutable counterparts, and they perform somewhat worse. The benefits of immutable data, which greatly ease not only concurrent programming but also ease programming large systems in general, often outweigh the costs. However, sometimes you really do need that extra performance, usually in a tight loop in a part of the program that is frequently called.

Focused Mutability shows how to use mutable data in these situations by creating functions that take in some immutable data structures, operate on mutable data inside of the function, and then return another immutable data structure. This lets us get more performance without letting mutability muck up our programs, since we're confining it inside a function, where nothing else can see it.

One consideration we need to make when using Focused Mutability is what the cost of translating a mutable data structure into an immutable one is. Clojure provides first-class support here with a feature called transients. Transients let us take an immutable data structure, convert it into a mutable one in constant time, and then convert it back into an immutable one when we're done with it, also in constant time.

In Scala, it's a bit trickier, since there's no first-class support for something like Clojure's transients. We have to use the mutable versions of Scala's data structures and then convert them into immutable ones using conversion methods on the collections library. Thankfully, Scala can do this conversion quite efficiently.

Code Sample: Adding to Indexed Sequence

Let's start off with a look at a very simple sample, adding a range of numbers to an indexed sequence. This isn't a particularly useful thing to do in practice, but it's a very simple example, which makes it easy to do some basic performance analysis.

For this example, we'll compare the time it takes to add a million elements to a mutable indexed sequence and then translate it into an immutable one with the amount of time it takes to build up the immutable sequence directly. This involves some microbenchmarking, so we'll do several trial runs of each test to try to spot outliers caused by garbage collection, caching issues, and so on.

This certainly isn't a perfect way to perform a microbenchmark, but it's good enough so that we can get a feel for which solutions are faster and by how much.

In Scala

In Scala, we'll compare the results of adding elements to an immutable Vector directly to the results of adding them to a mutable ArrayBuffer and then converting it into an immutable Vector. In addition to our test functions, which add elements to a Vector and an ArrayBuffer, we'll need a bit of infrastructure code to help out with timing and test runs.

Let's take a look at the immutable piece first. The following code defines a function, testImmutable(), which appends count elements to an immutable Vector and updates a reference to point at the new vector each time a new element is appended:

ScalaExamples/src/main/scala/com/mblinn/mbfpp/functional/fm/FocusedMutation.scala
```scala
def testImmutable(count: Int): IndexedSeq[Int] = {
  var v = Vector[Int]()
  for (c <- Range(0, count))
    v = v :+ c
  v
}
```

Now let's take a look at testMutable(), which is similar except that it appends elements to a mutable ArrayBuffer, which is a bit like a Java ArrayList. The code is here:

ScalaExamples/src/main/scala/com/mblinn/mbfpp/functional/fm/FocusedMutation.scala
```scala
def testMutable(count: Int): IndexedSeq[Int] = {
  val s = ArrayBuffer[Int](count)
  for (c <- Range(0, count))
    s.append(c)
  s.toIndexedSeq
}
```

Now we just need a way of getting timing information from runs of our test functions. We'll time runs by recording system time before the test run and after. Instead of embedding this in the test functions themselves, we'll create a higher-order function that can do the timing, time(), and another one, timeRuns(), that will run multiple tests at a time. Here is the code for both:

ScalaExamples/src/main/scala/com/mblinn/mbfpp/functional/fm/FocusedMutation.scala
```scala
def time[R](block: => R): R = {
  val start = System.nanoTime
  val result = block
  val end = System.nanoTime
  val elapsedTimeMs = (end - start) * 0.000001
  println("Elapsed time: %.3f msecs".format(elapsedTimeMs))
  result
}

def timeRuns[R](block: => R, count: Int) =
  for (_ <- Range(0, count)) time { block }
```

With the pieces in place, we can run some tests. Let's try five test runs with a count of one million against our immutable version:

```scala
scala> val oneMillion = 1000000
scala> timeRuns(testImmutable(oneMillion), 5)
Elapsed time: 127.499 msecs
Elapsed time: 127.479 msecs
Elapsed time: 130.501 msecs
Elapsed time: 142.875 msecs
Elapsed time: 123.623 msecs
```

As we can see, the times range from around 123 milliseconds to about 142 milliseconds. Now let's give it a shot with our mutable version, which only converts to an immutable data structure when modifications are done:

```
scala> timeRuns(testMutable(oneMillion), 5)
Elapsed time: 98.339 msecs
Elapsed time: 105.240 msecs
Elapsed time: 88.800 msecs
Elapsed time: 65.997 msecs
Elapsed time: 54.918 msecs
```

Here, the times range from around 54 milliseconds to around 105 milliseconds. Comparing the shortest run from our immutable version, 123 milliseconds, with the shortest run from our mutable version, 54 milliseconds, yields about a 128 percent improvement. Comparing the longest runs, 142 milliseconds with 105 milliseconds, yields an improvement of about 35 percent.

While your mileage may vary somewhat depending on your machine, on your JVM version, on your garbage collection tuning, and so forth, this basic microbenchmark suggests that the mutable version is generally faster than the immutable one, as we'd expect.

In Clojure

Clojure has built-in support for Focused Mutability through a feature named transients. Transients allow us to magically transform an immutable data structure into a mutable one. To use it, the immutable data structure is passed into the transient! form. For example, this would get us a transient, mutable vector, (def t (transient [])).

As the name suggests, transients are supposed to be, well, transient, but in a very different way than the transient keyword in Java means. Transients in Clojure are transient in the sense that you use them briefly inside a function and then transform them back into an immutable data structure before passing them around.

Transients can be appended to with a special version of conj called conj!. Using an exclamation point for operations on mutable data is an old Lisp convention meant to convey that you're about to do something exciting and dangerous!

Let's take a look at our basic Focused Mutability example, which has been rewritten to use Clojure's transients. First off, we need our mutable function. In Clojure, we'll build up our sequence of numbers with a recursive function that passes a vector through the call chain and conjes a single number to the vector in each call. The code is here:

ClojureExamples/src/mbfpp/functional/fm/examples.clj
```clojure
(defn test-immutable [count]
  (loop [i 0 s []]
    (if (< i count)
      (recur (inc i) (conj s i))
      s)))
```

Our mutable version looks almost identical; the only difference is that we create a transient vector using transient to be modified internal to the function. Then we convert it back to an immutable data structure with persistent! when done, as the code shows:

ClojureExamples/src/mbfpp/functional/fm/examples.clj
```clojure
(defn test-mutable [count]
  (loop [i 0 s (transient [])]
    (if (< i count)
      (recur (inc i) (conj! s i))
      (persistent! s))))
```

Finally, we need a way to time our examples. Clojure has a built-in time function that's much like the one we wrote for Scala, but we still need a way of running multiple trials in one shot. The somewhat cryptic-looking macro here fits the bill. If Lisp macros aren't in in your bag of tricks yet, we discuss them in Pattern 21, *Domain-Specific Language*, on page 218.

ClojureExamples/src/mbfpp/functional/fm/examples.clj
```clojure
(defmacro time-runs [fn count]
  `(dotimes [_# ~count]
    (time ~fn)))
```

Now we can put our Clojure solution through its paces. First, here's the immutable version:

```
=> (time-runs (test-immutable one-million) 5)
"Elapsed time: 112.03 msecs"
"Elapsed time: 114.174 msecs"
"Elapsed time: 117.223 msecs"
"Elapsed time: 114.976 msecs"
"Elapsed time: 300.29 msecs"
```

Next, the mutable one:

```
=> (time-runs (test-mutable one-million) 5)
"Elapsed time: 84.752 msecs"
"Elapsed time: 73.398 msecs"
"Elapsed time: 196.601 msecs"
"Elapsed time: 70.859 msecs"
"Elapsed time: 70.402 msecs"
```

These times are fairly similar to the Scala times, which isn't surprising since Scala's immutable data structures and Clojure's immutable data structures are based on the same set of techniques. Comparing the shortest and longest runs of both versions gives us a speedup of about 50 percent for the mutable version, which isn't too shabby.

One other interesting thing to note about this example is that the two outliers, 300.29 ms for the immutable run and 196.601 ms for the mutable one, are both twice as slow as the fastest run for their respective solutions.

A bit of digging into these examples with a profiling tool reveals that the culprit here is indeed a major garbage collection that ran during those samples and not the others. The effects of garbage collection on this example might be reduced with tuning, but that, alas, would be a book in itself!

Code Sample: Event Stream Manipulation

Let's take a look at an example with a bit more weight. Here, we'll process a stream of events that represent purchases. Each event contains a store number, a customer number, and an item number. Our processing will be straightforward; we'll organize the stream of events into a map keyed off of the store number so that we can sort purchases by store.

In addition to the processing code itself, we'll need a simple way of generating test data. For that, we'll use Pattern 18, *Lazy Sequence*, on page 186, to generate an infinitely long sequence of test purchases, from which we'll take as many as we need. Let's take a look!

In Scala

Our Scala solution starts with a Purchase case class to hold on to our purchases. We'll also need a sequence of test purchases, as well as the immutable and mutable versions of our test functions. In both cases, we'll go through our test purchases in a for comprehension, pull out the store number from the purchase, and add it to a list of other purchases from that store, which we'll then put into a map keyed off of by store number.

For timing, we'll reuse the same code from the above example. Let's start with the Purchase class, a straightforward case class:

ScalaExamples/src/main/scala/com/mblinn/mbfpp/functional/fm/FocusedMutation.scala
```scala
case class Purchase(storeNumber: Int, customerNumber: Int, itemNumber: Int)
```

Generating our test data can be done with an infinitely long lazy sequence, from which we'll take as many samples as we need. It's okay if you don't understand the details here; they can be found in Pattern 18, *Lazy Sequence*, on page 186. The upshot for our current example is that we can easily generate test data with infiniteTestPurchases(), from which we can use take(). Here's the code:

```
ScalaExamples/src/main/scala/com/mblinn/mbfpp/functional/fm/FocusedMutation.scala
val r = new Random
def makeTestPurchase = Purchase(r.nextInt(100), r.nextInt(1000), r.nextInt(500))
def infiniteTestPurchases: Stream[Purchase] =
  makeTestPurchase #:: infiniteTestPurchases
```

If we wanted to take, say, five items from our infinite sequence, we do so with take(), like this:

```
scala> val fiveTestPurchases = infiniteTestPurchases.take(5)
fiveTestPurchases: ...

scala> for(purchase <- fiveTestPurchases) println(purchase)
Purchase(71,704,442)
Purchase(23,718,87)
Purchase(39,736,3)
Purchase(33,3,233)
Purchase(86,985,152)
```

Now that we've got a way of generating test data, let's put it to good use in our immutable solution, immutableSequenceEventProcessing(). This function takes the number of test purchases, obtains the test purchases from our infinite sequence of test data, and adds them to a map indexed by store, as described earlier.

To add a new purchase to the map, we pull the store number out of the purchase and attempt to get any existing purchases for that store from the map. If they exist, we add the new purchase to the existing list and create a new map with the updated key. The code to do so is here:

```
ScalaExamples/src/main/scala/com/mblinn/mbfpp/functional/fm/FocusedMutation.scala
def immutableSequenceEventProcessing(count: Int) = {
  val testPurchases = infiniteTestPurchases.take(count)
  var mapOfPurchases = immutable.Map[Int, List[Purchase]]()

  for (purchase <- testPurchases)
    mapOfPurchases.get(purchase.storeNumber) match {
      case None => mapOfPurchases =
        mapOfPurchases + (purchase.storeNumber -> List(purchase))
      case Some(existing: List[Purchase]) => mapOfPurchases =
        mapOfPurchases + (purchase.storeNumber -> (purchase :: existing))
    }
}
```

Our mutable version is quite similar to the immutable version, except that we modify a mutable map and then turn it into an immutable one when done, as this code shows:

ScalaExamples/src/main/scala/com/mblinn/mbfpp/functional/fm/FocusedMutation.scala
```scala
def mutableSequenceEventProcessing(count: Int) = {
  val testPurchases = infiniteTestPurchases.take(count)
  val mapOfPurchases = mutable.Map[Int, List[Purchase]]()

  for (purchase <- testPurchases)
    mapOfPurchases.get(purchase.storeNumber) match {
      case None => mapOfPurchases.put(purchase.storeNumber, List(purchase))
      case Some(existing: List[Purchase]) =>
        mapOfPurchases.put(purchase.storeNumber, (purchase :: existing))
    }

  mapOfPurchases.toMap
}
```

So how do these two solutions perform? Let's take a look by running it over 500,000 samples, starting with the immutable version first:

```
scala> timeRuns(immutableSequenceEventProcessing(fiveHundredThousand), 5)
Elapsed time: 647.948 msecs
Elapsed time: 523.477 msecs
Elapsed time: 551.897 msecs
Elapsed time: 505.083 msecs
Elapsed time: 538.568 msecs
```

And now here's the mutable one:

```
scala> timeRuns(mutableSequenceEventProcessing(fiveHundredThousand), 5)
Elapsed time: 584.002 msecs
Elapsed time: 283.623 msecs
Elapsed time: 546.839 msecs
Elapsed time: 286.259 msecs
Elapsed time: 568.298 msecs
```

As we can see, the mutable version is only a tiny bit faster. A bit of profiling reveals that this is largely because much of the time in the example was spent generating test data, and not manipulating the map.

If we were reading the events off the filesystem or over the network, this overhead would be even greater, and the difference between the two solutions even smaller! On the other hand, even a tiny amount of time shaved off of each event processing may end up mattering if the data set is big enough.

In Clojure

Our Clojure solution is fairly similar to the Scala one. Just as in Scala, we'll use Pattern 18, *Lazy Sequence*, on page 186, to generate an infinite sequence of test purchases from which we'll take a finite number. We'll examine two implementations of our test functions. The first uses a normal, immutable map, and the second a mutable, transient one.

Let's get started with a look at the code that lets us generate test data. We can use a function named repeatedly, which, as the name suggests, calls the function multiple times and uses the results to create a lazy sequence. Outside of that, we just need a function to create the test purchases themselves. Here's the code for both:

ClojureExamples/src/mbfpp/functional/fm/examples.clj
```
(defn make-test-purchase []
  {:store-number (rand-int 100)
   :customer-number (rand-int 100)
   :item-number (rand-int 500)})
(defn infinite-test-purchases []
  (repeatedly make-test-purchase))
```

Now we need our test functions. We'll use reduce to turn a sequence of purchases into a map indexed by store number. Just as in the Scala example, we'll use take to take a finite number of test purchases from our infinite sequence of them. Then we'll reduce over that sequence, building up our map of purchases indexed by store number.

As before, we need to handle the case when we first see the store number, which we can do by passing in a default empty list to get. The code is here:

ClojureExamples/src/mbfpp/functional/fm/examples.clj
```
(defn immutable-sequence-event-processing [count]
  (let [test-purchases (take count (infinite-test-purchases))]
    (reduce
      (fn [map-of-purchases {:keys [store-number] :as current-purchase}]
        (let [purchases-for-store (get map-of-purchases store-number '())]
          (assoc map-of-purchases store-number
                 (conj purchases-for-store current-purchase))))
      {}
      test-purchases)))
```

Since Clojure has handy-dandy transients, the mutable solution looks very similar, save that we need to transform our map to and from a transient and that we need to use assoc! to add to it, as the code shows:

ClojureExamples/src/mbfpp/functional/fm/examples.clj
```
(defn mutable-sequence-event-processing [count]
  (let [test-purchases (take count (infinite-test-purchases))]
```

```
  (persistent! (reduce
    (fn [map-of-purchases {:keys [store-number] :as current-purchase}]
      (let [purchases-for-store (get map-of-purchases store-number '())]
        (assoc! map-of-purchases store-number
                (conj purchases-for-store current-purchase))))
    (transient {})
    test-purchases))))
```

Now let's give it a whirl, starting with the mutable version:

```
=> (time-runs (mutable-sequence-event-processing five-hundred-thousand) 5)
"Elapsed time: 445.841 msecs"
"Elapsed time: 457.66 msecs"
"Elapsed time: 452.743 msecs"
"Elapsed time: 374.041 msecs"
"Elapsed time: 403.498 msecs"
nil
```

Now on to the immutable one:

```
=> (time-runs (immutable-sequence-event-processing five-hundred-thousand) 5)
"Elapsed time: 481.547 msecs"
"Elapsed time: 413.121 msecs"
"Elapsed time: 460.379 msecs"
"Elapsed time: 441.686 msecs"
"Elapsed time: 445.772 msecs"
nil
```

As we can see, the differences are fairly minimal, but the mutable version is a bit faster.

Discussion

Focused Mutability is an optimization pattern. It's the sort of thing that the old advice to avoid premature optimization is all about. As we've seen from this chapter, Scala and Clojure's immutable data structures perform very well—not much worse than their mutable counterparts! If you're modifying several immutable data structures in one go and if you're doing it for large amounts of data, you're likely to see a significant improvement. However, immutable data structures should be the default—they're usually plenty fast.

Before using Focused Mutability or any small-scale performance optimization, it's a good idea to profile your application and make sure you're optimizing in the right place; otherwise, you might find that you're spending time optimizing a section of code that is rarely called, which will have little effect on the overall performance of the program.

Pattern 20

Customized Control Flow

Intent

To create focused, custom-control flow abstractions

Overview

Using the right control flow abstraction for the job can help us write clearer code. For instance, Ruby includes an unless operator, which can be used to do something unless a conditional is true. Good Ruby code uses this operator over if and the not operator, since it's clearer to read.

No language has every useful control flow abstraction built in, though. Functional programming languages give us a way to create our own using higher-order functions. For instance, to create a control flow structure that executes a piece of code n times and prints out the average time for the runs, we can write a function that takes another function and invokes it n times.

However, just using higher-order functions leaves us with a verbose syntax for our custom control flow. We can do better. In Clojure we can use the macro system, and in Scala we've got a bag of tricks that include *blocks* and *by name* parameters.

Sample Code: Choose One of Three

Let's start off with a look at a basic custom control structure, choose, which chooses between three different options. We'll explore two different implementations: the first will use higher-order functions and the second will explore how we can improve on our first solution by providing some syntactic sugar.

In Scala

Our choose() function takes an integer between 1 and 3 and three functions. It then executes the corresponding function, as the following code shows:

ScalaExamples/src/main/scala/com/mblinn/mbfpp/functional/ccf/Choose.scala
```scala
def choose[E](num: Int, first: () => E, second: () => E, third: () => E) =
  if (num == 1) first()
  else if (num == 2) second()
  else if (num == 3) third()
```

This is a straightforward use of higher-order functions. Let's take a look at how we'd use it:

```scala
scala> simplerChoose(2,
     | () => println("hello, world"),
     | () => println("goodbye, cruel world"),
     | () => println("meh, indifferent world"))
goodbye, cruel world
```

It works as we'd expect; however, the need to wrap our actions up in functions is cumbersome. A better syntax would be if we could just pass naked expressions into the choose(), as we do in the following imaginary REPL session:

```scala
scala> simplerChoose(2,
     | println("hello, world"),
     | println("goodbye, cruel world"),
     | println("meh, indifferent world"))
goodbye, cruel world
```

Let's see how to make this syntax real, starting with a very simple case. In the following REPL output, we define a test() function with a single argument, expression. The body of the function just attempts to execute the expression. We then call test() with the single argument println("hello, world").

```scala
scala> def test[E](expression: E) = expression
test: (expression: Unit)Unit

scala> test(println("hello, world"))
hello, world
```

It appears that this works and our expression is evaluated, since "hello, world" is printed to the console. But what happens if we try to execute our expression twice? Let's find out in the following REPL snippet:

```scala
scala> def testTwice[E](expression: E) = {
     | expression
     | expression
     | }
testTwice: (expression: Unit)Unit

scala> testTwice(println("hello, world"))
hello, world
```

The string "hello, world" is only printed to the console once! This is because Scala will, by default, evaluate an expression at the time it's passed into a function and then pass in the value of the evaluated expression. This is known as *pass by value*, and it's usually what we want and expect. For instance, in the following example, it prevents the expression from being evaluated twice:

```
scala> def printTwice[E](expression: E) = {
     | println(expression)
     | println(expression)
     | }
printTwice: [E](expression: E)Unit

scala> printTwice(5 * 5)
25
25
```

However, this is the opposite of what we need when writing custom control structures. Scala gives us an alternative calling semantic called *pass by name*. Using pass by name means that we pass a name for the expression into the function rather than the evaluated value of the expression. We can then refer to that name inside the function body to have it be evaluated on demand.

To make a function argument pass by name rather than by value, we can use => after the parameter name and before the type annotation. The following REPL snippet rewrites our test function to use pass-by-name calling:

```
scala> def testByName[E](expression: => E) {
     | expression
     | expression
     | }
testByName: [E](expression: => E)Unit

scala> testByName(println("hello, world"))
hello, world
hello, world
```

Now that we understand the difference between pass by value and pass by name, we can write a simplerChoose() function that takes naked expressions. The following code snippet does so:

ScalaExamples/src/main/scala/com/mblinn/mbfpp/functional/ccf/Choose.scala
```
def simplerChoose[E](num: Int, first: => E, second: => E, third: => E) =
  if (num == 1) first
  else if (num == 2) second
  else if (num == 3) third
```

Now we can use our naked expression syntax, as in the following REPL output:

```
scala> simplerChoose(2,
     | println("hello, world"),
     | println("goodbye, cruel world"),
     | println("meh, indifferent world"))
goodbye, cruel world
```

Clojure's approach to custom control flow is quite different and involves its powerful macro system. Let's take a look!

In Clojure

Let's start off our Clojure sample with a look at a simple version of choose that relies on higher-order functions. We take three functions and an integer indicating which one to run, as the following code shows:

ClojureExamples/src/mbfpp/functional/ccf/ccf_examples.clj
```
(defn choose [num first second third]
  (cond
    (= 1 num) (first)
    (= 2 num) (second)
    (= 3 num) (third)))
```

To use it, we pass in our integer and function arguments:

```
=> (choose 2
         (fn [] (println "hello, world"))
         (fn [] (println "goodbye, cruel world"))
         (fn [] (println "meh, indifferent world")))
goodbye, cruel world
nil
```

However, we'd like to avoid the need to wrap our actions up into functions and instead write code that looks like the following REPL session:

```
=> (choose 2
         (println "hello, world")
         (println "goodbye, cruel world")
         (println "meh, indifferent world"))
goodbye, cruel world
nil
```

To see how we can get there, we'll need to take a short detour into one of Clojure's most powerful features, its macro system. Along the way, we'll answer the age-old question of why Lisp has such a different syntax.

Clojure Macros

Macros are a form of metaprogramming: they are pieces of code that transform other pieces of code. This concept has surprising depth in Clojure and other Lisps.

To see why, let's do a thought experiment. The builder we introduced in Pattern 4, *Replacing Builder for Immutable Object*, on page 62, is verbose to write. One way to cut down on verbosity is to create a skeletal Java class with nothing but attributes in it, and then write code to generate the builder based on those attributes.

A block diagram of this approach is described in the following figure:

Figure 15—Metaprogramming in Java. Code generating a Builder class

Here, the builder creator is a piece of code that's responsible for taking in a skeletal Java class with nothing but attributes and producing a builder based on it. This is much like the support that IDEs have to generate getters and setters.

To do so, the builder creator needs some understanding of the input Java code. For such a simple task, the builder creator can just treat the file as text and read the input file line by line, figuring out which lines correspond to variable declarations as it goes.

However, what if we needed to manipulate our input Java code in a more complex way? Say we wanted to modify certain methods to log out the time they were invoked. This would be difficult to do: how do we know when a method starts and ends if we're just going through the file line by line?

The difficulty is that our simple code generator is treating the Java file as plain text. Complicated language applications like compilers will go through a series of passes to generate an *abstract syntax tree* or *AST*. The following diagram is a simplified representation of this process.

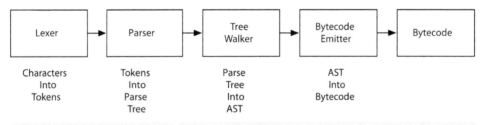

Figure 16—Simplified Compiler. Stages in a simplified compiler

The AST represents code at a more abstract level in terms of things like methods and classes, rather than as simple text data. For instance, a Java compiler written in Java might have Method and VariableDefinition classes as parts of its AST, among other things.

This makes the AST representation of code the most convenient representation to manipulate programmatically. However, in most programming languages, the AST is hidden away inside the compiler and requires intimate knowledge of the compiler to manipulate.

Lisps, including Clojure, are different. The syntax of Clojure is defined in terms of core Clojure data structures, like lists and vectors. For instance, let's take a close look at a humble function definition:

```
(defn say-hello [name] (println (str "Hello, " name)))
```

This is just a list with four elements in it. The first is the symbol defn, the second is the symbol say-hello, the third is a vector, and the fourth is another list. When Clojure evaluates a list, it assumes that the first element is something that can be called, like a function, a macro, or a compiler built-in, and it assumes that the rest of the list is made of arguments.

Other than that, it's just a list like any other! We can see this by using a single quote, which turns off evaluation on the form it's applied to. In the following snippet we take the first element from two lists—the first list is a list of four integers, the second is the function definition we just introduced:

```
=> (first '(1 2 3 4))
1
=> (first '(defn say-hello [name] (println (str "Hello, " name))))
defn
```

Since Clojure code is just Clojure data, it's very easy to write code to manipulate it. Clojure's macro system provides a convenient hook to do this manipulation at compile time, as the figure shows.

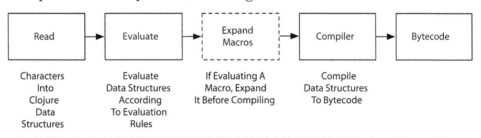

Figure 17—Read, Evaluate, Compile. Going from Clojure text to bytecode

Let's dig into this process in a bit more depth. In Clojure, the process of going from a sequence of characters to data structures is called *reading*, as described in the first box in the diagram. Instead of being some magic hidden away inside of the compiler, it's a facility that's available to the programmer.

Some forms are available that will read from various sources, such as files or strings. Here, we use the string version of read to read a vector from a string and take its first element:

```
=> (first (read-string "[1 2 3]"))
1
```

The read form has a partner, eval, as shown in the second step of the diagram. This takes a data structure and evaluates it according to a simple set of evaluation rules we discuss in Section 2.4, *TinyWeb in Clojure*, on page 28. In the following snippet, we use eval to evaluate a def after we've read it in from a string:

```
=> (eval (read-string "(def foo 1)"))
#'user/foo
=> foo
1
```

You may have seen eval in languages like Ruby or Javascript; however, there's a crucial difference between that eval and the one Clojure has. In Clojure and other Lisps, eval operates on data structures that have been read in, rather than on strings.

This means it's possible to do much more sophisticated manipulations, since we don't have to build up our code using raw string manipulation. The macro expansion step as described in the diagram provides a convenient hook for us to do exactly this.

A macro is just a function with a few key differences. The arguments to a macro are not evaluated, just like the call-by-name arguments we used in Scala in *In Scala*, on page 206. A macro is run before compile time, and it returns the code to be compiled. This gives us a formal, built-in way of doing the sort of manipulations we introduced in our Java builder-generator thought experiment.

We define a macro with the defmacro built in. In addition, a few other Clojure features help us build macros by controlling evaluation. These are the back-tick, `` ` ``, also known as the *syntax quote*, and the tilde, ~, also known as *unquote*.

Together, these features let us build up code templates for use in macros. Syntax quote turns evaluation off inside the form it's applied to, and it expands any symbol name out to be fully qualified by its namespace. Unquote, as the name suggests, lets us turn evaluation back on inside a syntax quote.

In the following snippet, we use syntax quote and unquote together. The symbol foo and form (+ 1 1) don't get evaluated, but since we apply unquote to number-one, it does.

```
=> (def number-one 1)
#'mbfpp.functional.ccf.ccf-examples/number-one
=> `(foo (+ 1 1) ~number-one)
(mbfpp.functional.ccf.cff-examples/foo (clojure.core/+ 1 1) 1)
```

The output looks a bit noisy because syntax quote has namespace-qualified foo and +.

Now that we've introduced macros, let's see how we can use them to simplify choose. We do so by writing a macro, simplerChoose. The simplerChoose macro takes in a number and three forms, and it returns a cond expression that evaluates the appropriate form. The code for simplerChoose is in the following snippet:

ClojureExamples/src/mbfpp/functional/ccf/ccf_examples.clj
```
(defmacro simpler-choose [num first second third]
  `(cond
     (= 1 ~num) ~first
     (= 2 ~num) ~second
     (= 3 ~num) ~third))
```

Before running it, we can use macroexpand-1 to see what code the macro generates, as we do in the following REPL session:

```
=> (macroexpand-1
     '(simpler-choose 1 (println "foo") (println "bar") (println "baz")))
(clojure.core/cond
  (clojure.core/= 1 1) (println "foo")
  (clojure.core/= 2 1) (println "bar")
  (clojure.core/= 3 1) (println "baz"))
```

As we can see, the macro expands out to a cond statement, as we'd expect. Now if we run it, it works as we'd expect, without the need to wrap our actions up in functions!

```
=> (simpler-choose 2
                   (println "hello, world")
                   (println "goodbye, cruel world")
                   (println "meh, indifferent world"))
goodbye, cruel world
nil
```

Clojure's macro system is one of its most powerful features, and it explains why Clojure has the syntax it does. In order for the magic to work, Clojure code has to be written in terms of simple Clojure data structures, a property known as *homoiconicity*.

Sample Code: Average Timing

Let's take a look at a more involved instance of Customized Control Flow. Here we'll create a custom control abstraction that executes an expression a given number of times and returns the average time of the executions. This is handy for quick and dirty performance testing.

In Scala

In Scala, our solution is two functions. The first, timeRun(), takes an expression, runs it, and returns the time it took. The second, avgTime(), takes an expression and a number of times to evaluate it and then returns the average time it took. It uses timeRun() as a helper function.

The code for our Scala solution follows:

ScalaExamples/src/main/scala/com/mblinn/mbfpp/functional/ccf/Choose.scala
```scala
def timeRun[E](toTime: => E) = {
  val start = System.currentTimeMillis
  toTime
  System.currentTimeMillis - start
}
def avgTime[E](times: Int, toTime: => E) = {
  val allTimes = for (_ <- Range(0, times)) yield timeRun(toTime)
  allTimes.sum / times
}
```

As advertised, this gives us a way to get the average runtime for a statement:

```scala
scala> avgTime(5, Thread.sleep(1000))
res0: Long = 1001
```

Let's break this down a bit more using the REPL. The meat of avgTime() is the following expression:

```scala
val allTimes = for (_ <- Range(0, times)) yield timeRun(toTime)
```

If we substitute some expressions in by hand, we can see this generates a sequence of run times. The underscore in the for binding indicates that we don't actually care about what the values of the Range expression are bound to, since we're just using it to run our statement a set number of times:

```scala
scala> val allTimes = for (_ <- Range(0, 5)) yield timeRun(Thread.sleep(1000))
allTimes: scala.collection.immutable.IndexedSeq[Long] =
        Vector(1000, 1001, 1000, 1001, 1001)
```

From there, we use sum() to calculate the sum of all runtimes, and we divide by the number of runs to get the average:

```scala
scala> allTimes.sum / 5
res2: Long = 1000
```

One other interesting element of this solution is how we pass a by-name parameter through two different functions. The toTime parameter is passed into avgTime(), and from there into timeRun(). It's not evaluated until it's used in timeRun().

The ability to chain together calls using by-name parameters is important because it lets us break up the code for more complicated instances of Customized Control Flow.

In Clojure

In Clojure, our solution consists of a macro, avg-time, and a function, time-run. The avg-time macro generates code that uses time-run to time runs of the passed-in statement and then calculate its average.

The code for our Clojure solution follows:

ClojureExamples/src/mbfpp/functional/ccf/ccf_examples.clj
```
(defn time-run [to-time]
  (let [start (System/currentTimeMillis)]
    (to-time)
    (- (System/currentTimeMillis) start)))

(defmacro avg-time [times to-time]
  `(let [total-time#
         (apply + (for [_# (range ~times)] (time-run (fn [] ~to-time))))]
     (float (/ total-time# ~times))))
```

Here, we use it to calculate the average time for a test statement:

```
=> (avg-time 5 (Thread/sleep 1000))
1000.8
```

Let's dig into how time-run works in a bit more detail, starting with a Clojure feature we introduce in this sample: automatic generated symbols, or *gensyms*. To avoid accidental variable capture in macros, whenever we need a symbol in our generated code, we need to generate a unique symbol.

The way we do this in Clojure is to append a symbol name with a hash sign when we use one inside of a syntax quote. As the snippet below shows, Clojure will expand the gensym out to a fairly unique symbol:

```
=> `(foo# foo#)
(foo__2230__auto__ foo__2230__auto__)
```

We use gensyms for total-time and _. The second one might seem a little strange, since we're just using underscore to indicate that we don't care about the values in range, just as we did in Scala.

If we don't make it a generated symbol, Clojure will qualify the symbol in the current namespace, but making it a gensym causes Clojure to generate a unique symbol for it. We demonstrate this below:

```
=> `(_)
(mbfpp.functional.ccf.ccf-examples/_)
=> `(-#)
(-__1308__auto__)
```

Now let's examine the heart of avg-time. The following syntax-quoted let statement serves as a template for the code that the macro will generate. As we can see, the meat of the solution is a for statement that wraps the expression in to-time in a function and runs it through time-run the requested number of times:

```
`(let [total-time#
   (apply + (for [_# (range ~times)]
               (time-run (fn [] ~to-time))))] (float (/ total-time# ~times))))
```

To test this out, we can use macroexpand-1 to look at the code it generates, as we do in the following REPL session:

```
=> (macroexpand-1 '(avg-time 5 (Thread/sleep 100)))
(clojure.core/let
 [total-time__1489__auto__
  (clojure.core/apply
   clojure.core/+
   (clojure.core/for
    [__1490__auto__ (clojure.core/range 5)]
    (mbfpp.functional.ccf.cff-examples/time-run
     (clojure.core/fn [] (Thread/sleep 1000)))))]
 (clojure.core/float (clojure.core// total-time__1489__auto__ 5)))
nil
```

Since all the symbols are either gensyms or are fully qualified by their namespace, this can be a bit hard to read! If I'm having trouble understanding how a macro works, I like to manually convert the output from macroexpand-1 into the code that I'd write by hand. To do this, you generally just need to remove the namespaces from fully qualified symbols and the generated part of gensyms. I've done so in the following code:

```
(let
  [total-time
   (apply + (for [n (range 5)] (time-run (fn [] (Thread/sleep 100)))))]
  (float (/ total-time 5)))
```

As you can see, this cleaned-up output is much simpler to understand. I've also found that the process of going through the generated code by hand will help any bugs in the macro to surface.

Discussion

Both Scala and Clojure let us create customized control flow abstractions, but the way they go about doing so is very different. In Scala, they're runtime abstractions. We're just writing functions and passing statements into them. The trick is that we can control when those statements are evaluated using by-name parameters.

In Clojure we use the macro system, which takes advantage of Clojure's homoiconic nature. Macros are a compile-time concern rather than a runtime one. As we saw, they allow us to fairly easily write code that writes code by using syntax quote as a template for the code we want to produce.

Clojure's approach is more general, but that's only possible because of Clojure's homoiconicity. In order to approximate Clojure-style macros in a nonhomoiconic language like Scala, the language would have to provide hooks into the compiler that let a programmer manipulate ASTs and other compiler artifacts.

This is a difficult task, but Scala does have experimental support for this sort of compile time macro in Scala 1.10. Using this style of macro is more difficult than using a Clojure-style macro, since it requires some knowledge of compiler internals.

Since Scala macros are experimental, and since Scala provides other ways to implement Customized Control Flow, we won't cover them here.

Pattern 21

Domain-Specific Language

Intent

To create a miniature programming language tailored to solve a specific problem

Overview

Domain-Specific Language is a very common pattern that has two broad classes: external DSL and internal DSL.

An external DSL is a full-blown programming language with its own syntax and compiler. It's not intended for general use; rather, it solves some targeted problems. For instance, SQL is an instance of Domain-Specific Language targeted at data manipulation. ANTLR is another, targeted at creating parsers.

On the other hand, we've got internal DSLs, also known as *embedded languages*. These instances of the pattern piggyback on some general-purpose language and live within the constraints of the host language's syntax.

In both cases, the intent is the same. We're trying to create a language that lets us express solutions to problems in a way that is closer to the domain at hand. This results in less code and clearer solutions than those created in a general-purpose language. It also often allows people who aren't software developers to solve some domain problems.

In this section, we'll look at building internal DSLs in Scala and Clojure. The techniques we'll use to build a DSL are very different in these two languages, but the intent remains the same.

In Scala

The current crop of Scala DSLs rely on Scala's flexible syntax and several other Scala tricks. The Scala DSL we examine here will take advantage of several of Scala's advanced abilities.

First off, we'll see Scala's ability to use methods in the postfix and infix positions. This lets us define methods that act as operators.

Second, we'll use Scala's implicit conversions, introduced in Pattern 10, *Replacing Visitor*, on page 113. These appear to let us add new behavior to existing types.

Finally, we'll use a Scala companion object as a factory for the class it's paired up with.

In Clojure

Internal DSLs are an old Lisp technique that Clojure carries on. In Clojure and other Lisps, the line between Domain-Specific Language and frameworks or APIs is very blurry.

Good Clojure code is often structured as layers of DSLs, one on top of the other, each of which is good at solving a problem on a particular layer of the system.

For example, one possible layered system for building web applications in Clojure starts with a library called Ring. This provides an abstraction over HTTP, turning HTTP requests into Clojure maps. On top of that, we can use a DSL named Compojure to route HTTP requests to handler functions. Finally, we can use a DSL named Enlive to create templates for our pages.

Clojure's DSLs are generally built around a core set of higher-order functions, with macros providing syntactic sugar on top. This is the approach we'll use for the Clojure DSL we examine here.

Code Sample: DSL for a Shell

I sometimes find myself cutting and pasting from a shell into a REPL when programming in Scala and Clojure. Let's take a look at a simple DSL to make this more natural by letting us run shell commands directly in a REPL.

In addition to running commands, we'll want to capture their exit status, standard output, and standard error. Finally, we'll want to pipe commands together, just as we can in a normal shell.

In Scala

The end goal of this example is to be able to run shell commands in a natural way inside of a Scala REPL. For individual commands, we'd like to be able to run them like this:

```
scala> "ls" run
```

And we'd like to run pipes of commands like so:

```
scala> "ls" pipe "grep some-file" run
```

Let's take our first step on our shell DSL journey by examining what we want a command to return. We need to be able to inspect a shell command's status code and both its standard output and error streams. In the following code, we packaged those pieces of information together into a case class named CommandResult:

ScalaExamples/src/main/scala/com/mblinn/mbfpp/functional/dsl/Example.scala
```scala
case class CommandResult(status: Int, output: String, error: String)
```

Now let's see how to actually run a command. We can dip into Java's Process-Builder class for this.

The ProcessBuilder class constructor takes a variable number of string arguments, representing the command to run and its arguments. In the following REPL snippet, we create a ProcessBuilder that will allow us to run ls -la :

```scala
scala> val lsProcessBuilder = new ProcessBuilder("ls", "-la")
lsProcessBuilder: ProcessBuilder = java.lang.ProcessBuilder@5674c175
```

To run the process, we call start() on the ProcessBuilder we just created. This returns a Process object that gives us a handle on the running process:

```scala
scala> val lsProcess = lsProcessBuilder.start
lsProcess: Process = java.lang.UNIXProcess@61a7c7e7
```

The Process object gives us access to all the information we need, but output from standard out and standard error are inside of InputStream objects rather than inside strings. We can use the fromInputStream() on Scala's Source object to pick them out, as we demonstrate in the following code:

```scala
scala> Source.fromInputStream(lsProcess.getInputStream()).mkString("")
res0: String =
"total 96
drwxr-xr-x  12 mblinn  staff     408 Mar 17 10:23 .
drwxr-xr-x   8 mblinn  staff     272 Apr  6 15:12 ..
-rw-r--r--   1 mblinn  staff   35583 Jun  9 16:35 .cache
-rw-r--r--   1 mblinn  staff    1200 Mar 17 10:10 .classpath
-rw-r--r--   1 mblinn  staff     328 Mar 17 10:08 .project
drwxr-xr-x   3 mblinn  staff     102 Mar 16 13:29 .settings
drwxr-xr-x   9 mblinn  staff     306 Jun  9 15:58 .svn
drwxr-xr-x   2 mblinn  staff      68 Mar 13 20:34 bin
-rw-r--r--   1 mblinn  staff     262 Jun  9 13:12 build.sbt
drwxr-xr-x   6 mblinn  staff     204 Mar 13 20:33 project
drwxr-xr-x   5 mblinn  staff     170 Mar 13 19:52 src
drwxr-xr-x   6 mblinn  staff     204 Mar 16 13:33 target
"
```

Notice how the method that gets us the output from standard out is somewhat confusingly called getInputStream()()? That's not a typo; the method name seems to refer to the fact that standard out is being written into a Java InputStream that the calling code can consume.

Now we can put our Command class together. The Command takes a list of strings representing the command and its arguments and uses it to construct a ProcessBuilder. It then runs the process, waits for it to complete, and picks out the completed process's output streams and status code. The following code implements Command:

ScalaExamples/src/main/scala/com/mblinn/mbfpp/functional/dsl/Example.scala
```scala
class Command(commandParts: List[String]) {
  def run() = {
    val processBuilder = new ProcessBuilder(commandParts)
    val process = processBuilder.start()
    val status = process.waitFor()
    val outputAsString =
      Source.fromInputStream(process.getInputStream()).mkString("")
    val errorAsString =
      Source.fromInputStream(process.getErrorStream()).mkString("")
    CommandResult(status, outputAsString, errorAsString)
  }
}
```

To make Command classes a bit easier to construct, we add a factory method that takes a string and splits it into Command's companion object:

ScalaExamples/src/main/scala/com/mblinn/mbfpp/functional/dsl/Example.scala
```scala
object Command {
  def apply(commandString: String) = new Command(commandString.split("\\s").toList)
}
```

As the following REPL session demonstrates, this gets us a bit closer to our desired syntax for running a single command:

```scala
scala> Command("ls -la").run
res1: com.mblinn.mbfpp.functional.dsl.ExtendedExample.CommandResult =
CommandResult(0,total 96
drwxr-xr-x  12 mblinn  staff     408 Mar 17 10:23 .
drwxr-xr-x   8 mblinn  staff     272 Apr  6 15:12 ..
-rw-r--r--   1 mblinn  staff   35592 Jun  9 16:57 .cache
-rw-r--r--   1 mblinn  staff    1200 Mar 17 10:10 .classpath
-rw-r--r--   1 mblinn  staff     328 Mar 17 10:08 .project
drwxr-xr-x   3 mblinn  staff     102 Mar 16 13:29 .settings
drwxr-xr-x   9 mblinn  staff     306 Jun  9 15:58 .svn
drwxr-xr-x   2 mblinn  staff      68 Mar 13 20:34 bin
-rw-r--r--   1 mblinn  staff     262 Jun  9 13:12 build.sbt
drwxr-xr-x   6 mblinn  staff     204 Mar 13 20:33 project
drwxr-xr-x   5 mblinn  staff     170 Mar 13 19:52 src
drwxr-xr-x   6 mblinn  staff     204 Mar 16 13:33 target
,)
```

To get the rest of the way there, we'll use the implicit conversions we introduced in Pattern 10, *Replacing Visitor*, on page 113. We'll create a conversion that turns a String into a CommandString with a run() method. A CommandString turns the String it's converting into a Command that its run() method calls. It's implemented in the following code:

```
ScalaExamples/src/main/scala/com/mblinn/mbfpp/functional/dsl/Example.scala
implicit class CommandString(commandString: String) {
  def run() = Command(commandString).run
}
```

Now we've got our desired syntax for running single commands, as we demonstrate with the following REPL output:

```
scala> "ls -la" run
res2: com.mblinn.mbfpp.functional.dsl.ExtendedExample.CommandResult =
CommandResult(0,total 96
drwxr-xr-x  12 mblinn  staff     408 Mar 17 10:23 .
drwxr-xr-x   8 mblinn  staff     272 Apr  6 15:12 ..
-rw-r--r--   1 mblinn  staff   35592 Jun  9 16:57 .cache
-rw-r--r--   1 mblinn  staff    1200 Mar 17 10:10 .classpath
-rw-r--r--   1 mblinn  staff     328 Mar 17 10:08 .project
drwxr-xr-x   3 mblinn  staff     102 Mar 16 13:29 .settings
drwxr-xr-x   9 mblinn  staff     306 Jun  9 15:58 .svn
drwxr-xr-x   2 mblinn  staff      68 Mar 13 20:34 bin
-rw-r--r--   1 mblinn  staff     262 Jun  9 13:12 build.sbt
drwxr-xr-x   6 mblinn  staff     204 Mar 13 20:33 project
drwxr-xr-x   5 mblinn  staff     170 Mar 13 19:52 src
drwxr-xr-x   6 mblinn  staff     204 Mar 16 13:33 target
,)
```

Let's extend our DSL to include pipes. The approach we'll take is to collect our piped command strings into a vector and run them once we've constructed the full chain of pipes.

Let's start off by examining the extensions we need to make to CommandString. Remember, we'd like to be able to run a pipe of commands like so: "ls -la" pipe "grep build" run. This means we need to add a pipe() method, which takes a single string argument, to our CommandString implicit conversion. When it's called, it'll take the string it's converted to a CommandString and the argument it was passed, and it'll stuff them both into a Vector. The code for our expanded CommandString follows:

```
ScalaExamples/src/main/scala/com/mblinn/mbfpp/functional/dsl/Example.scala
implicit class CommandString(firstCommandString: String) {
  def run = Command(firstCommandString).run
  def pipe(secondCommandString: String) =
    Vector(firstCommandString, secondCommandString)
}
```

Now our conversion will convert "ls -la" pipe "grep build" into a vector with both shell commands in it.

```scala
scala> "ls -la" pipe "grep build"
res2: scala.collection.immutable.Vector[String] = Vector(ls -la, grep build)
```

The next step is to add another implicit conversion that converts a Vector[String] into a CommandVector, much as we've already done for individual strings. The CommandVector class had a run() and a pipe() method.

The pipe() method adds a new command to the Vector of commands and returns it, and the run() method knows how to go through the commands and run them, piping the output from one to the next. The code for CommandVector and a new factory method on the Command companion object used by CommandVector follows:

```scala
ScalaExamples/src/main/scala/com/mblinn/mbfpp/functional/dsl/Example.scala
implicit class CommandVector(existingCommands: Vector[String]) {
  def run = {
    val pipedCommands = existingCommands.mkString(" | ")
    Command("/bin/sh", "-c", pipedCommands).run
  }
  def pipe(nextCommand: String): Vector[String] = {
    existingCommands :+ nextCommand
  }
}
object Command {
  def apply(commandString: String) = new Command(commandString.split("\\s").toList)
  def apply(commandParts: String*) = new Command(commandParts.toList)
}
```

Now we've got our full DSL, pipes and all! In the following REPL session, we use it to run some piped commands:

```scala
scala> "ls -la" pipe "grep build" run
res3: com.mblinn.mbfpp.functional.dsl.ExtendedExample.CommandResult =
CommandResult(0,-rw-r--r--   1 mblinn  staff    262 Jun  9 13:12 build.sbt
,)

scala> "ls -la" pipe "grep build" pipe "wc" run
res4: com.mblinn.mbfpp.functional.dsl.ExtendedExample.CommandResult =
CommandResult(0,       1      9     59
,)
```

A couple of notes on this DSL. First, it takes advantage of Scala's ability to use methods as postfix operators. This is easy to misuse, so Scala 2.10 generates a warning when you do so, and it will be disabled by default in a future version of Scala. To use postfix operators without the warning, you can import scala.language.postfixOps into the file that needs them.

Second is a simple DSL, suitable for basic use at a Scala REPL. Scala has a much more complete version of a similar DSL already built into the scala.sys.process package.

In Clojure

In Clojure, our DSL will consist of a command function that creates a function that executes a shell command. Then we'll create a pipe function that allows us to pipe several commands together using function composition. Finally, we'll create two macros, def-command and def-pipe, to make it easy to name pipes and commands.

Before we jump into the main DSL code, let's take a look at how we'll interact with the shell. We'll use a library built into Clojure in the clojure.java.shell namespace, which provides a thin wrapper around Java's Runtime.exec().

In the following REPL session, we use the sh function in clojure.java.shell to execute the ls command. As we can see, the output of the function is a map consisting of the status code for the process and whatever the process wrote to its standard out and standard error streams as a string:

```
=> (shell/sh "ls")
{:exit 0, :out "README.md\nclasses\nproject.clj\nsrc\ntarget\ntest\n", :err ""}
```

This isn't very easy to read, so let's create a function that'll print it in a way that's easier to read before returning the output map. The code to do so follows:

ClojureExamples/src/mbfpp/functional/dsl/examples.clj
```
(defn- print-output [output]
  (println (str "Exit Code: " (:exit output)))
  (if-not (str/blank? (:out output)) (println (:out output)))
  (if-not (str/blank? (:err output)) (println (:err output)))
  output)
```

We can now use sh to run ls -a and get readable output:

```
=> (print-output (shell/sh "ls" "-a"))
Exit Code: 0
.
..
.classpath
.project
.settings
.svn
README.md
classes
project.clj
src
```

```
target
test
```

```
{:exit 0,
:out ".\n..\n.classpath\n.project\n.settings\n.svn\n
        README.md\nclasses\nproject.clj\nsrc\ntarget\ntest\n",
:err ""}
```

Let's move on to the first piece of our DSL, command function. This function takes the command we want to execute as a string, splits it on whitespace to get a sequence of command parts, and then uses apply to apply the sh function to the sequence.

Finally, it runs the returned output through our print-output function, wraps everything up in a higher-order function, and returns it. The code for command follows:

ClojureExamples/src/mbfpp/functional/dsl/examples.clj
```
(defn command [command-str]
  (let [command-parts (str/split command-str #"\s+")]
    (fn []
      (print-output (apply shell/sh command-parts)))))
```

Now if we run a function returned by command, it'll run the shell command it encapsulates:

```
=> ((command "pwd"))
Exit Code: 0
/Users/mblinn/Documents/mbfpp/Book/code/ClojureExamples
```

If we want to name the command, we can do so using def:

```
=> (def pwd (command "pwd"))
#'mbfpp.functional.dsl.examples/pwd
=> (pwd)
Exit Code: 0
/Users/mblinn/Documents/mbfpp/Book/code/ClojureExamples
```

Now that we can run an individual command, let's take a look at what it'll take to pipe them together. A pipe in a Unix shell pipes the output from one command to the input of another. Since the output of a command here is captured in a string, all we need is a way to use that string as input to another command.

The sh function allows us to do so with the :in option:

```
=> (shell/sh "wc" :in "foo bar baz")
{:exit 0, :out "       0       3      11\n", :err ""}
```

Let's modify our command function to take the output map from another command and use its standard output string as input. To do so, we'll add a second arity to command that expects to be passed an output map.

The command function destructures the map to pluck out its output and passes it into sh as input. The code for our new command follows:

ClojureExamples/src/mbfpp/functional/dsl/examples.clj
```
(defn command [command-str]
  (let [command-parts (str/split command-str #"\s+")]
    (fn
      ([] (print-output (apply shell/sh command-parts)))
      ([{old-out :out}]
        (print-output (apply shell/sh (concat command-parts [:in old-out])))))))
```

Now we can define another command, like the following one that greps for the word README:

```
=> (def grep-readme (command "grep README"))
#'mbfpp.functional.dsl.examples/grep-readme
```

Then we can pass the output of our ls command into it, and the ls output will be piped into grep. Each command will print its output to standard out, as the following REPL session shows:

```
=> (grep-readme (ls))
Exit Code: 0
README.md
classes
project.clj
src
target
test

Exit Code: 0
README.md

{:exit 0, :out "README.md\n", :err ""}
```

With our modified command function, we can create a pipe of commands by composing together several commands with comp. If we want to write the commands in the same order as we would in a shell, we just need to reverse the sequence of commands before we compose them, as we do in the following pipe implementation:

ClojureExamples/src/mbfpp/functional/dsl/examples.clj
```
(defn pipe [commands]
  (apply comp (reverse commands)))
```

Now we can create a pipe of commands, as we do in the following REPL session:

```
=> (def grep-readme-from-ls
     (pipe
       [(command "ls")
        (command "grep README")]))
#'mbfpp.functional.dsl.examples/grep-readme-from-ls
```

This has the same effect as running the ls command and passing its output into grep-readme:

```
=> (grep-readme-from-ls)
Exit Code: 0
README.md
classes
project.clj
src
target
test

Exit Code: 0
README.md

{:exit 0, :out "README.md\n", :err ""}
```

Now that we can define commands and pipes, let's use macros to add some syntactic sugar to make things easier. For an introduction to Clojure's macros, see *Clojure Macros*, on page 209. First we'll create a def-command macro. This macro takes a name and a command string and defines a function that executes the command string. The code for def-command follows:

ClojureExamples/src/mbfpp/functional/dsl/examples.clj
```
(defmacro def-command [name command-str]
  `(def ~name ~(command command-str)))
```

Now we can define a command and name it with a single macro invocation, as we do in the following REPL output:

```
=> (def-command pwd "pwd")
#'mbfpp.functional.dsl.examples/pwd

=> (pwd)
Exit Code: 0
/Users/mblinn/Documents/mbfpp/Book/code/ClojureExamples

{:exit 0, :out "/Users/mblinn/Documents/mbfpp/Book/code/ClojureExamples\n", :err ""}
```

Now let's do the same for our piped commands as we did for single commands with the def-pipe macro. This macro takes a command name and a variable number of command strings, turns each command string into a command, and finally creates a pipe with the given name. Here's the code for def-pipe:

ClojureExamples/src/mbfpp/functional/dsl/examples.clj

```
(defmacro def-pipe [name & command-strs]
  (let [commands (map command command-strs)
        pipe (pipe commands)]
    `(def ~name ~pipe)))
```

Now we can create a pipe in one shot, as we do below:

```
=> (def-pipe grep-readme-from-ls "ls" "grep README")
#'mbfpp.functional.dsl.examples/grep-readme-from-ls
=> (grep-readme-from-ls)
Exit Code: 0
README.md
classes
project.clj
src
target
test

Exit Code: 0
README.md

{:exit 0, :out "README.md\n", :err ""}
```

That wraps up our look at Clojure's DSLs!

Discussion

Currently, Scala and Clojure take a very different approach to Domain-Specific Language. Scala uses a flexible syntax and a variety of tricks. Clojure uses higher-order functions and macros.

Clojure's approach is more general. In fact, most of the Clojure language itself is written as a set of Clojure functions and macros! Advanced Scala DSL writers may bang up against the limitations of Scala's current approach.

For this reason, macros are being added to Scala. However, as noted in the *Discussion*, on page 217, they're much harder to implement and use without the simple syntax and homoiconicity available in Clojure and other languages in the Lisp family.

Related Patterns

Pattern 20, *Customized Control Flow*, on page 206

For Further Reading

DSLs in Action [Gho10]

CHAPTER 5

The End

That wraps up our look at patterns in functional programming. Hopefully now you see how functional programming tools can help you write shorter and clearer code and how immutable data can remove large sources of error from your programs.

I hope you've also gotten a taste for both Scala and Clojure. Even though they both include functional features, they're quite different from each other. By seeing examples written in both Scala and Clojure, you've been exposed to a wide range of functional techniques.

Most of all, I hope you can apply what you've learned in this book to make your day-to-day programming experience better.

Thanks for reading!

Bibliography

[AIS77]   Christopher Alexander, Sara Ishikawa, and Murray Silverstein. *A Pattern Language: Towns, Buildings, Construction*. Oxford University Press, New York, NY, 1977.

[Blo08]   Joshua Bloch. *Effective Java*. Addison-Wesley, Reading, MA, 2008.

[FBBO99]   Martin Fowler, Kent Beck, John Brant, William Opdyke, and Don Roberts. *Refactoring: Improving the Design of Existing Code*. Addison-Wesley, Reading, MA, 1999.

[FH11]   Michael Fogus and Chris Houser. *The Joy of Clojure*. Manning Publications Co., Greenwich, CT, 2011.

[GHJV95]   Erich Gamma, Richard Helm, Ralph Johnson, and John Vlissides. *Design Patterns: Elements of Reusable Object-Oriented Software*. Addison-Wesley, Reading, MA, 1995.

[Gho10]   Debasish Ghosh. *DSLs in Action*. Manning Publications Co., Greenwich, CT, 2010.

[Goe12]   Brian Goetz. *JSR 335: Lambda Expressions for the Java Programming Language*. Java Community Process, http://jcp.org, 2012.

[HB12]   Stuart Halloway and Aaron Bedra. *Programming Clojure*. The Pragmatic Bookshelf, Raleigh, NC and Dallas, TX, Second, 2012.

[Lip11]   Miran Lipovaca. *Learn You a Haskell for Great Good!: A Beginner's Guide*. No Starch Press, San Francisco, CA, 2011.

[MRB97]   Robert C. Martin, Dirk Riehle, and Frank Buschmann. *Pattern Languages of Program Design 3*. Addison-Wesley, Reading, MA, 1997.

[Nor92]   Peter Norvig. *Paradigms of Artificial Intelligence Programming: Case Studies in Common Lisp*. Morgan Kaufmann Publishers, San Francisco, CA, 1992.

[Sub09]   Venkat Subramaniam. *Programming Scala: Tackle Multi-Core Complexity on the Java Virtual Machine*. The Pragmatic Bookshelf, Raleigh, NC and Dallas, TX, 2009.

[Sue12]   Joshua Suereth. *Scala In Depth*. Manning Publications Co., Greenwich, CT, 2012.

Index

Put the "Fun" in Functional

Elixir puts the "fun" back into functional programming, on top of the robust, battle-tested, industrial-strength environment of Erlang.

You want to explore functional programming, but are put off by the academic feel (tell me about monads just one more time). You know you need concurrent applications, but also know these are almost impossible to get right. Meet Elixir, a functional, concurrent language built on the rock-solid Erlang VM. Elixir's pragmatic syntax and built-in support for metaprogramming will make you productive and keep you interested for the long haul. This book is *the* introduction to Elixir for experienced programmers.

Dave Thomas
(240 pages) ISBN: 9781937785581. $36
http://pragprog.com/book/elixir

A multi-user game, web site, cloud application, or networked database can have thousands of users all interacting at the same time. You need a powerful, industrial-strength tool to handle the really hard problems inherent in parallel, concurrent environments. You need Erlang. In this second edition of the best-selling *Programming Erlang*, you'll learn how to write parallel programs that scale effortlessly on multicore systems.

Joe Armstrong
(548 pages) ISBN: 9781937785536. $42
http://pragprog.com/book/jaerlang2

The Joy of Math and Healthy Programming

Rediscover the joy and fascinating weirdness of pure mathematics, and learn how to take a healthier approach to programming.

Mathematics is beautiful—and it can be fun and exciting as well as practical. *Good Math* is your guide to some of the most intriguing topics from two thousand years of mathematics: from Egyptian fractions to Turing machines; from the real meaning of numbers to proof trees, group symmetry, and mechanical computation. If you've ever wondered what lay beyond the proofs you struggled to complete in high school geometry, or what limits the capabilities of the computer on your desk, this is the book for you.

Mark C. Chu-Carroll
(282 pages) ISBN: 9781937785338. $34
http://pragprog.com/book/mcmath

To keep doing what you love, you need to maintain your own systems, not just the ones you write code for. Regular exercise and proper nutrition help you learn, remember, concentrate, and be creative—skills critical to doing your job well. Learn how to change your work habits, master exercises that make working at a computer more comfortable, and develop a plan to keep fit, healthy, and sharp for years to come.

This book is intended only as an informative guide for those wishing to know more about health issues. In no way is this book intended to replace, countermand, or conflict with the advice given to you by your own healthcare provider including Physician, Nurse Practitioner, Physician Assistant, Registered Dietician, and other licensed professionals.

Joe Kutner
(254 pages) ISBN: 9781937785314. $36
http://pragprog.com/book/jkthp

Seven Databases, Seven Languages

There's so much new to learn with the latest crop of NoSQL databases. And instead of learning a language a year, how about seven?

Data is getting bigger and more complex by the day, and so are your choices in handling it. From traditional RDBMS to newer NoSQL approaches, *Seven Databases in Seven Weeks* takes you on a tour of some of the hottest open source databases today. In the tradition of Bruce A. Tate's *Seven Languages in Seven Weeks*, this book goes beyond your basic tutorial to explore the essential concepts at the core of each technology.

Eric Redmond and Jim R. Wilson
(354 pages) ISBN: 9781934356920. $35
http://pragprog.com/book/rwdata

You should learn a programming language every year, as recommended by *The Pragmatic Programmer*. But if one per year is good, how about *Seven Languages in Seven Weeks*? In this book you'll get a hands-on tour of Clojure, Haskell, Io, Prolog, Scala, Erlang, and Ruby. Whether or not your favorite language is on that list, you'll broaden your perspective of programming by examining these languages side-by-side. You'll learn something new from each, and best of all, you'll learn how to learn a language quickly.

Bruce A. Tate
(330 pages) ISBN: 9781934356593. $34.95
http://pragprog.com/book/btlang

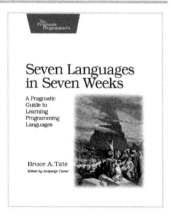

The Pragmatic Bookshelf

The Pragmatic Bookshelf features books written by developers for developers. The titles continue the well-known Pragmatic Programmer style and continue to garner awards and rave reviews. As development gets more and more difficult, the Pragmatic Programmers will be there with more titles and products to help you stay on top of your game.

Visit Us Online

This Book's Home Page
http://pragprog.com/book/mbfpp
Source code from this book, errata, and other resources. Come give us feedback, too!

Register for Updates
http://pragprog.com/updates
Be notified when updates and new books become available.

Join the Community
http://pragprog.com/community
Read our weblogs, join our online discussions, participate in our mailing list, interact with our wiki, and benefit from the experience of other Pragmatic Programmers.

New and Noteworthy
http://pragprog.com/news
Check out the latest pragmatic developments, new titles and other offerings.

Save on the eBook

Save on the eBook versions of this title. Owning the paper version of this book entitles you to purchase the electronic versions at a terrific discount.

PDFs are great for carrying around on your laptop—they are hyperlinked, have color, and are fully searchable. Most titles are also available for the iPhone and iPod touch, Amazon Kindle, and other popular e-book readers.

Buy now at *http://pragprog.com/coupon*

Contact Us

Online Orders: *http://pragprog.com/catalog*
Customer Service: *support@pragprog.com*
International Rights: *translations@pragprog.com*
Academic Use: *academic@pragprog.com*
Write for Us: *http://pragprog.com/write-for-us*
Or Call: +1 800-699-7764

Milton Keynes UK
Ingram Content Group UK Ltd.
UKHW032133210823
427243UK00009B/556